# CUBAN MUSIC

## MAYA ROY

Translated by
Denise Asfar and Gabriel Asfar

The translation of this book into English was supported by a grant from the French Ministère de la Culture et de la Communication.

For information write to:
Markus Wiener Publishers, 231 Nassau Street, Princeton, NJ 08542

Book design by Cheryl Mirkin
Cover design by Maria Madonna Davidoff
Chapter title illustrations by Sigfried Kaden
Cover photo courtesy of Holger Pöhlmann and Anthrovision, Munich, Germany
This book has been composed in Stone Serif

Library of Congress Cataloging-in-Publication Data
Roy, Maya.
    [Musiques cubaines. English]
    Cuban music/Maya Roy; translated by Denise Asfar
        and Gabriel Asfar.
    Includes bibliographical references and discography.
    ISBN 1-55876-281-7 (hc)
    ISBN 1-55876-282-5 (pb)
    1. Popular music—Cuba—History and criticism.  I. Title.
    ML3486.C8 R69 2002
    780'.97291—dc21     2001056846


Published in the United Kingdom by the Latin America Bureau
1 Amwell Street, London EC1R 1UL
www.lab.org.uk
A CIP catalog record for this book is available from the British Library
ISBN 1899365 54 0

The Latin American Bureau is an independent research and publishing organization. It works to broaden public understanding of issues of human rights and social and economic justice in Latin America and the Caribbean.

Distributed in the Caribbean by Ian Randle Publishers
11 Cunningham Avenue, Box 686, Kingston 6
A catalogue record for this book is available from the National Library of Jamaica


Printed in the United States of America on acid-free paper.

# Table of Contents

# Acknowledgments

My thanks go to all those who supported and encouraged me, with special thanks to Rodolfo Chacón, Roberto Bello, Miké Charroppin, and William Tanifeani.

The photographs in this text were reproduced courtesy of the National Museum of Music, Havana. The author and publisher would especially like to thank Ileana Baisines for her expertise and professionalism in helping select appropriate illustrations.

To those who first guided me along the path of Cuban music: Argeliers León, Ezequiel Rodríguez and María Teresa Linares, Leonardo Acosta, and Radamés Giró. To all the musicians who gave me their time, their music, and sometimes their friendship. Whether alive or gone, they remain in my heart, and this modest book owes everything to them.

—MAYA ROY

It should be known—and let us repeat that this is the first objective of this book—that what is available today to a European sensibility weary and in need of new invigoration, like an invention likely to set off its hidden springs, is by no means an improvisation intended to attract tourists, but rather a spiritual creation developed by a people struggling for four centuries to find its own expression.

—EMILIO GRENET
*Música popular cubana,*
Secretaría de Agricultura, Havana, 1939

# Preface

BY JUAN FLORES

The American love affair with Cuban music goes back a long way, and its roots run deeper than the commercial hype would have us believe. The current infatuation with the Buena Vista Social Club is but the latest echo of a love song that began over 150 years ago with "Ojos Criollos" by Louis Moreau Gottschalk, considered America's first musical composer. The "Spanish tinge," Jelly Roll Morton's proverbial phrase for the crucial Cuban infusion to the inception of jazz, has resonated in the steady string of crazes through the decades of American popular music: "rhumba," conga, mambo, cha cha, salsa, household words in the 20th-century cultural lexicon. Not so trova, guaguancó, son montuno, charanga, punto guajira, and countless other styles and rhythms that constitute the history of Cuban music.

Where do Americans and others with tropical fever go? Who would know more about this seductive cultural source? How to get beneath the glittery surface and trivial distortions and gain a sense of the profound social meanings and striking creative ingenuity of Cuba's rich musical traditions? Major Cuban writers like Fernando Ortíz, Alejo Carpentier, Leonardo Acosta, María Teresa Linares, and Argeliers León have produced a wealth of historical documentation and analysis, and other studies shed valuable light on important aspects of the many styles, traditions, and musical artists. But for an introductory overview, which gleans this earlier scholarship and presents the main contours of that history in an informed and well-conceived presentation, I would recommend the present work, Maya Roy's newly translated book, *Cuban Music*.

—*New York, July 2002*

# Introduction

Cuban popular music is closely tied to the history of the entire area of the West Indies—a history marked by colonization, the almost complete eradication of its indigenous peoples, and slavery. The islands of the Caribbean archipelago, at stake in the rivalries among European powers, developed according to different patterns that were imposed by the colonizers. But everywhere the wealth of colonial society depended on the labor of the slaves imported from Africa. With the passing of time, and to varying degrees, the mixing of the African and European resulted in a culture that was no longer either European or African, but in itself remarkable and belonging distinctly to the particular country in question. An authentically Cuban music could only develop after a national identity had been formed within the colonial society by means of political and social claims and two wars of liberation from Spanish rule, an identity whose cultural form is expressed in the concept of "Cuban-ness" (*"cubanidad"*).

This book deals primarily with the various types of popular music, including dance music and other types of music, while leaving aside one important aspect: There is a type of concert music, specifically Cuban, that crystallized in the mid-nineteenth century around the emergence of the national feeling, and whose Cuban nature was nourished precisely by the integration of themes borrowed from types of popular music that were already mixed. This Creole quality is expressed, for example, in quadrilles and in the dances of Manuel Saumell (1817–1870) and Ignacio Cervantes (1847–1905). In the early twentieth century, in connection with the literary and artistic movement of an elite group claiming to be the exponents of "Afrocubanism," Amadeo Roldán (1900–1939) and Alejandro García Caturla (1906–1940) continued this trend toward "Creolization" in greater depth. With "Overture on Cuban themes," Roldán goes further to integrate Cuban instruments that, until then, had been used only in dance music, thus facilitating the osmosis between concert music and popular music.

Musical theater also reflects this permeability. Little by little, characters typical of Cuban society (the mulatto, the peasant, the black person) replaced in the theater of the burlesque the Spanish *zarzuelas* characters that were regularly portrayed in the theaters; the music that accompanied them would give birth to different types of Cuban song, such as the *guaracha.\** The 1930s saw the flowering of Cuban *zarzuelas*, which—while maintaining the overall structure of the Spanish genre—were characterized by themes and music typically Cuban. The composers Gonzalo Roig (1890–1970), Ernesto Lecuona (1896–1963), and Rodrigo Prats (1909–1980) followed this trend, along with Jorge Anckermann (1877–1941), Moises Simons (1890–1945), Eliseo Grenet (1893–1950), and his brother Emilio (1908–1941). All composed tunes for dance bands. Roig and Lecuona founded the first symphony orchestra of Havana in 1922.

This mingling of musical styles, played in different places for distinctly different audiences, was also found in the urban expression of what we will call (for lack of a better term) "popular" music. The city was the melting pot where the truly Cuban dance genres came together by means of the progressive "Creolization" of a European musical foundation under the influence of musicians of African origin.

---

*Terms followed by an asterisk are explained in the glossary at the end of the book.

## The Interracial Musical Mix

Colonization did not begin with the first arrival of the Spanish conquerors in 1492, but rather in 1511, westward from the east coast, with the founding of the cities of Baracoa, Bayamo, Sancti Spíritus, Trinidad, Puerto Principe (present-day Camagüey), and, at the end of 1514, of Santiago de Cuba, the island's first capital. When Havana became the headquarter of the Spanish governor in 1552, it challenged the supremacy of Santiago de Cuba; as a result of the business monopoly that it retained until 1765, Havana occupied a strategic place between Spain and her colonies on the continent. Later, another zone of economic importance developed with the port of Matanzas as its center.

The first contingents of Spanish colonists belonged to the army, the Church, and the royal bureaucracy. The types of music they developed in urban settings symbolized their power: military music, religious music, and court music. The rapid rise in the cities of a Creole bourgeoisie stimulated the proliferation of musical entertainment, particularly in the eighteenth century. By the same token, popular events that, in the Spanish tradition, accompanied large religious celebrations, such as Corpus Christi, gave rise to masquerades and street theater, the precursors of light comedy (Carpentier, 1985, pp. 53–54). This is how traditional Spanish folk music spread to the cities.

In both the city and the countryside, this tradition spread to the rhythm of the successive waves of immigration from all regions of the Iberian Peninsula. Andalusia and the Canary Islands were a source of constant immigration; but Extremadura, Castille, Leon, Navarre, and the Basque region also contributed to this musical legacy, as did Asturias, Galicia, and Catalonia, in the nineteenth century. Besides the string instruments they brought with them, the Spaniards brought a repertoire of sung poetry, enriched by the traditions of Arab versification and song, the popular stanza of four octosyllabics versus (or *copla*), seguidillas, *tiranas*, and ballads, as well as an entire series of dances mentioned in historical chronicles, such as the *zapateado*.\*

In the cities, these traditions fused with Creole rhythms, songs, and dance tunes. In the countryside, the low population density and the isolation of the regions slowed the evolution of the music and furthered much closer ties with its Spanish roots, at least in western Cuba. The rural music varied according to the origin of the Spanish colonists, as well as their type of business and the geographic and demographic structure of the area in which they settled. In eastern Cuba, the presence of a significant black minority and a steady trade between farms—even those that were relatively isolated—and with the markets in the small neighboring villages, stimulated a more marked cross-fertilization of cultures, which was expressed in the *son*.\* From the inception of Cuba's colonization, the native populations had been reduced to slavery to extract and pan for gold and their numbers had been decimated within a few decades to a degree that they left very little mark on the musical development. The instruments the Spanish chroniclers cited at the time of the Indian holidays and later described as "Indian" also existed in Africa—instruments such as calabashes, which were hollowed out and filled with seeds like *maracas*,\* or the *mayohuacán*, a hollowed-out tree trunk, which was struck with wooden sticks. All one can say is that the first African slaves, who coexisted on the island with the native population that survived into the sixteenth century, would have used these instruments because they were already familiar with them.

The music the slaves played in relation to the African cosmogonies were present in two very different contexts. The slave trade, which was officially banned in 1820, continued illegally until 1873, reaching its height between 1790 and 1841, when the large-scale plantation economy was developing. The total number of slaves imported to Cuba is estimated at about 930,000. Slavery was not abolished until 1886. Thus the plantations were a constantly renewing source for systems of worship, of which colonial society, on the whole, remained unaware until slavery was abolished; indeed, ignorance of the slaves' systems of worship persisted even after the abolition of slavery, since racial discrimination remained a feature of Cuban society after independence.

Beginning in the sixteenth century, the cities were inhabited by large numbers of freedmen, mulattos, and blacks, employed as artisans or in light construction (carpenters, masons, shoe-menders, and tailors). The slaves, whose masters frequently farmed out their labor for hire, took over unskilled tasks in heavy construction, packing and handling at the ports and commercial firms, and copper mining in the eastern regions. According to colonial legislation, the African-born slaves, or *bossales*, were grouped together into *cabildos*, these were organizations within which the slaves were permitted to cultivate their traditions. On the plantations and in the cities, all of the slaves' activities were closely supervised, but the permanent contact of the members of the *cabildos* with the dominant European culture and with the slaves and freedmen born in Cuba had an appreciable impact on urban music.

## The Army and the Church: The First Music Schools

Military bands were the crowning glory of all official celebrations, such as births in the royal or princely family, or religious holidays. The bands played concert music, symphonies, and musical entertainments that integrated "classical" arrangements of popular themes. Even though black people could not hold military office, there were numerous blacks and mulattos in the army in separate battalions of people of color. There they were introduced to the European instruments of the military bands—brass, clarinets, fifes, and drums —as well as to all genres of European music.

The Church too needed singers and instrumentalists to accompany the liturgy, which was based on that of the Church of Seville. Choral traditions, which remain strong in Cuba, developed from the performance of church songs, such as motets, hymns, and holy stories. Next to the organ, sacred music also incorporated the harp, the bassoon, the viola da gamba, and the violin. The churches became veritable concert halls, where instrumentalists and singers "of color" were especially appreciated. Besides European music, works by Cuban composers were also heard there. One such significant example is that of Esteban Salas y Castro (1725–1803), director of the music chapel and of the cathedral of Santiago de Cuba. He composed not only liturgical music (masses, requiems, litanies, psalms, passions), but also compositions sung in Spanish, a highly unusual practice in the religious context of the era. These vernacular works included pastoral poems, *villancicos*, and various songs for several voices. Besides the instruments already cited, he used the flute, the oboe, and the French horn. Moreover, as Alejo Carpentier notes, certain characteristics of Salas's music could still be detected in the methods of composing the *danzón* in the late nineteenth century (1985, p. 82).

## The Status of Musicians

With the growth of entertainment activities, there also developed concert groups as well as dance bands that accompanied the kind of social dancing that imitated European figure dancing. By the late eighteenth century, Havana had fifty public dance halls, segregated by the color of the clientele. More sensual types of dances also developed on the island: chaconnes, fandangos, saltarellos, tarantellas, and congo minuets.

Since music was considered a profession that offered no

Benny Moré during the show;
on the right, with her guitar, is María Teresa Vera.

guarantee for a steady livelihood, it quickly became the exclusive domain of "people of color," along with manual activities; these were generally referred to as mechanical and liberal arts. In 1800, Antonio Valle Hernández stated: "The arts which, in other countries, are the occupation of respected, well-born white people, here are the near-monopoly of people of color" (Torres-Cuevas, Reyes, 1986). For most of the musicians of color, the boundaries between classical, religious, and popular music were blurred, since they were proficient in all three types. With their instrumental expertise and their own musical heritage, musicians of color created original scores with a typical Creole flavor that won over the popular public, and then fashionable high society as well. It is from this Creolized music that the properly Cuban genres, such as the *danzón,* developed. The first bands described as "typical" (*"orquestas típicas"*) performed the Creole quadrilles using the brass instruments of military bands and the timpani of the symphonic orchestra; the *Charanga a la francesa** orchestras, which came later, took on violins, flute, and piano.

## The Internationalization of Cuban Rhythms

The Ten Years' War, from 1868 to 1878, revealed the existence of a national consciousness, but from 1823, with the Monroe Doctrine, the United States had been asserting its commercial claims in the region. Independence was definitively attained in 1898—at the end of a three-year war against Spain—with the armed intervention of the United States, which then occupied the Cuban territory until 1902. Until the revolution of 1959, the Cuban Republic remained a quasi-U. S. colony, ruled by the Platt Amendment.

It was mainly during this second phase that Cuban rhythms became international. The first audio recordings were made in 1877. The record industry originated simultaneously in Europe and in the United States in 1894; radio broadcasting expanded rapidly in the 1920s. Cuba had almost immediate access to the recording industry thanks to the wealth of its musical output and its proximity to the United States. With the help of Latin America's linguistic unity, the market for records developed very rapidly.

This context had contradictory effects. Broadcast widely by large U.S. companies, popular music invaded the international market and bands multiplied. Havana attracted performers of all nationalities who, for a time, integrated Cuban bands. The *son* triumphed throughout the Caribbean. In the United States, non-Cuban musicians, such as the Catalan Xavier Cugat, popularized debased forms of rumbas and salon congas. Exoticism triumphed. However, from the 1930s, many black musicians, having been victims of racism, went outside Cuba to seek their fortunes, and many composers, whose music had traveled around the world, would die destitute.

Distinctive historic features, musical vitality, and business politics undoubtedly explain how, despite its insularity, Cuba was more successful than the other Caribbean islands in preserving, exporting, and gaining recognition through the present day for its great variety of rhythms.

# I

# Ritual Music

Cuba is a country where African cosmogonies, rituals, and the cultural practices linked to them remain very much alive. This African heritage impregnates all of Cuban culture, beyond the population concerned with the various cults. This is one of the matrices that sustain popular music, a knowledge that has been transmitted and transformed across generations since the period of slavery. Even today, many Cuban musicians, percussionists in particular, are initiated into at least one of the systems of worship. They know all the ways that make the drums speak, and this knowledge constantly enriches the musical art.

## Slavery and Colonial Society

Traditionally, when studying ritual music, people refer to the different origins of the slaves brought to the Americas. The Spanish administration used the term "nation" (*nación*) to designate the principal groups who were thought to belong to the same ethnic or language group. The slaves were grouped under generic names such as *lucumí** (identified with Yoruba), *congo** (identified with Bantu), and *carabalí* (which comes from Calabar). However, the designations under which the slave traders listed the slaves were often erroneous or were simply taken from the port of embarkation once the slaves had been captured inland (Martínez Furé, 1979). Under the name Minas, for example, which was taken from a slave-trading port in the Gold Coast (present-day Ghana) of that name, one actually finds slaves of Ashanti, Fanti, Twi, and Éwé origin.

The Yoruba cultural area covered Nigeria and the east of Benin, as far as the kingdom of Ketu. The Bantu inhabited the south of Cameroon, Gabon, the Congo (formerly Congo-Brazzaville), Burundi, Rwanda, Congo-Zaïre, and Angola, as far as the north of Namibia. Calabar stretched between Nigeria and Cameroon, from the coast to Lake Chad. The Ararᇱ were from the Kingdom of Allada, in the south of Dahomey, not far from the slave-trading port of Ouidah. Other ethnic groups were also represented, such as those who were often called Gangas, but actually belonged to the Mandé (Mandingo, in colonial vocabulary), an immense ethnic-linguistic group whose place of origin stretched from the bend of the Niger to the Atlantic Ocean, from Senegal to Liberia. The Gangas also included slaves of Pulaar and Soninké origin.

As a survival tactic, these uprooted groups, who had been deported en masse to the Americas, reconstituted their cosmogonies and their systems of interpreting the world. To keep the slave under control and to improve their labor output, their masters allowed them, under certain conditions, to observe their holidays.

The plantation was a world unto itself largely dependent on the good will of the slave masters. The slaves were permitted to meet on Sundays and to "beat the drum" according to whichever ethnic group was the most numerous, but periodic bans on drumming were imposed as punishment for such infractions as rebellion and escape attempts. Despite its precarious nature, this context for the Sunday drum beating assured the survival of many songs, dances, and music as part of the cultural system. The presence of different ethnic groups on the same plantation may have facilitated the diffusion of cosmogonies. However, due to the exceptionally long duration of the slave trade, sizable contingents of slaves were arriving, up until the end of the nineteenth century, with their native culture intact, and thus they renewed the traditions that otherwise might have been dulled after two centuries of oral transmission. When slavery was abolished, these slaves streamed to the cities and were integrated into societies that grouped them together as "people of color."

## From "*Cabildos*" to Entertainment Associations

In the cities, the grouping together of only African-born slaves by "nation" was institutionalized in *cabildos*, which were organizations derived from medieval Spanish guilds. Fifteenth-century Seville already had *cabildos* of Gypsies and of African slaves or freedmen. (Spain and Portugal had been practicing slavery since the eighth century.) The *cabildos*, which had been introduced into the Americas after the conquest, provided the colonial authorities with a means to control rivaling groups of the rising number of slaves.

The *cabildos* served as mutual aid societies and for protection, as well as religious brotherhoods in which an embryonic social and religious organization of ethnic groups was being

Dance inside a Havana "cabildo"

formed; each group elected a king or queen as its head, to safe-guard the traditions and the proper order, as well as a treasur-er and an entire hierarchy. Besides the festivities that were held on their own premises, *cabildo* members were also al-lowed to go out into the streets in their costumes, with their masks and drums, during certain religious feasts of the Catho-lic calendar, such as Epiphany or Corpus Christi.

After the official abolition of slavery, the *cabildos* were banned. In 1887, they were forced to submit to fellowship leg-islation that transformed them into mutual aid societies open to everyone, each society under the aegis of a patron saint. They were affiliated with the Catholic Church, which also would claim a group's funds in case of its dissolution. The persecution of the population of African descent and of its culture turned these associations into cells of resistance, and the *cabildos* became, indisputably, the melting pot that enabled the cosmogonies, languages, music, songs, and dances related to these systems of worship to preserve their life and significance.

## General Character of the Systems of Worship

The mass transports of Africans to the Americas brought about a radical break with ancient lineages, hierarchies, and roles, which were destroyed by the dispersion of ethnic groups and by the very nature of slavery. The Africans and their descendants then had to re-create their systems of worship by adapting them to their new circumstances: They reconstructed their drums, but with materials found in their new location; they reformed a "horizontal" rather than a pyramidal order of brotherhoods and ritual families that were relatively independent of one another. Their native languages were modified and their practices were adapted to new situations. Since African cosmogonies are by nature open, they assimilated outside elements that arose according to the interaction between the different systems and social necessities. These systems do not constitute a domain outside everyday life. Rather they are an entire body of knowledge and set of values, transmitted orally and through customary practice, stretching from the colonial era to the present day. They are part of an ethical code and norms of conduct intended to facilitate the integration of the individual into the various types of society in which he or she participated. Alongside the perpetuation of traditions, which correspond to those still found in Africa, exists an entire series of modifications that prove these religions have undergone the process of "transculturation" as defined by Fernando Ortiz.

In this context, music (instruments, songs, and dances) represents a veritable language, integrated into a vision of the world in which the dead are always present among the living, and in which the demarcation between the sacred and the profane is blurred since social acts are inseparable from the sacred dimension. Music, a privileged means of communication with the divinities, involves the active, collective participation of all present—the invisible participants as well as the visible. Each rhythm played by the drums has a definite context with a given function and objective, according to a specific rule, for the consecrated drum is the preeminent link between people and their divinities, between the living and the spirits of their ancestors.

It is not our concern here to describe in detail the rituals or the cosmogonies that underlie them. We will simply try to underscore the principal elements of the ritual music, focusing on those that passed, directly or indirectly, into other manifestations of Cuban culture.

## Music of Yoruba Origin

The *lucumí* form the majority group. Their system of worship, the *regla de ocha ifá*,* is better known under the name of *santería*,* in reference to a supposed syncretism with the Catholic Church. Although correspondences can be effectively established between the African divinities and certain Catholic saints, and the initiates go to church on certain occasions, one can tell, through the music, that the Catholic influence is practically nonexistent, except in a special type the so-called "hybrid" cults where, for example, the Spanish language intervenes.

The most commonly practiced form, the *regla de ocha*, is structured around the ritual family; the house of each initiate constitutes a temple-house (*ile-ocha*), which includes a room where sacred objects representing the venerated divinities (*orisha*) are kept. There are many types of ceremonies: initiation (which lasts several weeks), in various stages; feasts with a fixed date in honor of certain *orisha*; commemorations related to the life of each initiate; and holidays with broader participation—such as a simple thanks to a deity for his beneficial "work" or a feast offered to an *orisha* demanding tribute.

The sacred drums are the three *batá* drums [*see picture below*], which were double-headed, in the shape of a clepsydra, beaten by hand on each side. They are carved from the trunks of either cedar or mahogany trees. The drumheads, of different diameters, are stretched, lengthwise and crosswise, by a

The three batá drums

leather lacing. The largest of these is called the *iyá*. Each rim is surrounded by small bronze bells called *shaworó*, which complement and modify the drum's sound. The drum with the middle register is called *itótele*; the smallest and higher-pitched drum is the *okónkolo*. With six initial notes, the *batá* have the most complex sound system of all the ritual drums. Since the two drumheads are united, the tones and sounds vary according to location and intensity of impact from the hand, and also according to the pressure on the other drumhead. The *iyá* is the lead drum in the group. It opens the ritual in calling the particular *orisha* being invoked; this is followed by the *itótele*, to the left of the first drummer, who responds to him; the *okónkolo* plays the basic rhythmic pattern. Sacred and consecrated instruments, holders of a "secret" (*aña*), these drums speak; they are the voice that calls the deities, and the divinities speak through the drums. Initially, the combination of rhythmic patterns, melodic inflections, and timbres reproduced the tonal sequences of the Yoruba language.

There is a special musical language of the drums that corresponds to each divinity, as well as special songs and dances. Ceremonies always open and close with words of praise to Eleguá, the deity in charge of opening and closing paths in life. The *olubatá* who play the sacred drums—the only ones authorized to ritually consecrate them—have passed down, over the centuries, an extremely complex body of knowledge: a multitude of melodic/rhythmic patterns, as well as the skill of making the transition from one rhythmic pattern to another in a conversation with the same divinity or in going from one invocation to another.

Certain parts of rituals call for the drums only, such as the *oru de igbodu*, an initial salute to each deity with the corresponding rhythms. Others include invocation chants, accompanied by drums, generally in tongue (i.e., in languages of African origin), where soloist and chorus alternate. The soloist (*akpwón\**), guardian of the tradition and responsible for transmitting it, intervenes before the start of each ritual and invokes the spirits of the ancestors and the deities. He starts singing various chants, which correspond to each *orisha* or to the various aspects of the deity's narrative. This structure, in the form of a dialogue with the chorus, underscores the collective character of a type of music that is part of the ritual whose purpose goes beyond that of mere background or distraction. The ritual is, in itself, an active force intended to invite those divinities that, at the time, are incarnated in one of the initiates, to "come down." The songs follow the modal system, and they move from high notes to low notes by a sequence of segments or units of varying intensity, which always ends in a low register. The chorus enters as an element of contrast in the timbres, partly repeating the phrase indicated by the soloist, or linking it to a different motif (León, 1974, pp. 50–51). Besides Merceditas Valdés (who died in 1996), the best-known *akpwón* in Cuba is Lázaro Ros, who teaches this art today to young children.

The dances accompanying the group are also part of the ritual: each *orisha* and each of its incarnations (*caminos*) has its own dances.

### *Iyesá\** Drums

The *iyesá* drums, which were brought by the Yoruba who had come from the Oyo Kingdom (present-day Nigeria), are also sacred. They survive in the regions of Matanzas, Cienfuegos (Palmira), and Santa Clara (Placetas). Three of the drums in use today are considered by the priests to be authentic *iyesá*. They are cylindrical, of different sizes, double-headed and stretched by lacing.

The drums are struck on one side with wooden sticks, and the performer exerts pressure, with the hand, on the other side of the drum, to modify the tone. The fourth drum, which is beaten with a bare hand, was added later for use in secular ceremonies. Sometimes it is replaced by a *tumbadora.** These drums are accompanied by metallic percussion instruments called *agogo*, whose shape and tone differ according to the deity being celebrated, and by the chants that always alternate between soloist and chorus.

### Güiro* and Bembé*

Certain ceremonies—for example, the anniversary of the initiate's rebirth or an offering of thanks—are part of the cult practice without being sacred rituals.

In Havana, a kind of entertainment offered to the divinities is called *güiro*; there are three *shekere*—which are large, hollowed-out gourds, of varying size, shape, and thus tone, enmeshed in a net of glass beads. It is open-ended on one side, and the instrument is beaten on the surface with a flattened hand on the lower part. The orchestral principle is still the same: the biggest *shekeré*, which is again the lowest in register, performs the variations; the two others mark the distinct but constant rhythms. When they have a religious usage, these instruments are not consecrated, as are the drums used in solemn rituals. That is why it is often said that these instruments are part of the secular musical culture of the *lucumí*.

The *bembé* feasts are considered within the same context. The three *bembé* drums, generally cylindrical in form, are not consecrated. Their size and construction vary with the region. Originally made from the wood of a palm tree or an avocado tree, they have a single drumhead, which is nailed onto the instrument. Some have three feet on the open part; *bembé* drums made in the center of the island are double-headed. Today all sorts of secular drums are in use; some of these derive from the *iyesá* drums, accompanied by a tumbadora and a flat metallic percussion instrument called *guataca*.*

## Music of Bantu Origin

The slaves who were designated as *congos* in Cuba were mainly concentrated in the present-day provinces of Matanzas and Las Villas, the large sugar plantations of the Colón plain, Cienfuegos, and Trinidad. After the Ten Years' War (1868–1878), their settlements followed the expansion of the sugar industry into the eastern regions, where slaves were already present. In Havana, one *cabildo* of the colonial era best known for the prestige of its Epiphany-day procession was the *cabildo de los congos reales* (the Cabildo of the royal Congos), consisting of slaves the king of Spain had assigned to shipbuilding. Sources also attest to their presence in large numbers at Regla and Guanabacoa. In the region of Pinar del Río, one finds traces of traditional Congo celebration in isolated mountain villages in the center of this province, where the runaway *cimarrones*—slaves who had fled the coffee and sugar cane plantations—had created their *palenques*.* After the abolition of slavery, Congo groups, refusing to create associations and braving the authorities' bans, founded villages where participation in celebrations was open to all.

These particularities may explain why certain feasts and instruments were preserved until recently, in their original form, whereas elsewhere they have disappeared (Linares, discographic notes, *Anthologie*, 1981, V).

In the cities, the Congo people gathered around temple-houses. At the head of these were the *tata-nganga*, who officiated in the rites of initiation, commemoration, and funerals. *Nganga* refers to the spiritual power of the ancestor who presides at all magic rites. *Regla de Palo* or *regla congo* are the generic names of their systems of worship, which are divided into various branches. Cubans have often referred to this religious community of *paleros* by the pejorative term *brujos* (sorcerers), that is, supposedly dangerous people around whom an entire legend of cruelty has developed, because of the power of their magic rites which are considered to serve evil ends.

### The Instruments

The Bantu songs and dances have been less well preserved and the interplay of the drums is less complex than in music of Yoruba origin. Originally, the ritual drums were very diverse, differing by ethnic origin, while still bearing the generic Bantu name *ngoma*.*

The *kinfuiti** is a sacred drum, ritually consecrated, and must remain hidden from the view of the uninitiated. The drum's sound is produced by internal friction. The vibration of the drumhead occurs by means of a small string, to which is attached, at the center of the drumhead, a wooden stick that goes down into the drum's interior. The performer sits on the ground, with the open side of the drum turned toward him, and performs a rubbing motion along the stick, thus transmitting the vibrations to the drumhead, while never actually touching it directly. Depending on the speed of the performance and the chosen site, the performer produces raucous sounds that range from a moan to a howl. In Africa, this technique is always used with instruments that have religious significance (Brandily, 1997, p. 66). These particular sounds can be found in popular music, where the *bongó* drummers and even the *tumbadora** drummers produce them by rubbing

Makuta dance on a Cuban plantation

the drumhead (in their case, directly), using a glissando technique.

The *makuta** may also have been sacred in origin. Today *makuta* refers to a profane feast offered to the divinities as a type of entertainment (Ortiz, III, 1952, pp. 430–445; Cabrera, 1979, p. 76). There are three *yuka** drums, of different sizes, which are called—from largest to smallest—*caja*, *mula*, and *cachimbo*, and which are still used in rural areas today. These drums are made from the trunk of a fruit tree, often an avocado tree; the trunk is hollowed out and a single membrane is nailed to it, to serve as the drumhead. Disappearing in Palmira and in the province of Havana, these feasts still take place in the Congo villages in the center of the province of Pinar del Río. The drums are accompanied by one or more metallic percussion instruments, which are of the hoe variety. Sometimes they are also accompanied by a *marímbula,** which is a tuned idiophone made of metal strips mounted on a sounding board and is derived from *sanza** or *mbila*, a Bantu heritage that has passed into Cuban popular music, where it is used for performing the *son*.

Of all the dances that are part of these feasts, the most frequently mentioned is the *baile de makuta* (the *makuta* dance) during which a man and a woman face each other. The choreography imitates the man's amorous pursuit—dodged by the woman—using a series of pelvic girations that imitate sexual possession. This dance has been integrated into a present-day dance movement, the *guaguancó,** part of the entirely profane rumba. Engravings and epic narratives also prove the existence of a dance now disappeared, the *baile de maní*, whose descriptions are evocative of the *capoeira* of Brazil, where two men imitate a battle, dancing to the rhythm of the *yuka* drums.

## Abakuá Music

*Aquel que no tiene de congo tiene de carabalí* (Whoever has no congo in him, has some *carabalí*). This popular expression, intended to remind people of the closeness of their black ancestors, refers to the third "nation"—Efik and Efor—native to the former territory of Calabar. Organized as secret societies into which only men are admitted, the *carabalí** practice a cult with a complex ritual centered on a founding myth—the great secret of the magic voice of the fish Tanze. The term *abakuá* designates both the secret societies and their initiated disciples, who are also called *ñanigos*. These societies are structured, within the various branches, into brotherhoods called *potencias* or *juegos*, with a strict hierarchy of dignitaries, laws, and a code of honor. Besides a hermetic spoken language—even

more esoteric than that of the Congo, the *Abakuá* have preserved a graphic language made of signatures, seals, and sacred
signs, utterly unique in the Americas and of great artistic
value. These associations, which are also mutual aid societies,
play a very important role in the protection of their members,
especially those in the port cities (from Matanzas to the bay of
Cárdenas, in Havana, and its surrounding area, Marianao,
Regla, and Guanabacoa) and the workers in the stockyards and
tobacco factories.

The sacred *abakuá* drum, the *ekwé*, must remain hidden
from view, as is the case for the sacred drum used in Congo rituals. This is a rubbing drum, which is rubbed on the outside.
The rubbing motion on the thin stick that penetrates the
drumhead is performed, from the outside of the drumhead, by
the dignitary empowered to make the drum talk, and the
sound thus produced embodies the great secret of the founding myth, the voice of the sacred fish. The body of the drum,
generally made of cedar, ends in three feet; the drumhead is
stretched by a lacing controlled by wooden pegs set into the
sides. Four other sacred drums appear beside the *ekwé*. These
are smaller drums, open on one side, with a single drumhead:
*empegó, ekueñon, enkríkamo,* and *eribó* (Ortiz, IV, 1954, pp.
42–66; Léon, 1974, p. 82). These four drums do not "speak";
the dignitaries beat them at certain moments to make a point
or to indicate, in a symbolic manner, a particular moment in
the ritual. One of the peculiarities is the plume of rooster
feathers attached to the lacing on one side. The last drum even
has four of these placed on its perimeters: each one "personi-
fies" a superior entity belonging to the body of narratives per-
taining to this religion.

Another set of drums, which accompanies songs in tongue
and dances in a secular context, is known by the name

*biankomeko* and is arranged in the same order. Of these four single-head drums, *biankomé, obiapá, kuchiyeremá,* and *bonkó enchemiyá,* only the latter "speaks" and improvises. They are accompanied by the *ekón,* a metallic percussion instrument related to the Egyptian sistrum; the instrument is made of two triangular-shaped metal plates, welded on the sides and struck with a metallic stick; they are accompanied too by two *erikundi* (conical rattles). The *erikundi* are woven from vegetable fibers, closed off by a half gourd, decorated with seeds, and wrapped in lively colored cloth. Two small wooden drumsticks were added, for beating the outside of the *bonkó.* This ensemble accompanies and leads the dance of the *íreme,\** which are the incarnations of the ancestral spirits; these characters, totally masked and dressed in cloth and vegetable fibers, are led by the song "in tongue" of a soloist who alternates with the chorus, which narrates the founding myths. The dance of the *íreme* is still found today in carnivals, with a bouncing choreography and symbolic gestures whose meaning is not understood by the layperson.

In the eastern region, particularly in Santiago and Guantánamo, the tradition of the *carabalí* also continues within the *cabildos* which are mentioned as early as 1884 in the area of Santa Lucía. In 1894 the Cabildo Carabalí Isuama was founded; the Cabildo Carabalí Olugo followed later. These institutions, which persist today, have barely been studied until now. They were secret societies as well as public associations. Their main event is the display of the *comparsa\** on feast days. From the number and function of each type of instrument, the *comparsa carabalí* of Santiago resembles its counterpart in the western part of the island: four drums, two rattles, and two wooden drumsticks; to this ensemble was added a small, three-holed wooden flute made of cane, similar to the one once used by certain brotherhoods. However, under the influence of particular local traditions, the drums are completely different in the way they are made and the method of percussion: double-headed and beaten on both sides, with the drumheads stretched by lacing; the *ekón* became the hoe of a plow, and the rattles were replaced by the *chachá*, borrowed from the *tumba francesa*.*

## Arará Music

The *Arará* groups of the Allada kingdom (present-day Benin), which were numerous in Matanzas and its surrounding region in the nineteenth century, nonetheless remained in the minority. They experienced a fairly important interpenetration between their own system of worship, which was close to the origin of the *radá* ritual of Haitian voodoo (which also originated in Dahomey), and the system of worship of the Yoruba groups. In the old *cabildos*, the members made a distinction among *arará sabalú*, *arará magino*, and *arará dajomé*. Today, there are a few descendants of the old *cabildos* at Jovellanos, Perico, Agramonte, Cárdenas, and Matanzas, and they are structured around temple-houses.

The *Arará* introduced the drum with a single drumhead into Cuba. The oldest of these were built in the nineteenth century and are preserved in the Music Museum of Havana and in the *Casa de Africa* (House of Africa), still showing their multicolored decoration. Cut from an entire trunk, sculpted on the upper part, and often separated from the second part of the body of the drum by an ornamental design in broken lines, these drums have a base of a smaller diameter, cylindrical in form and painted in contrasting colors, which accentuate the effect of its separation from the body of the drum. The drumhead is stretched by ropes that are attached to wooden posts stuck into the body of the drum.

There are three ritual drums that accompany the songs and dances. They have different names, but each one contains the syllable *hun*, which, depending on its intonation, can mean "drum" or "blood." The mother drum, *hunga*, is played using a wooden drumstick, alternating with the bare hand, on the drumhead and the body of the drum. The *hunguedde* and the *huncito* generally are beaten with two drumsticks. All three drums are supported on a small wooden bench, so that the performer can stand astride the body of the drum (Linares, *Anthology*, IV, 1981). A smaller, fourth drum held between the legs was recently added in festive ceremonies of a secular nature. In the region of Havana, where the traditional drums have practically disappeared, the *arará* feasts are accompanied by *tumbadoras* that are beaten with drumsticks. Metallic idiophones are included with the drums: two metal cattle-bells and the *oggán*, which is made of two metal plates, semi-oval or triangular in shape, joined at the edges. The plates of the *oggán* are beaten with a metal drumstick. This instrument is also found in Haiti, under the same name.

The *Arará* have bequeathed a large variety of songs, always in the same responsive mode, but they also have songs performed *a cappella*, accompanied only by the clapping of hands.

## Continuance of Ritual Music

The instrumental formats used in the celebration of the various cults bear many similarities. All unite the three domains of animal (i.e., the leather of the drumheads), vegetable (i.e., the wood), and mineral (i.e., the metal). The orchestral group is structured around the rhythmic dialogue between the instruments (leader, response, improvisation) and the super-imposition of different tones and timbres, with the instruments and modal song coming together to form a whole. This polyrhythmic and polyphonic language, which is specifically African, is found, with some modifications and in varying degrees, in all of Cuban folk music.

Yet, the very existence of this African imprint has been called into question in the course of the twentieth century.

Merceditas Valdés, a great figure in Afro-Cuban music

During the period of the pseudo-Republic, everything African was considered by the dominant elite to be lowly, vulgar, and uncultured. Nonetheless, part of this heritage survived among the most disadvantaged strata of society, thanks to its oral transmission in spite of repression and an outright ban of the cults. Increasing impoverishment has brought the poor of all colors closer together, thus broadening the social base of the followers. When the drums were banned, people resorted to subterfuge: They modified the drums' structures; they built them from crates and barrels; they invented or "hijacked" instruments once considered as belonging exclusively to the white people.

A small number of Cuban intellectuals working against the dominant trend also contributed to the valorization of this legacy. Fernando Ortiz, who published his first criminological study in 1906, focused his sociological work on slavery, the condition of black people, and then on their artistic expression and their contribution to Cuban culture. He presented in 1937 at the Hispanoamerican Cultural Institute and in the early 1940s at the Havana University a group of batá drummers including great performers such as Jesús Pérez, accompanied by Merceditas Valdés, nicknamed La Pequeña Aché (the Little Aché), or Lázaro Ros. He also collaborated with renowned anthropologists and ethnologists such as Romulo Lachatañeré and Lydia Cabrera.

After the Revolution in 1959, the fieldwork and conceptualization continued at various institutions, such as the Popular Music Seminar directed by Odilio Urfé. The students of the pioneers Argeliers León, María Teresa Linares, and Isaac Barrial continued their investigation, transcribing the collected music and beginning the job of archiving and publishing. The Academy of Sciences was founded together with the Institute of Ethnology and Folklore, as well as a seminar that brought together researchers of different areas of specialization: historians; specialists in the colonial period, such as Zoila Lapique; specialists in slavery, such as Miguel Barnet (author of *Biografía de un cimarrón* [Biography of a Runaway Slave]); and Rogelio Martinez Furé, who, in 1962, participated in the founding of the Conjunto Folklórico Nacional de Cuba [National Folkloric Group of Cuba]. The government demonstrated its intention to preserve and valorize the heritage of popular culture, especially that with African antecedents which had been most sorely underappreciated. At the same time, however, the government's official atheism, with its concomitant dismissal of religions and beliefs it considers "superstitions," has denied the symbolic dimension of the music and its link to the sacred—elements that cannot be dissociated from the everyday life of that culture. Despite all this, thanks to the power of oral transmission, and because this symbolic order is an integral part of Cuban-ness (*cubanidad*), these living roots will never become fossilized.

# II

# Comparsas and Congas:
## THE "CARNIVAL" CELEBRATION

### Colonial Origins

Traditionally, the feast of the Epiphany ushers in the period of carnival festivities, which continues until Lent. In Europe, these are the vestiges of ancient pre-Christian agrarian rites, symbolizing the struggle between winter and spring and the return of death in rebirth. Traces of these are found in the wearing of disguises, of electing a king of fools, and the unbridled revelry in a topsy-turvy world. In Cuba, the Spaniards perpetuated the tradition of cavalcades and street processions, whereby the dictates of the agricultural calendar sometimes prevailed over the Christian calendar.

In the colonial period, the feast of the Epiphany was the only day when the members of the *cabildos de nación* were per-

Diablito ñañigo.
Illustration by Victor Landaluze
circa 1870

mitted to parade through the city. With their costumes, their songs and their dances, their instruments, both traditional and ritual, they were permitted to march to the governor's residence or that of his representatives, to pay homage to the colonial authorities. This pageantry was generally referred to as "the black people's carnival." To the outside observer these exotic characters, instruments, ritual gestures, and dances were a carnival extravaganza. In reality, under the conditions imposed upon them, the slaves had reconstituted, on Cuban soil, the ancestral rites of purification and expulsion of evil spirits. In various African countries, as in Cuba and other islands of the West Indies, we find sacred characters in disguises, who generally embody the spirits of their ancestors (Ortiz, 1920, in 1984, p. 54–59). Through a process of assimilation, into their own tradition, of characters disguised as devils, the Spanish chroniclers of the period called the characters in Cuba *diablitos*, and this name remains today. However, among the Abakuá and the *lucumí*, they have a specific name: *íreme* among the former, *egungun* among the latter.

Abakuá dance of Íreme
Performed by the National Folk Dance Group of Cuba

These carnival processions were periodically prohibited, either as punishment for slave revolts or during wars of independence, when combatants took advantage of masquerades to obtain arms and spread news; they were definitively prohibited during the 1884 Feast of the Epiphany.

## Toward the Modern Era

After the abolition of slavery, and then under the Republic, the tradition of street processions was revived in the form of carnival *comparsas*. Each neighborhood makes up a formation that includes masks, music, song, and dance. Some classic characters are directly descended from figures presented in the *cabildos* processions, such as *"la culona,"* girded with a large ring decorated with dangling plant fibers. Ortiz tells us that certain horn-shaped ornaments evoke the crowns of the kings of Angola and the Congo.

To this day each neighborhood chooses a new theme for the *comparsas*, with a song specially composed for the occasion. The collective preparations take a long time and are carried out under the direction of the head of the *comparsa*. The participants put the final touches on the costumes, the choruses, and the choreography; these have to be perfectly coordinated, so that each detail of the dance is in harmony with the overall movement as seen from the gallery. The bearers of banners appear in the forefront, with the colors of the *comparsa* and giant lanterns, followed by the dancers and singers, then the musicians who bring up the rear.

At the time of the pseudo-Republic, successive governments repressed anything that might give rise to opposition on the part of those social strata most adversely affected by the government's policies and its rampant corruption. As it happened, the principal players in the carnivals were precisely the former slaves and their descendants, the mulattos and poor white people who lived side by side on the outskirts. The lyrics of the songs composed for the occasion of what amounted to popular demonstrations reflect the tradition of commentary on current events, either directly or through double meaning.

Cubans who have been through that period speak of "white

carnivals" as opposed to those from the black neighborhoods. The authorities sanctioned a "deluxe" carnival on the grand avenue of the Paseo del Prado, which was often underwritten by the manufacturers of alcoholic beverages, with marvelous carriages and *comparsas* with choreography that ressembled those of salon dances. On these occasions, the crowds were allowed to march only on the sidewalks. Visits among *comparsas* from one neighborhood to another were forbidden by order of the police, on the pretext that they might give rise to riots. Conscious of the popularity of the *comparsas*, the political parties made use of them in their electoral campaigns, though the ban on the African drums of the former *cabildos* was never lifted.

This state of affairs led to a change in the composition of orchestras. The popular spirit adapted. Fanfare instruments were used, and new ones were fashioned with everyday utensils, but the rhythm sections of these orchestras largely reproduced the sound structures of ritual music.

## Havana *Comparsas*

The names of the Havana *comparsas* still evoke their origins, for example, those of African totems such as El Gavilán (The Kestrel), La Culebra (The Serpent), or the famed Alacrán (The Scorpion) of the Cerro neighborhood. Inspiration is also drawn from the colonial period with Los Marqueses (the Ataré district), Los Mosqueteros del Rey (La Timba), or from local lore with Los Mambises (Lugano). Los Dandys (Belén) assert their dapper elegance in spite of prejudice. Others allude to the participants' professions: Los Boyeros (Los Sitios), Los Componedores de batea (Pueblo Nuevo). From the community of Regla, on the other side of Havana Bay, come two famous *comparsas*: Los Moros Azules and Los Guaracheros de Regla.

The *comparsas* orchestras include drums, metallic percussion instruments, and brass, whose number varies according to the size of the *comparsa*, since the orchestra, located behind, directs the dancers' ballet. The *redoblantes*, replicas of military kettle drums, punctuate the march. The *bombos*,* derived from bass drums, are narrower than their Spanish counterparts and are played differently: they are beaten on one side with a mallet; on the other, the musician modifies the sounds through the pressure of his hand on the drumhead. The last drums, entirely Afro-Cuban, are made out of casks; these *tumbadoras* are structured musically in threes, however many their number, according to the already well-known principle: The stable rhythm is executed by the *salidor*; the *tumbador** responds and fills in the gaps; the *quinto** improvises the rhythmic patterns and, when the choreography calls for a solo demonstration by a couple of dancers, creates a dialogue with them. Drums are added to these in the high register—various metal idiophones made out of everyday parts or utensils: the *cencerro*, a cow bell; the *reja*, a plowshare; the *llantas*, trucks' tire rims; and the *sartenes*, which are two frying pans mounted on a wooden support suspended from the player's neck. To complete the sounds of the rhythm section, all the fanfare brass instruments are included—trumpets, trombones, and saxophones. The trumpet, substituting for the solo singer, plays the melody, which is taken up by the participants in a chorus.

In the years following the revolution of 1959, the Havana carnivals remained synonymous with popular entertainment. The innumerable neighborhood *comparsas* followed different itineraries and converged on the galleries where the jury was seated, on the Malecón, the great seaside promenade. After the political campaign of 1969–1970 calling for a drastic increase in sugar cane output and the economic reorganization that followed the campaign's failure, the carnival was moved to the month of July to coincide with the national holidays of the new regime and to avoid wasting work hours. The festive pageants, accompanied by spontaneous crowds of fans, were restricted to the defined carnival area. The holiday celebrations in specially delineated outdoor dance spaces were animated by the performances of popular bands. Canceled for financial reasons in the early 1990s, the carnivals resurfaced in 1996 in debased caricature form as spectacles for tourists. Thanks to tourism and the dollar, they were returned to the original Christian calendar date and the former itinerary on the Paseo del Prado.

## Carnivals of the Eastern Region

As Cubans themselves have often stated, the only real carnivals are those of the eastern regions, especially those of Santiago de Cuba, which the oldest participants continue to call by their former name: *fiesta de mamarrachos* or *de máscaras*. These have always taken place during three days around the holiday of Saint James (July 24, 25, and 26) and have stretched until the holidays of Saint John (June 24) and of Saint Peter (June 29).

Three types of orchestras emerged for the carnival: the *comparsa* with its *conga*,* the *conga* alone, and the *paseo*. Of more recent vintage, the *paseos* are similar in their instrumentation to the *comparsas* of Havana, but their thematic content is rarely traditional; rather, they perform the biggest popular hits of the year, with a choreography adapted for the purpose. As for the *comparsas*, they are distinguished from those of Havana by specific musical influences that are reflected in the instrumentation and practices of the *conga*.

The *conga* is the musical formation that, on the night of the

The celebration of Diá de Reyes.
Illustrated by Patricio Landaluze, circa late 1870s

official July march, accompanies the *comparsa* of its neighborhood. However, from the June holidays on, the *congas* travel
alone through the city streets and wherever they go, crowds
form around them without any particular costume distinction. The rhythm that impels the followers' march is more sustained, more syncopated, with rhythmic figures of drums and
metallic percussion instruments different from those of the
western *comparsas*. The refrains, which are repeated by a chorus, comment on current events. The crowd moves to it with
a characteristic ungainly step, saving its energy by dragging its
feet on the ground somewhat, for the ordeal is harsh, in mid-
afternoon, when people climb and descend along the coast
under the blazing sun. In Santiago this is called *arrollar, venir
arrollando.*

Another tradition of the Santiago carnival underscores that the popular verdict and massive participation are at least as important as the jury's decision. This tradition is *la invasión*, a kind of ritual visit paid by the city's best-known formation to those of other neighborhoods. Formerly, the course was considerably longer than it is today, when the course, along with the date, is imposed by the authorities. Nevertheless, tradition demands that the *conga* of Los Hoyos visit at least Alto Pino, El Guayabito, San Agustín, and Paso Franco, four of the best-known neighborhoods. People greet each other, but they also measure each other up musically. The best *conga* is the one that, through the force of its music and songs alone, succeeds in assembling behind it the crowd that was following its competitors.

The instrument that primarily identifies the eastern carnival is the *corneta china*,* which originated in Canton (Millet, Brea, and Ruiz Vila, 1997). This tiny wind instrument, with an extremely sharp tonality and a nasal timbre, was introduced during the Chinese immigration of the second half of the nineteenth century—the Chinese immigrants became a quasi-enslaved workforce employed in the sugar refineries to make up for the ban on black slavery. From Havana and Matanzas, the instrument is said to have traveled the island with soldiers (Millet and Brea, 1989, p. 45) and with the migrant workers following the harvests. Sources agree that the first *corneta* appears in Santiago in 1915 with the *comparsa* Los Colombianos, which represented the Tivolí neighborhood; the following year, the rival neighborhood of Los Hoyos also included it in its *conga*. Ever since, it has remained the symbol of eastern carnivals, though, strangely enough, it was not adopted in the western region from where it came. This instrument carries the melody and launches *conga* and *comparsa*. The art

of the *corneta* is extremely difficult. Although the instrument
has only five basic notes, the skilled performer, through complex techniques transmitted from one generation to the next,
can turn it into a true solo instrument.

The metallic percussion instruments also have their regional originality. Under the generic term *campana** or *llanta* are
designated the drums made from very heavy, round truck
brakes that are beaten with a metal rod; these are even more
sonorous than the tire rims of tractors or trucks.

These drums also are distinguished from those of Havana.
The most numerous ones, the *bocúes,** are rather high, narrow,
and slightly stumpy. They include the *fondo*, which is superior
to the others in proportion, the *requinto*, which responds to it,
and the *quinto*, which is very emblematic and somewhat higher pitched. The drums play continuously, without any break
whatsoever in the sound. Beside these, three large drums closer to those of Havana, but tuned differently, function as a trio,
whatever their number. These are the two *galletas** (an allusion
to their narrow shape), which accompany the regular rhythm
set by the *pilón*. The last percussion instrument, which is indispensable to the *conga* of Santiago, is the *tambora;** this drum
was borrowed from the immigrants of the French colony of
Santo Domingo who flocked to this region between 1791 and
1804. The "French" influence, furthermore, is very important
in understanding the special characteristics of the eastern
region.

### The "French" Immigration

In Cuba, the term "French" is synonymous with white slave
masters, whether French people from France or Creoles, as
well as their slaves, most were native to the Gulf of Benin and
predominantly Fon and Bantu. They fled the revolution in

Santo Domingo and their arrival in large numbers, at the beginning of the nineteenth century, in Santiago de Cuba, Baracoa, and Guantánamo, radically modified the economic and cultural landscape of that region.

The colonists brought with them their knowledge of agricultural and agro-industrial techniques, which brought prosperity in a few years to the coffee plantations in the mountains surrounding Santiago. They developed orchards, cotton plantations, and indigo production, injecting a new vitality into the sugar cane plantations. They also continued the clandestine recruiting of other Haitian slaves (Chatelain, 1996, no. 45, p. 40), renewing thereby a cultural base very different from that of Cuba. In their magnificent residences, the colonists indulged in refinements previously unknown on the island, in forms of music and dance seldom performed until then by the local bourgeoisie: the minuet, the rigadoon, the gavotte, the passepied, and, especially, the quadrille.

In Santiago, the masters and their servants, freedmen and slaves alike, settled in the Tivolí district. Forming mutual aid and cultural organizations along the lines of the *cabildos de nación*, the "French Negroes" organized themselves into associations of *tumba francesa*.* With the Ten Years' War (1868–1878), which erupted in the eastern region, Céspedes and other large landowners freed their slaves, many of whom joined the armed struggle of the rebel Mambis. Most of the coffee plantations were burned down, the social structure disintegrated, and a large number of slaves freed de facto settled in the suburban areas of Santiago, making up the "French" population of the future district of Los Hoyos, where they mixed with the black Cuban population while retaining their own traditions.

Collection of Tumba Francesa instruments at the Carnival Museum in
Santiago de Cuba. Courtesy of Judith Bettelheim.

## The *Tumba Francesa*

First performed on the plantations, the *tumba francesa* festivals were later reconstituted into organizations of the same
name; beginning in 1887, they were transformed, like the
*cabildos*, into associations. The organizations multiplied and,
at the beginning of the twentieth century, there were about
thirty of them between Santiago and Guantánamo. Today,
only one such organization remains in each city. Guantánamo's is part of the tourist circuit and thus benefits from some
support. Santiago's, the most authentic, is also the most en-
dangered. Very much a part of the district of Los Hoyos, but
prey, like so many others, to the penury of the "special period," it no longer has the economic means to meet the needs
required by the art it seeks to perpetuate—for example, in providing costumes. Its "queen," Gaudiosa Yoya Venet Danger,

who died in 1997, was the heiress of a very long tradition: Her grandfather had been born a slave and fought in the army of General Maceo; her a mother, herself a "queen," was an expert in all the arts of the *tumba francesa* (*Géo*, no. 213).

The dances of the *tumba francesa* carry on the choreography of the eighteenth-century dances that were performed in the salons of the aristocracy and the bourgeoisie in the colony of Santo Domingo. However, the slaves performed them in their own manner, with their songs in Creole and their specific instruments, drums, *catá*,* and *chachá*. The festival opens with the song of the *composé*—a man or woman, who is the soloist and improviser; the chorus, generally made up of women, answers in alternation; the *composé* calls the *catá*, who sets the basic rhythm; then the drums begin to play. *Tumba* is the generic name of the festival, which is accompanied by three large drums with a single drumhead. The drums are played with the naked hand by the *tambouyés*: the *bulá** maintains a fixed rhythm while varying the sounds; the *segón** supports the rhythms,* and the *premier** (the first one), somewhat larger and lower pitched, is charged with the performance of the rhythmic variations and improvisations. Despite its name, the *premier* comes in last. The entire polyrhythm is organized around the playing of the *catá*, which is a drum of Bantu origin, made from a hollowed-out tree trunk, and which is struck with sticks. As for the *tambora*, used exclusively to accompany the *masón*,* it is smaller and double-headed; one side is struck with a skin-covered stick, while the other hand modifies the sounds by applying pressure on the other side. The polyrhythm is completed by the *chachá*, metallic shakers that are decorated with ribbons and shaken by the chorus.

The choreography is directed by a dance master, who may be male, *el mayor*, or female, *la mayora de plaza*. The dance master regulates the unfolding of the dances with the aid of a whistle, choosing the dancers—whether couples or soloists—as in the days of court dances. Two types of dances, each including several choreographed dances and percussion styles, survive today in Santiago: the *masón* and the *yubá*. The *masón* include the dances that allude to those of the masters—*carabiné*, *minué*, and rigadoon, or dance with ribbons braided around a central mast. The *yubá* is an older dance. It closes with a segment called *fronté*, where the *bulá* and *premier* drums are placed on the ground, and the drummer modifies the sounds by pressing against the drumhead with his foot while he beats it with his bare hand. As the rhythm grows faster, a dancer, who stands alone facing the drum, engages with the drummer in a sort of mutual challenge: The drum follows in its improvisations the dancer's steps, but with patterns that accentuate the rhythmic complexity and to which the dancer responds in turn—a situation that evokes other dances performed in the Caribbean, as well as a pattern of the rumba, the *columbia*.*

### *Tahona* and *Cocoyé**

Frequent marriages of descendants of French black people with Cubans facilitated exchanges between different traditions. The *tumba francesa* festivals retain the distinct character of salon parties and remain the prerogative of societies of the same name. But the "French" also join in the Saints' Day festivities of Santiago by putting together their own carnival groups (*tahona* or *tajona*) with often satirical songs and drums that play a marching rhythm, as well as a faster rhythm, which is also called *tajona*. The term thus designates the instrumental group, the dances, and a rhythm. As in all music from Santo Domingo, the rhythmic pattern of the *cinquillo** is fundamental. One of the *comparsas* of the district of Tivolí performed the famous tune of the *cocoyé* on that fateful day in 1836 when a Catalan musician heard it, transcribed it for a military brass band, and introduced it in Havana. In 1947, the *comparsa* of Los Hoyos symbolized how much it owed to this tradition by taking the name of Los Hijos del Cocoyé.

## The Main *Comparsas* of Santiago

When the oldest informants talk about *comparsas*, they always cite the *comparsa* of Tivolí, which was the great rival of Los Hoyos until 1938, when it split up to become Paso Franco, the *comparsa* of San Agustín, El Guayabito, Alto Pino, and San Pedrito, without forgetting the two *carabalí* groups already mentioned.

The Tivolí, cradle of the *cocoyé*, also originated a song later performed by any number of Cuban orchestras, *A la loma de Belén*, which evokes the work of those who manufacture and repair the indispensable water tubs. The *comparsa* of San Agustín always distinguished itself by imaginativeness in the creation of its costumes and its great capes decorated with colorful motifs and spangles. The *comparsa* of Los Hoyos, unanimously respected, has never known an interruption of its collective tradition, and it is sometimes nicknamed El Piano for the rhythmic and melodic richness of its *conga*. It is proud to have counted among its members one of the few female *campana* percussionists, Gladys Linares. Directed until his death in 1999 by Sebastián "Chan" Herrera, the *comparsa* of Los Hoyos is the veritable memory of the city. It plays an essential role in the oral transmission of this entire popular knowledge, which ranges from the manufacture and beating of drums to the creation of costumes and the constitution of a repertoire of songs.

# III

# The Rumba

The rumba is a strictly secular music that originated in the regions of Matanzas and Havana among "Negroes and persons of low condition." The crisis of the slave system and economic upheavals drove these people from the plantations and agricultural exploitation to the cities, where they swelled the ranks of freedmen and former urban slaves in neighborhoods "outside the walls" (Le Riverend, 1960, pp. 317–320). They lived in the *solares** which are buildings subdivided into crowded habitations around a spacious central courtyard. Here most domestic activities take place. This way of collective living is frequently rife with conflict. Some historians consider such living conditions barely better than those of the slaves in the *barracones** on plantations.

## An Afro-Cuban Expression

The courtyard of the *solar*, the port district, the bars, and the sidewalks of red-light districts were the locations where the rumba developed. Its three variants—the *yambú,** the *colum-bia*, and the *guaguancó*—reflect the urban as well as rural origins of the population from which hailed the musicians, singers, and dancers of the rumba. Beyond their differences, these styles present common characteristics. Musicologists and direct informants note a relationship with the non-religious manifestations of the Congo-Bantu system of worship where *yuka* drums are used. But the rumba underwent a transculturation demonstrated in the relationship in the structures of sound and rhythm. Whereas, in ritual music, the rhythmic improvisation is performed, as in Africa, on the low-pitched drums, in the rumba (as in the *comparsas* orchestras) the inverse is true. Due to European influence, the highest-pitched percussion instruments speak and play the virtuoso part. Nevertheless, the improvising drum always remains in the center, as in ritual music. By the same token, song remains fundamentally modal, with a responsive pattern (alternating soloist and chorus), but the improvisation of lyrics is done in quatrains or in octosyllabic ten-line verses—a Spanish legacy Africanized in the Cuban crucible.

## Instrumentation

The rumba remains so lively in Cuba largely because any pretext will serve to improvise a song, and not even a drum is needed to start a party. Any domestic object will do the trick: a table, a drawer, a leather-seated stool, spoons striking a bottle or a wooden surface—in short, anything that will allow communication through its world of sound. The rumba is the quintessential "street school," where a good many drummers and singers of note admit they received their education.

## Rumba de cajón*

The first "codified" percussion instruments were large wooden crates of varying shapes, known by the generic name of *cajón*. The musicians generally preferred the crates used for shipping codfish and, for the smallest instruments, the crates for packing candles. The wooden parts would be cut out and polished to improve their resonance; then they were rejoined with nails or glue (Ortiz, III, 1952, p. 152). Later, *cajones* were made for a specifically musical usage, in different sizes, whose forms might vary but generally go in sets of three according to the established arrangement of their rhythmic and sound relationship. In fact, this arrangement is the only criterion that permits a classification of these instruments, especially since the names given to them by musicians, according to their use, often vary.

The stable rhythmic pattern is established by the *tumbador* (or *salidor*), the largest of the *cajones*, which the musician plays seated. The instrument is beaten according to different styles (including with a closed fist) on the sides or on one side and on the front, with one hand playing in counterpoint to the other. The small *cajón*, also called *repicador*,* is used for improvising. The musician holds it in place by squeezing it between the knees. The last *cajón*, of a middle register, is called *tres-dos*,* or *tres golpes*\*; it is linked rhythmically to the *tumbador*.

To accompany these drums, the *rumberos* use the *guagua*,* a piece of hollowed-out tree trunk that is beaten with sticks in a sustained, forceful rhythm; sometimes these are replaced by a thick bamboo cane. Finally, there are the *claves*,* which mark the 2/4 or 4/4 time. These are two pieces of hardwood that are struck against each other, while forming a sound box with the hand; the pitch depends on where one of the *claves* strikes the other. They were originally made from the large dowels used for assembling the parts of boats under construction (Ortiz, 1935). The *claves* set the basic, unchanging rhythmic pattern, a true "key" around which most of this type of popular music is organized.

### Evolution Toward the *Tumbadoras*

Since the beginning of the twentieth century, the instruments have evolved, and calfskin drums have generally replaced the *cajones*. These *tumbadoras* were once made of wooden casks, which explains their slightly bulging shape, and the drumheads were nailed and tuned by means of heat—a mark of non-sacred drums. Today the *tumbadoras* are stretched by means of a system of keys.

The *tumbador* is the opening drum. The largest and lowest-pitched of the drums, it guides the band marking a sustained rhythm: "Without it we can do nothing, and it must be beaten in a special way, in the middle, like the *bombo* of the *comparsas*, for it to resonate as it ought to," says M.A. "Aspirina," a member of a great family of *rumberos* from Guanabacoa (interview, 1996). The *tres golpes* has a medium tone. It is the "slave" of the preceding drum to which it responds, always within the limits of a steady rhythm. The *quinto* is the drum that improvises; it gives all the variations and the most complicated rhythmic motifs while playing a melodic role in the higher register. Said to require great skill, the *quinto* engages in dialogue, not only with the other drums, but also with the solo singers and the chorus, without leaving any gaps in the orchestral sound. The instrumental group is completed by the *guagua* and, of course, the *claves*, according to the above description.

## The Styles of the Rumba

*La columbia*
*Oigo una voz que me llama*
*Arenilleo*
*Siento una voz que me dice*
*Malanga murió.*
*Unión de Reyes llora*
*A su timbero mayor,*
*Que se fue regando flores*
*Desde Matanzas a Morón . .*

The *columbia*
I hear a voice calling me
Arenilleo
I feel a voice telling me
Malanga is dead.
Unión de Reyes weeps
for his greatest *timbero*,
who has left, scattering flowers
from Matanzas to Morón . . .

This refrain, now a classic of Afro-Cuban music, immortalizes one of the legendary figures of the *columbia*, José Rosario "Malanga" Oviedo. Born in 1885 on a *finca* (a working farm) of the Alacranes region, he grew up in Unión de Reyes. Leading a nomadic life as a worker following the sugar-cane harvests, he disappeared mysteriously in the area of Morón in 1923 (Orovio, 1994, p. 145). The province of Matanzas, its sugar cane industry in full expansion in the nineteenth century and its small working farms devoted to local agriculture, was the cradle of this variation of the rumba in the period before

Rumbero, Cuba 1999

the abolition of slavery. Unión de Reyes, Alacranes, Sabanilla, Jovellanos, all hail from this rural world. The history of the passage of the *columbia* from the countryside to the city of Matanzas is also the history of the building of the railroad, which linked plantations, sugar refineries, and the ports shipping cargoes of sugar for export. The oldest *rumberos* of Matanzas recall that the *columbia,* considered the oldest element of the rumba, was born in a hamlet near Sabanilla.

The drums begin their dialogue to a very rapid tempo. Then the solo singer, often called *El Gallo* (The Rooster), which in proper Cuban parlance is synonymous with power and quality, chants an introduction, the *diana,** a series of meaningless syllables, used for rhythmic and expressive purposes, which are often compared to the sounds of the Andalusian *cante jondo*. Then he presents the theme of his song and begins the improvisation, with the chorus intervening in alternation during the refrain. This arrangement of the song is common to all three variants of the rumba, but it can vary according to region and the particular style of the solo singer.

The *columbia* nevertheless has certain distinguishing features. Its tempo is very rapid in Havana, slower in Matanzas. The speed shortens the *diana* to a point of sometimes giving the impression that it is missing altogether. But it is in the improvisation and in the soloist-chorus structure that the differences are most marked. The closeness to slavery and the rural origin of the genre are expressed, to this day, by the use of words, of fragments of sentences, and even entire sentences "in tongue," mixed with Spanish. These elements function as a code of recognition, linked directly to the lives of those who developed it. They also allow the soloist to complete the rhymes and assonances of the verses, for the singers improvise their songs in quatrains or in octosyllabic ten-line verses (*décimas**). The descendants of slaves appropriated this poetic form, which came from Spain and plays a dominant role in the *punto guajiro,** but they made it subject to contractions, expansions, and displacements characteristic of African sung poetry, which nonetheless were adjusted to the rhythms (Ortiz, 1981, pp. 205–207). Among the *columbia* singers, we also find the song with a descending structure observed in rituals, ending on the low register, and closer to the pentatonic scale than to the European tonality. It is also called *llanto*, that is to say a plaint, a lamentation, perhaps a reminiscence of Andalusia. The chorus often punctuates the soloist's song, beginning with the *diana* and the exposition. It briefly supports the end of a line and then provides a systematic alternating intervention by repeating a brief structure of two sequences.

The songs' themes evoke characters or situations, in a descriptive or satirical manner, with very fragmented sequences. Miguel Angel Aspirina, a stockyard worker and a prodigious improviser, recounted in 1996 an anecdote that illumines the atmosphere of the period:

Near where I lived, there was a *solar* where Macho
Jamaiquino lived—we called him that because his family had come from Jamaica—and when he took a drum,
we had to call him *maestro*. He was a celebrity of the
*comparsas*. On the *quinto* he was a phenomenon.
Throughout the week, they played the rumba in his
hovel in the *solar*. Me, I listened to him, and I learned.
I always preferred the *columbia* to the *guaguancó*. At his
place, *rumberos* from Havana's forty-three districts used
to gather. I was twelve years old. I would take the
"spoons," they would give me a bench so I wouldn't
get tired, and I sweated from playing for hours. One
day, one of the great *rumberos* from my neighborhood,
Diego Longina, who was the leader of the *comparsa* Los
Moros Azules of Regla, had a musical battle, as in the
*punto guajiro*, with another singer who was called El
Congo—he, too, was an old man, with a shaven head—
about the famous sacred big tree, the *ceiba* [kapok tree]
that one can still see in the Park of Fraternity, in Havana, and it went on for hours: when was it planted,
under which government, who was president, was the
earth that of seven nations? And each time he ended a
*décima*, he would say to Diego: *"Rabo de mono amarra a
Ramón."* I didn't understand what that meant, but
Diego never answered that line, and they went on and
on, and I was sweating from beating on my bench with
the spoons. At one point I had an inspiration, I got up
and said: *"Si rabo de mono amarra a Ramón, porque rabo
de mono no me amarra a mí."* And then I sat down full
of shame, because at twelve years of age one can't allow
oneself to interrupt like that. So El Congo stopped the
drums and asked me: "Where did you get that from?"
Me: "I don't know." "You don't know what you're saying?" And he gave me a peseta. Years later, Diego, who
was a *palero*, a *santero*, and an Abakuá, explained to me
that it was a *managua*, a formula used in the rumba as
in the *palo*, a kind of forced rest. And he said to me:

"Me, I didn't find the answer, and you, without know-
ing, you managed to finish."

The most impressive aspect of the *columbia* doubtlessly is
the dance, performed by a solo male dancer. He first salutes
the *quinto* drum, then breaks into the dance by moving according to various kinds of complex choreography. Many of
these include acrobatic movements in which the feet, the
shoulders, and the arms have a particular importance, in a
kind of rhythmic joust with the *quinto*, which he challenges
and which challenges him, one of them having to emerge the
victor in this duel. When a dancer has finished, he invites,
with an imperious gesture, another dancer to take his place in
the symbolic circle and to have his turn at demonstrating his
art, because it is also a duel among dancers. The most accom-
plished dancers perform very old dances balancing a glass of
water or a candle on their head. Sometimes they perform the
"dance of knives" or that of machetes, which requires great
skill. In this group of dances, we also find reminiscences of certain Congo dances and the abrupt, leaping movements of the
Abakuá *íreme*. We also find resemblances to the musical "battle" with the *premier* drum of the *fronté* of the *tumba francesa*,
since the region of Matanzas had experienced a "French"
immigration, if not as massive, from Santo Domingo in the
early nineteenth century, as well as from Louisiana. All these
influences came together during the development of the
*columbia* in an urban environment in the districts of Matanzas, Cárdenas, Havana, Regla, and Guanabacoa.

Popular recollection retains the memory of women, such as
the legendary Maria La O or Andréa Baró, who were famous
*columbia* dancers in its original rural phase. However, once it
had moved into an urban environment, this dance was per-

formed only by men. A complete list of dancers and singers would be too long, but we can cite two legendary figures, "Malanga," the supremely illustrious dancer discussed above, and the famous Papa Montero, legendary singer of Sagua la Grande.

### The *Yambú*

The *yambú* and the *columbia* are the oldest styles of rumba; the origin of the *yambú* is clearly urban. It is danced by couples, to a rather slow but measured tempo, "with an elegant sensuality," in the words of all informants. It is indeed a dance of seduction, but without any violent gesture of possession (*vacunao**), as is indicated in the *guaguancó*: "*En el yambú no se vacuna,*" according to the oft-repeated refrain. "Its first meaning," a musician from Matanzas told me, "is a sweet seduction where the woman has the essential role, and her partner pays homage to her grace. At the end he places his hands on the dancer's shoulders, like a true partner, to lead her back to the circle of spectators." One can think that the *yambú*, in its elegant and poised gestures, with its contained sensuality, preserved from the outset something of the stylized aspect of salon dances. There is another variant of the same rather slow tempo in the *rumba de tiempo España*, whose name directly suggests the colonial period. In this dance, the dancers mime situations of domestic life: *Lala no sabe hacer nada*, for example, is a pantomime of a woman who can do nothing—cannot do laundry, cannot iron clothes, and so on—while *Mama'buela* tells the story of the relationship between a disobedient child and an old woman who pursues and scolds him.

The *yambú* repertoire was played by bands, such as the Conjunto Folklórico Nacional of Havana, but excellent rumba bands, such as Los Muñequitos of Matanzas, and, in Havana,

Yoruba Andabo or Clave y Guaguancó, continue to create *yambú* dances. The *yambú* repertoire also remains a source of inspiration for dance orchestras that certain classics of the genre in their own arrangements, such as Elio Revé with, for example, *María Belén*, as well as the untarnishable *Ave María morena*, which in fact is titled *Yambú pa'los maribá*.

In the musical tradition, the *yambú* is played with only two *cajones*, *tumbador*, and *quinto*. It is the only rumba style in which the duple time set by the *claves* is played in the "3-2 direction," that is, the measure with three notes precedes the measure with two notes: |♩ ♪♩ ♩ |♩ ♩ ♩ | Here is no borrowing from African languages. The *diana* presents the melody, followed the exposition of the theme (often romantic) and the dialogue with the chorus, after which the dancers make their entry. Often the soloist punctuates the end of a verse by repeating some sounds, and certain sequences have become standard in time, for example, the variations on the syllables *Eh!/aé/eá*, or the phrase *Que bueno, que bueno, é*.

### The *Guaguancó*

The last-born of the rumba styles, the *guaguancó* appeared in the first decade of the twentieth century, also in the provinces of Matanzas and Havana. It too has a clearly urban character, combining elements of the legacy of the two other variants. It is by far the most frequently performed and the most popular of the *rumbero* cycle.

The tempo of the *guaguancó* is livelier than that of the *yambú*, and its modern evolution tends to accelerate it even more. The basic rhythm is set by the *claves*, but in 2-3 direction, the measure with two notes is first: |♩ ♩ ♩ |♩ ♪♩ ♩ | The three *tumbadoras* cover the same rhythmic and melodic functions as those described above. The musicians' art resides not only in their talent for improvising on the *quinto*, but also in their ability to vary the types of beating action to multiply the sounds. Moreover, every other timbre that enhances the sound registers is welcome—for example, metallic disks attached to the wrists of the player of the *quinto, shekeré*, maracas, and so on.

Here, too, the song opens with the *diana*. The theme may be presented with two voices, generally in thirds. The chorus also is characterized by polyphony: The first voice gives the tone; the second voice, lower-pitched, is placed at the bottom of the triad; the third voice is the highest pitched. Traditionally, the soloist improvises in ten-line stanzas (*décima*) or in quatrains (*cuarteta**), or else in free prose that always has rhythm and assonance.

The choreography, performed by a couple, is a highly erotic pantomime, where the man pursues the woman; in the *guaguancó*, the pursuit of the woman imitates not merely a seduction from afar, as in the *yambú*, but rather an act of complete sexual possession. The symbolic gesture of possession is the famous *vacunao*, which the man can bring forth at any moment and with any part of his body by miming penetration, while the woman dodges by covering her private parts and turning away slightly. Then she begins the dance of seduction, where feet and hips mark a different movement responding to the drumbeats, while her shoulders follow the *clave.** The movements are rapid, and the number of steps are virtually infinite, like an erotic game between partners, depending on the creativity of the dancers. If the woman lets herself be caught, the dance is interrupted and another couple comes on stage. If not, the man must admit defeat.

The thematic range of the songs is vaster even than that of the other variants. The practice of the *guaguancó* never abated;

it constitutes a kind of sung oral tradition that is anchored in the urban neighborhood and comments on aspects of society—big and small events, human relations—through which a popular memory has slowly developed. In this regard, Leonardo Acosta speaks of "the social chronicle of the dispossessed, the humble, the marginal" (Acosta, 1983, p. 54).

Only the *guaguancós* whose authorship has been identified have been codified and preserved, and these are far outnumbered by those in the collective and anonymous mass. One of the legendary figures associated with the *guaguancó* is the famous "Tio Tom," also known by his real name, Gonzalo Asencio Hernández, "the king of the *guaguancó*." He was born in 1919 in the district of Cayo Hueso (Acosta, 1983). Not only a composer, he was also a singer, dancer, and drummer. Like most of the musicians discussed in this book, he did all sorts of odd jobs, working as a shoeshine boy, newspaper vendor, construction worker, day laborer, and so on. His compositions have often been orchestrated in Cuba as well as beyond the island: *Changó ta'vení*, inspired by a religious feeling; *Consuelate como yo*, with its refrain *Por eso ahora, ya yo no vuelvo a querer* (This is why I shall never love again); *Siento que me regaña el corazón*, with its refrain, *Si tu me lo das, porqué me lo quitas* (Why do you take back what you gave me), inspired by unrequited love; *A la fiesta de los caramelos no pueden ir los bombones*, which ironically stigmatizes the prevalent racism, and many others as well. Mention must also be made of Chano Pozo, famous for having introduced Cuban percussion into American jazz, and author, among other pieces, of the famous *Blem blem blem*, and the four Abreu brothers, "Los Papines," must also be noted. But the majority of drum masters who are still alive today are known only in the rumba world (Angel Pelladito, Esteban "Chachá" Vega of Matanzas, Pancho Quinto, Mario "Aspirina" Jauregui of Guanabacoa). The same applies to the voices: Agustín "Flor de amor" Pina, Mario "Chabalonga" Dreke, Miguel Angel Aspirina, Calixto Callava, Amelia Pedroso, and Ines María Carbonell. The tradition continues with Los Muñequitos of Matanzas (since 1952, with the voices, in those days, of "Virulilla" and "Saldiguera"), in addition to Yoruba Andabo, Los Columbianos of Cárdenas, Clave y Guaguancó, and many others.

## Coros de Clave*

The polyphonic wealth of the *guaguancó* owes a great deal to its amateur groups, the *coros de clave.** During the nineteenth century, they roamed the streets singing *a cappella* during Christmas holidays and patron saints' days. Their repertoire included songs inspired by the lyric tradition of choral singing societies, a tradition that is highly developed in Cuba. With the urban expansion, they multiplied in the new neighborhoods and began to create and also perform in ten-line stanzas an entire repertoire of rumbas and specifically *guaguancós*. They accompanied themselves on the *claves*, with clapping, and with a small, portable instrument called a *viola*. This is a type of small tambourine (*pandero*) with a single membrane but without metallic disks; the membrane is mounted on two rather long handles, which are decorated with ribbons of the group's colors. Often the *viola* is made from a banjo whose strings have been removed.

It is in these groups that Ignacio Piñeiro, a native of the district of Jesús María and the future founder of the Septeto Nacional, had his first musical experiences. An improviser in the *coro de clave* El Timbre de Oro, he became the leader of the celebrated band Los Roncos, whose rivalry with Paso Franco is the theme of a number of *guaguancós* of the early twentieth century. Several of his compositions—*Sobre una tumba, una rumba, Papá Ogún, Donde estabas anoche*—were to become part of the national repertoire of Cuba, and part of the international repertoire as well.

The importance of the *coros de clave* derives primarily from the vocal polyphony and the manner in which the lines of the lyrics unfold. Female voices, especially sopranos, who are often chosen as soloists (*clarina*), played an important part in the further development of the *guaguancó*. These bands disappeared after 1940, but their repertoire continues in musical theater and in song.

Since its initial appearance, the rumba has spread across the whole island. The orchestras have caught on to it, and together with the *son*, the *guaguancó* has become the rhythm that has left its most distinct mark on contemporary Cuban music. This musical genre displays certain essential features of Afro-Cuban music: a world where percussion is at once rhythm and melody; where song, instrument, and dance are in constant dialogue and interaction; where individual improvisation is an integral part of the performance. Next to the *son*, the rumba expresses most profoundly the cross-fertilization of people and cultures—the richness and the flavor of Cuban-ness (*cubanidad*). Through the artistry and inspiration of the drummers and singers, each piece becomes a unique experience, expressing emotion and pleasure. Some rumba songs are as poignant as a bolero.

# IV

# Punto and Tonadas of the Rural Regions

*Punto guajiro* and *música campesina* are often conflated. However, the *punto* is only one of numerous musical expressions encountered in the Cuban countryside. It is performed in the western area and the center of the island; the farther east one goes, the less it is present.

The *punto guajiro* was one of the first native musical forms originating in the late eighteenth century. It also preserved the most markedly Spanish characteristics. In 1836, the musical dictionary of Esteban Pichardo distinguished the *punto*, which designates the instrumental accompaniment, from the *¡Ay!* or *El ¡Ay!*, also called *llanto*, which defines singing. Alongside the entry for this non-dance genre, the dictionary also notes the existence of dances such as the *zapateo*,* with a specific musical accompaniment (Pichardo, 1875, 1985). The *zapateo* was performed less and less frequently in the twentieth century, while the *punto* continued to develop by acquiring styles that were distinctive from region to region.

## Social Function of the *Punto*

The *punto* was originally rooted in the tobacco plantations of western Cuba, where immigrants from the Canary Islands predominated. It then followed the expansion of the tobacco industry toward the center of the island. The dispersed habitat and the lack of communication with the exterior reinforced the importance of the *guateques*,* spontaneous celebrations between neighbors, or during particular celebrations, such as anniversaries, marriages, and baptisms. These collective festivities gradually established the essential characteristics of the two great musical styles of the *punto guajiro*, with their instrumentation, their melodies, and the *tonadas*,* their particular songs.

## Origins and General Characteristics of the *Punto*

The experts agree that the two most recognizable influences on these musical forms of the Cuban countryside come from Andalusia and the Canary Islands, two of the most constant sources of immigration throughout the colonial period. The *guajiro* was originally the white peasant who had come from Spain in search of land. But the population of the Cuban countryside is not exclusively "white." Though black people and mulattos are minority groups outside the plantations, they are nonetheless present. The Hispanic antecedents may well be more marked in the *punto* than in other Cuban musical genres, but this is also a musical form that has been re-created and transculturated in Cuba, a music that has evolved over the centuries. In her two studies devoted to rural music, María Teresa Linares (1957 and 1972) points out a kinship with Andalusian genres such as the *bulería* and the *seguidilla*, certain modes predating the major and minor keys, and the use of high-pitched and nasal tonalities that she relates to popular songs of the Canary Islands. But she also emphasizes that it is impossible to identify precisely the totality of influences present in this repertoire, since settlers from each Spanish province brought with them a musical heritage that then was assimilated into Cuban music. The predominance of Hispanic roots is marked nonetheless by the fact that, contrary to the majority of Cuban music, the *punto* has retained a compound beat.

## The Instruments

From the beginning, the Spaniards brought with them a series of string instruments; some of them remain characteristic of the *punto* accompaniment. Certain songs today sometimes evoke instruments that have disappeared, such as the harp, *vihuela*, *bandurria* (mandola, an ancestor of the mandolin), or *tiple*, besides those that are used today—such as the lute, the guitar, and the *tres*.*

Probably introduced into Spain by the Arab conquerors, the lute underwent multiple transformations in Cuba. The most common of these includes the use of a pear-shaped sound box, and twelve strings, tuned in pairs that are played with a plectrum. The lute is used as a solo instrument or for accompaniment. The guitar, with six strings, has a figure-eight-shaped sound box, with a small opening. The *tres*, which is derived from the Spanish guitar, is smaller in size and has three sets of double strings; this instrument is specifically Cuban and also is used to accompany other types of music, particularly the *son*, from the eastern to western regions of the island. To these string instruments are traditionally added the *claves*, the *güiro*,* and the maracas, which proves that the *punto* also underwent a "transculturation."

## Sung Poetry

The songs that these instruments accompany are an improvised form of poetry, composed according to the literary form of the *décima*, a stanza of ten octosyllabic lines. The *décima* was known in formal Spanish poetry as early as the fifteenth century; it was soon adopted in sung forms of popular poetry, as is shown in a number of collections of songs of the sixteenth and seventeenth centuries, along with quatrains of the popular *copla*. In Cuba, the *décima* shares similarities with the sung *décima* of the Andalusian repertoire. In the Andalusian version, there is a pause after the fourth line, which is indispensable to the singing and can be considered a combination of the two forms—the traditional *décima* and the quatrains of the *copla* (Orta Ruiz, 1980, pp. 28–37). The very name *repentista** (improviser) that is given to the singer is significant, because it puts the emphasis not on the quality of the voice, but on the ability to improvise creatively. Since there is no intervention from a chorus, the singer is essentially a versifier, charged with telling a story within a given literary form. Just as local family gatherings occur spontaneously, this Cuban tradition of sung poetry has developed among itinerant entertainers, who travel from community to community, improvising as a way of spontaneous commenting on news from other villages or from the cities.

## The *Controversia**

The tradition of the *controversia*, a sung argument—a dispute in verse around a given theme—continues today to constitute one of the high points of gatherings among neighbors from one locality or region. Two poet-singers confront each other, but the joust can take on various forms. On a given theme, the first singer performs the entire ten-line stanza; his adversary must then turn his opponent's last line into the first line of his own ten-line stanza and then develop a contrary idea. Often, too, the first singer delivers a first quatrain (*cuarteta*), and the opponent must then complete the next six lines; the rules require that the singers who follow each other impose rhyme as well as versification on their opponents. The public is the judge of these poetic jousts; here the art of improvisation, the spirit of appropriateness, and humor are the decisive factors in determining the winner—the one who will deserve, more than anyone else, his title of poet. Tradition has preserved for us the memory of a prominent *repentista* from the region of Sagua and Camajuan, in the center of the island: Juan R. Delgado Limindoux, *"El Negro cantor"* (the black singer), capable of holding his own against his adversaries for a whole night (Orta Ruiz, 1980). He had learned to read and, using knowledge found in almanacs, filled his verse with references to Genesis, the Milky Way, the Greek gods, and legends from around the world.

The most common themes of these sung arguments are those that are opposites at the outset: men and women; bachelors and married men; love and money; the beauty of women, according to their skin color; the argument between trees charged with symbols, such as the palm tree and the kapok tree. Whether or not it fits into the framework of a dispute, the thematic content of rural forms of music is indeed vast: commentary on events, criticism of social and living conditions, satire on the physical or moral shortcomings of characters known in the immediate vicinity or incarnating certain stereotypes, but also the more universal themes of love, other feelings, the divine, natural scenery, the universe, destiny, eternity.

## The *Punto Guajiro* and Its Regional Variants

Here is how one can summarize the general features of the *punto guajiro*: First there is a musical introduction, which is usually played on the lute, backed up by the *tres*, with the guitar playing fixed rhythmic patterns. Then the singer introduces a theme in four lines. Next comes a musical interlude, which is dominated by the lute's melodic variations and accompanied by the percussion instruments and by two other string instruments. The *tres* fills in the gaps left by the guitar. Then the singer continues and concludes on the previous theme by improvising the six remaining lines in the stanza. Sometimes the first two repeat those of the first stanza and the improvisation once again focuses on a *cuarteta*, with a brief instrumental rest. The final stretch is reserved for the instruments, and the lute plays a free improvisation on the melody. Among the percussion instruments, the *clave* rhythmically accompanies the voice of the singer, with no fixed pattern. The melody (*tonada*) is generally in a major key, but all sorts of variations are possible.

Historically, two styles of *punto* developed, and they could be differentiated according to the relationship between the singing and the musical accompaniment. In the western provinces of Pinar del Río, Havana, Matanzas, and Cienfuegos, the *punto libre* dominated; in the more central regions of Camagüey and Las Villas, populated later and influenced by the Oriente province (in the eastern region), the *punto fijo* took hold. But with the development of radio broadcasts and the record industry, both these styles spread across Cuba, and today both can be heard, from the eastern to the western parts of the island.

### Punto Libre

In the western region, the melody (*tonada*) is not subject to a fixed tempo; the beat strictly follows the oratorical rhythm of the lyrics, which are delivered rather slowly by elongating the final cadences. This is the *punto libre*, also called the *punto pinareño* or *punto vueltabajero*, in a reference to the regions in question—Pinar del Río and Vuelta Abajo. The melodies of the *punto libre* are fluid, rather slow, and independent of the musical accompaniment. The instruments are used in the manner of a countermelody, emphasizing a passage with chords from the guitar or the *tres*; the lute follows the unexpected movements of the melodic line of the singing, by establishing a kind of dialogue with the soloist; the *claves* do not intervene. In the interludes, the instruments again take up a fixed 3/4 meter.

### Punto fijo

In the island's center, on the other hand, the singer intones his melody according to a fixed and constant beat, which explains the name *punto fijo*, also called *punto en clave* or *camagüeyano*. In *punto fijo*, melody and beat are invariable, the instrumental accompaniment is permanent, and the rhythm is set by the *claves*.

One of the variants of the *punto fijo*, the *punto cruzado*, is characterized by syncopated singing, while the accompaniment keeps stability reinforced by the percussion, in compound meter. The tension resulting from the rhythmic difference between voice and instruments precipitates frequent displacements of the beat of the prosody. This variant is played in 3/4, in 3/8, or in a 6/8 meter.

## Specificity of Certain Singing Modalities

Each style includes a great variety of melodies. Those *tonadas* that have remained in the repertoire independently of accompaniment are sometimes classified separately and they can even be performed *a cappella*. In the region of Sancti Spíritus, singing is in two voices, generally in thirds or sixths, and this *tonada spirituana*, influenced by the *coros de clave*, is most often performed according to the fixed rhythm of the *punto fijo*.

Within the free style are melodies in a minor key—the only ones in the entire *punto* genre—which are called *tonada carvajal* or *tonada española*, and which show traces of the Phrygian mode, as in certain songs of Andalusia and the Canary Islands (Alen Rodríguez, 1994).

Certain *tonadas* combine characteristics of both styles, like those that incorporate a refrain at the beginning, at the end, or in the middle of the ten-line stanza. Often, the singing begins in free style, then slides toward a fixed meter in 3/4, and the refrain is performed by the chorus according to the exact meter of the *punto fijo* (Eli, Gómez, 1989).

## The *Punto* Today

The orchestras that today accompany peasant celebrations borrowed some of their instruments from the *son* groups. In the western region, we find the lute and/or the *tres*, the guitar, the *claves*, the *güiro*, and also the maracas and the *tumbadora*. The *marímbula* joined in later (later replaced by the double bass), as well as the *bongó* and the *paila criolla*.* The lute has an essentially melodic function; it executes free rhythmic patterns, as does the *tres*, while the guitar has a harmonic function and plays fixed rhythmic patterns (Eli, Gómez, 1989). In the provinces of east-central Cuba, the high register of the lute has practically disappeared from the *punto fijo*, and the melodic function is provided by the *tres*, which the guitar reinforces harmonically; *claves*, *güiro*, maracas, *bongó*, and *tumbadora* are the most frequently used instruments, reinforced by the *marímbula* or the double bass.

## Radio and Record Production

The discography of Cuban music through 1925 established by Díaz Ayala reveals a significant number of *puntos guajiros* recorded by big U.S. companies such as Victor or Columbia, especially between 1908 and 1920. In the earliest recordings, the accompaniment is played on the *bandurria* or on the lute, then only the lute with guitar accompaniment. The names of singers that are repeated most often are those of Antonio Morejón, Martin Silveira, a *congo* native of Wajay, and Juan Pagés, nicknamed "El Cojo," composer of a famous melody baptized *guambán*, an onomatopoeia that concluded each line by imitating guitar chords (Linares, 1957, no. 17). As for the instrumentalists, their names almost never appear in the archives consulted.

Political and social themes occupy a large place. The most frequently cited themes are crises in tobacco production, the condition of female workers in factories, the extreme poverty of the small peasant, corruption, direct attacks against government abuses, and U.S. meddling. The tone, satirical or elegiac, is always violently contentious, and one can wonder how record companies broadcast these compositions. The market was doubtless lucrative, and, adds Díaz Ayala, the sound engineers did not understand Spanish! Furthermore, he cites a similar example concerning recordings in Cajun in New Orleans, where the only imperative was "no obscenities" (Díaz Ayala, 1994). Radio played an important role in the dissemination of the *punto* as of the mid-1920s, with broadcasts not only to large audiences in the country's interior but also in urban areas to which many unemployed peasants had emigrated. From the 1930s to the 1950s, it was radio that allowed the *punto* to keep a national audience, while the record industry turned toward dance music. Thus artists were able to improvise their *décimas* live.

## Since the Revolution

From the earliest years, there developed in Cuba an amateur movement that benefited from radio sound studios, from festivals organized on the island, such as the *Noches campesinas*, and from workshops that cultivated the *punto*, such as the *Talleres de la décima*. On television, the program *Palmas y Cañas* has featured not only well-known artists, but also regional talents, and some orchestras, such as Campo Alegre and Palmas y Cañas, were formed specifically to appear on the program. Among the best-known performers are Ramón Veloz, his companion Coralia Fernández, Luis Martínez ("Luis Gómez"), a native of Cienfuegos, and two celebrities, improvisers specializing in the *controversia*, Justo Vega, from Matanzas, and Adolfo Alfonso. We should also mention Jesús Orta Ruiz, better known as "El Indio Naborí"; a native of San Miguel de Padrón, a renowned performer of the *punto* until the time of the Revolution, when he became a journalist and writer. In

Celina González (born 1929),
the queen of folk music

recent decades, a new generation has emerged, showcased on television, but small in number: it includes Ramoncito Veloz, María Victoria Rodríguez, and, before she left Cuba, Albita Rodríguez.

The most illustrious woman's voice is that of Celina González, known the world over as "the queen of folk music." Even though her repertoire is not strictly that of the *punto*, it is profoundly anchored in this tradition and constitutes a link between the various musical expressions of the rural environment. Born near Jovellanos, in the province of Matanzas, she grew up in Santiago, in a family that cultivated the *décima*; her older sister plays the *tres* and her brother the lute. It was during a *guateque* that she met the man who would become her husband, Reutilio, a native of Guantánamo; with Reutilio she created first an amateur duo, then a professional one. In 1947, they sang together on a program of Radio Cadena Oriental:

> We started together in a broadcast called *Atalaya campesina*, which criticized all the misdeeds of the

then-current regime, and which enjoyed great success
for thatreason. I had been improvising ten-line stanzas
since the age of six, of course not as beautiful as those
of Justo Vega or of El Indio Naborí, but I held my own;
and Reutilio sang back-up in certain songs. We were
always told that in Santiago the public didn't like the
*punto*; its culture was rather the *trova*. So we weren't at
all sure of our success. And barely two weeks after our
débuts on Radio Cadena Oriental, were hired for a big
concert at the Maceo stadium in Santiago, with two
Mexican artists who were famous at the time. They
were sumptuously dressed. As for me, I had on a simple
dress; I really looked like a poor peasant girl. Reutilio
hardly looked better, with his hat made of *guano* (palm
fibers) and his shirt. There were seven to eight thousand people in the stadium, and someone kindly pointed out to us that we looked pathetic and that the public might throw cigarette butts at us. That's how they
drove artists off the stage when they failed to please!
But hardly had the announcer said that we were the
duo who had appeared on *Atalaya campesina*, when the
people stood up and started a frenzied applause. And I
improvised on the spot a part of the repertoire to con-
vey my emotion to this public that was welcoming us
with such warmth (interview, July 1988).

Their success brought them an engagement in Havana on
November 2, 1948, on Radio Cadena Suaritos. Celina then
composed in *décimas* the song *A Santa Bárbara*, which has
since been around the world under the title of *Que viva
Changó*; however, Celina makes clear that "at the time, I had
no idea what was an Afro song derived from Yoruba music.
I wrote as usual my ten-line octosyllabic stanzas. The only
Yoruba reference was the refrain and the homage to the
Changó divinity (*ibid.*)."

After her separation from Reutilio in 1961, Celina continued alone, with one of her sons, Lázaro Domínguez. The
orchestra that accompanied her then included *bongó*, *tumbadora*, *güiro*, *claves*, double bass, guitar, lute, *tres*, and maracas.
During the 1980s, she added a *marímbula* on certain occasions,
thus re-creating within a modernized band the sounds of the
first rural expressions of the *son*. Celina González is among
those who consider that rural musical forms constitute a unity,
and that she herself is a product of all those influences, from
the *punto* in all its varieties to the *son montuno** or *guajiro*. She
states, "The *son* that the peasants perform and dance in their
manner, differs from that of the city." And if she and Reutilio
composed in 1950 *Yo soy el punto cubano*, at a time when they
were financially secure, it was out of solidarity with the other
performers of this music and with peasants in general, who are
excluded, scorned, and miserable. It is also a reminder to
everyone that the liberators of Cuba, the Mambis, sang the
*punto cubano* in their resistance hideouts, and that this musical form is in itself an integral part of Cuban-ness.

# V

# The Danzón:

## PREHISTORY AND POSTERITY
## FROM THE QUADRILLE
## TO THE CHA-CHA-CHA

With the history of the *danzón*, we enter a different universe: The salons of the aristocracy, where court dances reign beside concert music, bourgeois salons that imitate the aristocratic styles, and musicians of color who creolize these forms of European music. At the end of this process, we see the appearance, in the late nineteenth century, of the *danzón*, the first dance rhythm considered authentically Cuban.

The dancing craze was a major feature of colonial society. Dances such as the minuet, rigadoon, and above all the quadrille were all the rage. Public dances were officially authorized, starting in 1792 in Havana, and this prompted a notable rise in the number of musicians. Toward the end of the eighteenth century, the first "academias de baile" (segregated dance halls) appeared and proliferated in the nineteenth century. In the humbler neighborhoods, the *bailes de cuna** were frequented by common people as well as by well-born sons who would "go slumming" there. The image of the mulatto beauty showing off her dancing skills in the company of

La Mulata de Rumbo
Illustration by Patricio Landaluze, showing a typical mulatto woman
of the "baile de cuna" (late 18th to early 19th century)

a well-to-do young man appears in all the contemporary chronicles.

## European Music and Musicians "of Color"

Precarious as it may be, the status of musician offered "people of color" the possibility of upward social mobility, to move beyond manual labor to which they were otherwise restricted. They acquired a thorough grounding and mastery in the European instruments of classical music, which are prevalent in the orchestration of dance music as well and provided the accompaniment for figure dances at high-society balls. Toward the late eighteenth century, we witness the appearance of famous black and mulatto concert musicians—violinists, cellists, flutists, double-bass players, and even organists, besides composers and dance masters. Though high society may have bowed to their talent, the colonial system reminded them of their place, as was seen in the repressive measures taken against them after the slave revolts in the region of Matanzas and in the Staircase Conspiracy in 1844. Poets and musicians of color were the first to be tortured and shot (Carpentier, 1985, p. 136).

## From the European Quadrille to the Havana *Contradanza*

The majority of Cuba specialists believe that the quadrille was introduced into Cuba by the French settlers of Santo Domingo at the end of the eighteenth century. But Alejo Carpentier asserted as early as 1946: "When we speak of *contradanza\* cubana*, we must not forget that there existed, at the same time, two specific types of this dance throughout the early nineteenth century, that of Santiago and that of

Havana," whereby he considered the Havana version closest to the minuet (1985, p. 120).

In Europe, the English country dance appeared in the seventeenth century, took root in France, beside the minuet, at the court of Louis XIV, and spread through Europe as the French quadrille. Thus it is not surprising that it would then be practiced, like the minuet and other figure dances, in the French colonial salons of Santo Domingo and New Orleans. Some of those who fled to Santiago de Cuba from the Haitian revolution in 1791 left for Louisiana and returned to Cuba only after 1812, since the French colony Louisiana was sold to the United States in 1803. They would then settle in the region of Matanzas (Yacou, no. 23, 1994, p. 71).

Now sources prove that the quadrille was known in Cuba as early as the mid-eighteenth century, indicating that it arrived from Spain with the incessant traffic of naval fleets between the Peninsula and its colony. With the accession of the Bourbons to the Spanish throne in 1700, "the art of dancing in the French style" became all the rage at court, as it was in the salons. Musical scores of European quadrilles, printed in France, England, and Spain, as well as the many brochures published in Spain, beginning in 1733, that describe the complicated steps of figure dances, allow us to follow the evolution of orchestration, rhythm, and choreography in Europe from 1714 to 1791 (Galán, 1983, pp. 69–78; Lapique, in Giró, 1996, pp. 156–157). In Spain, starting in 1755, quadrilles appear that are called "new," where one notes—in the melody as in the bass accompaniment—a rhythmic pattern known by the name *tango*\* $|\frac{2}{4}$ ♪ ♪♪ ♪$|$ which had become obsolete in Parisian quadrilles of that period (Lapique, in Giró, 1996). The origin of this pattern remains subject to debate among musicologists, who have identified it in many types of Arab, Arabo-

Andalusian, and African Bantu music (Ibid.). In Cuba, its presence gave rise to greater syncopation and to a dance that was
closer to popular taste. Sensuality triumphed over European
rigidity, which was denounced, in accounts from 1770 to
1790, as immoral and lascivious.

A final possible influence may have come from the occupation of Havana by the British fleet, from the summer of 1762
to the end of spring 1763. The British brought with them
another type of quadrille, already creolized in Guadaloupe,
which they took from the French in 1759 (Galán, 1983).

All of these influences would come together in practice with
the development of public dances. The interracial and inter-
cultural cross-fertilization became prominent in the rhythm,
reinforced by the progressive addition of typically Cuban
instruments such as the *güiro*. At the turn of the twentieth century, the quadrille, thus modified, carried the name Creole or
Cuban. Outside the island, in other countries of the Americas
and in Spain, it was called *contradanza habanera** (Havanan) to
differentiate it from the European versions that existed at the
same time—hence the confusion of terms with another
modality, the sung *habanera,** which appeared in Havana in
1841 and is still practiced in Spain and in other Latin
American countries, particularly Mexico (Lapique, in Giró,
1996, pp. 167–191).

The first *contradanza cubana* to have reached us dates from
1803: *San Pascual bailón*, an anonymous piece in two parts, in
2/4 time. The duple meter, better adapted to the rhythmic
habits of musicians of color and to urban dance, prevailed in
Cuba over the original compound rhythms. In addition to the
use of horns, this piece is characterized by the constant presence in the bass of the rhythmic pattern of the *tango*. The
black and mulatto composers of the western part of the island

(Tomás Buelta y Flores, Ulpiano Estrada, Claudio Brindis de Salas, dance master and father of the famous violin virtuoso, and even the "father of national music," Manuel Saumell) still had no idea what would renew the art of the quadrille and its derivatives, in particular, the *cinquillo*.

## Eastern Quadrille

With the arrival of the French settlers from Santo Domingo, another way of playing the quadrille arose in eastern Cuba. This technique had already been "contaminated" by the interpretation given by their slaves in the brilliant French colony. They brought a rhythmic novelty, the *cinquillo*, which is a group of syncopated notes: $|\frac{2}{4} \, ♪ \, ♫ \, ♫ \, |$ Santiago orchestras then adopted this rhythm and the "French" style of playing.

Present in the music of the *tumba francesa*, the *cinquillo* passed into the tradition of *comparsas-congas* of the *mamarrachos* celebrations. According to Santiago tradition, one evening in August 1836, a Catalan musician, Juan Casamitjana, was seated at a table in the *Venus* café, watching one of these famous *comparsas* go by. It was the *cocoyé comparsa*, led by two of the city's famous mulatto women, María de la Luz González and María de la O. Soguendo. The tune pleased Casamitjana so much that he transcribed it and composed a score that was played a few days later by the brass band of the Catalonia regiment.

In 1849, Julián Reynó, another Catalan musician, also composed a version of it for the brass band of the regiment of Isabella II, based in Bayamo. Transported from one brass band to another, the *cocoyé* became one of Havana's most popular tunes. On April 1, 1852, the press insisted on the fact that, for the first time, the theme would be played on a *marímbula*, a *güiro*, and other instruments "used by people of color for their dances" in the *cabildos* (Lapique, pp. 168–170). Combined with other brief rhythmic patterns, the *cinquillo* created a new style of quadrilles that, according to the *Gaceta de La Habana* of July 18, 1852, had "a notable superiority over the old quadrilles, because they do away with the monotony that once used to be characteristic of accompaniment, especially in the bass" (Lapique, *id.*).

The orchestra that performs the quadrille, the *orquesta típica*, was generally made up of two violins, two clarinets, one double bass, a cornet, a trombone, and one ophicleide, to which were added the timpani and the *güiro*. The choreography was modified, slowly abandoning figure dancing (dancing according to the form of court dances such as the quadrille) in favor of dancing as an intertwined couple, definitively codified in the *danzón*. The term *danza,** which gradually replaced the term *quadrille*, reflects this evolution; the term also designates a type of semi-classical musical composition, written in 6/8 time, sometimes in two parts—one in simple meter, and the other in compound meter. The principal innovation of the *danzón* was precisely to free itself from the bipartite division of the *contradanza/danza*, in order to get closer to the tripartite one of the rondo.

## From the *Danza* to the *Danzón*

The *danzón* originated neither in Santiago nor in Havana, but in Matanzas, on the northern coast. By 1830, the artistic radiance of the city was so great that it was nicknamed "the Athens of Cuba." In 1929, seven years after Havana's, Matanza's Philharmonic Orchestra was founded. The city already had several symphony orchestras, made up primarily of mulatto musicians who also played in dance orchestras. In Havana, as everywhere else on the island, everyone dances.

Traditionally, the birth of the *danzón* is dated January 1, 1879, when the composer Miguel Failde Pérez, a native of Caobas Limonar, near Matanzas, officially presented *Las Alturas de Simpson*, named after a relatively elegant neighborhood of the period. The piece was performed in the Club de Matanzas, a future *Liceo* that has since become the José-White Hall. Failde was the son of a Spanish trombone player from Galicia and a freed mulatto woman. Failde formed his own orchestra in 1871 with his brothers, Eduardo (on clarinet), and Cándido (on trombone), with himself on the cornet (Rodriguez, 1967, p. 17).

In reality, the name *danzón* appears much earlier in the provincial archives. In an article entitled "Ball with *Danzón*," the April 7, 1860, issue of the newspaper *Aurora del Yumurí* relates an evening sponsored by people of color, intended to raise money for the war against Morocco. The featured dance of the evening was "a *danzón* with garlands of flowers," a custom that seems to have begun in Matanzas (León, 1974, p. 257). But the structure of these *danzas* remained identical with that of the already Cubanized quadrille: four steps of eight measures each, the first two, *paseo* and *cadena* with a slow rhythm, the others, *sostenido* and *cedazo*, with a livelier rhythm. The innovations involved only the repetition of certain steps, called for by the frenzy of the dancers who "give tips to the orchestra in order to prolong the music" (Léon, 1974).

The *danzón* of Failde, at least his second version presented in 1879, made the first clean break with this scheme, since it is in three parts and is danced by an intertwined couple, to a much slower rhythm. Furthermore, it definitively establishes the 2/4 meter. It opens with an introduction of eight measures, during which the dancers hold each other by the arms, miming a walk, and greet each other in passing; this step is repeated in the course of the dance and serves as a transition between the danced parts. These parts include sixteen or thirty-two measures; each part has its own distinct harmony and melody, and each part is dominated by a particular instrument. In the performance of a typical orchestra, the clarinet section is followed by the more melodic violin section; the last part, with a livelier tempo, develops rather quickly from a section dominated by the brass toward a free orchestration. One dances practically without moving, "on a tile," with a haughty elegance and a contained sensuality.

Despite the obligatory return to the introduction, it is possible to add as many parts as fancy might dictate. Thanks to this flexibility, the *danzón* reigned supreme in Cuban popular dance until the 1920s. As it developed further, the "typical" orchestra was replaced by a new orchestral format and elements from the new musical genre, the son, were added early in the twentieth century.

## The *Charanga a la Francesa* Orchestra

From the late nineteenth century, "typical" orchestras began to compete with an orchestral format whose name betrays its origins: the *charanga a la francesa*. It included instruments reserved up to that point for concert or chamber music and became the perfect vehicle of the *danzón*. The clarinet continued to be used for a while, but the brass disappeared in favor of the piano and the ebony five-hole flute, in conjunction with the violins, the double bass, and the *guiro*. The timpani were most often replaced by the *paila criolla (timbales criollos)*, two small Creole kettledrums with single drumheads, fastened together and placed on one foot, and beaten with a combination of sticks and the hand.

The addition of the piano to the *charanga* formation can be dated to approximately 1899 (Orovio, 1994, p. 103). It appeared in the orchestra of the pianist Antonio Toroella (Rodríguez, 1967, p. 97). In the same period, the flutist Leopoldo Cervantes invited the pianist Antonio María Romeu to join his orchestra. These modifications radically altered the timbre of the *danzón* orchestras. The violins, the flute, and the piano dominated the various sections, and the quality of the solo performances henceforth acquired special importance. The number of sections of the *danzón* multiplied without any one of them being identical to the preceding one, and the composers acquired the habit of adapting and including fashionable melodies borrowed from a variety of musical genres: opera overtures and arias, tunes from operettas, and songs taken from *zarzuelas* in vogue at the theater, as well as from the popular repertoire.

The titles of recordings prior to the 1930s show that, despite its purely instrumental character, the *danzón* considered itself as a medium grappling with contemporary events: the Chinese immigration, the construction of the great central roadway linking eastern Cuba to the capital, the inauguration of the automatic long-distance telephone, the appearance of radio, the dawn of aviation, sports, the (negative) role of the press, and equally critical references to various governments through animal nicknames given to presidents. The compositions also paid homage to the carnival and to other types of music, especially the rumba and the *coros de clave*. The black-oriented themes were very much in evidence, because the majority of the great masters of the *danzón*, who were composers as well, were black or mulatto (Díaz Ayala, 1994, pp. 103–160).

One of the most famous of the "typical" orchestras was that

of the trombone player Raimundo Valenzuela. After his death, his brother Pablo Valenzuela, a cornet player, famous for his exceptional tone, led the orchestra until his own death in 1926. There was also the orchestra of the double-bass player José Alemán, that of the cornet player Enrique Peña, with the famous duo of the clarinet players José Belén Puig and José Urfé, who later joined the *típica* of Félix González, and that of Felipe Valdés, one of the "typical" orchestras that recorded the largest number of *danzones* before 1920 (Ibid.). Among the earliest of the *charanga* orchestras, we find that of the flutist Octavio "Tata" Alfonso, in which several instrumentalists, who would go on to fame, had their debuts. These rising stars included the pianist Jesús López, the *timbalero* Ulpiano Díaz, and Abelardo Valdés on the *güiro*. The orchestra that dominated from this period on and evolved further in the course of the history of the *charangas* was that of Antonio María Romeu, one of the most prolific of *danzón* composers.

## First "Contamination" by the *Son*

Before the uncontested reign of *charangas* orchestras in the late 1920s, it is to José Urfé, a clarinet player in the orchestra of Enrique Peña, that we attribute one of the most notable transformations of the *danzón* after 1910: the addition of a last part, even more rhythmic and fast, in *montuno* form, inspired by the *son*. Díaz Ayala asserts that, in a 1909 recording, the *danzón* titled *Mamá Teresa* by Pablo Valenzuela already included this kind of final part. However, according to the official history, this distinction belongs to the famous *El Bombín de Barreto*, inaugurated in 1910 and recorded later by all the *danzón* orchestras of Cuba. Inspired by an anecdote during a concert in the small eastern town of Puerto Padre, José Urfé's composition anticipated the rhythm craze that was just reaching Havana, but that had long been at home in the eastern part of the island.

Beginning in the 1920s, all the *danzón* orchestras were faced with a problem: How should they respond to the tidal wave of the *son*, with its contagious rhythm and specific orchestration, which relegated to the background the delicacy and refinement of their own music. Most of the orchestras adapted themes in a *danzón* rhythm, as they had done before with all types of music. One famous example is that of Antonio María Romeu's *danzonera* version of the *son* titled *Tres lindas Cubanas* (Three Pretty Cuban Women) (1926), which, it is said, inaugurated a new tradition of piano solos. However, in spite of these esthetic refinements and the possibility of varying the number of sections, the *danzón* evolved little, compared to the *son*, which became popular because it was music not just to be sung, but to be danced to as well.

## An Innovation in the Guise of a Parade: The *Danzonete**

Aniceto Díaz, the father of the *danzonete*, was a native of Matanzas. A shoemaker in love with music, he played the ophicleide in the orchestra of Miguel Failde, then learned to play the flute and the piano, composed *danzones*, and ended up creating his own orchestra in 1914. One day in May 1929, in Alacranes, where he alternated playing at a dance with a *son* sextet, the dance floor remained almost empty while his orchestra played. Humiliated and worried about his future, he invented a new musical form (Rodríguez, 1979). On June 8, 1929, the first *danzonete*, *Rompiendo la rutina*, was presented at the Spanish casino of Matanzas. Aniceto Díaz kept the introduction, the violin section, and the repetition of the introduction. But then the *güiro* player grabbed a pair of maracas—

a familiar *son* instrument never used in the *danzón* until then—and the orchestra played two of the parts that ordinarily were entirely sung: One part was performed more slowly, with the tempo of a *bolero-son*, and the last part was performed faster, with the tempo of a *guaracha-son*. This proved to be a great innovation. Certain previous *danzones*, such as *La Mora* of Eliseo Grenet, already included brief sung sequences. With the *danzonete*, however, the presence of the solo singer became indispensable.

The *danzonete* had an ephemeral life of roughly ten years, but thanks to radio, its singers became known throughout the island: Paulina Álvarez (1912–1965), "the empress of the *danzonete*," who sang with the orchestra of Neno González before forming her own, and Pablo Quevedo, the singer in the orchestra of Cheo Belén Puig, much loved by listeners. Quevedo passed away in 1936 without having made any recordings. Thus the *danzón* orchestras regained some popularity.

## A New Stage: The Sung *Danzón*

From then on, all the *charanga* orchestras hired singers. The orchestra of Cheo Belén Puig distinguished itself with Pablo Quevedo, then with Alfredito Valdés and Vicentico Valdés; the Orquesta Gris hired Fernando Collazo; and the name of Barbarito Diez is associated with the orchestra of Antonio María Romeu. Besides their own new creations, these orchestras often adapted hits of other sung genres of the same period— song, bolero, *guaracha* or *guajira-son*, Argentinean tango, which had been very much in fashion since the 1920s, and even U.S. musical comedies. The traditional structure exploded: The instrumental part between sections may or may not be repeated; the sung section became lyrical. But in spite of these innovations, the *danzón* had a hard time resisting the modifications of the musical atmosphere of the period—the soaring interest in Cuban and international song, the explosion and evolution of the *son* and its instrumentation, and the proliferation of jazz-band-type orchestras. This context explains the decisive rhythmic and instrumental innovations that came into play at the end of the 1930s and paved the way to a new style, the *danzón nuevo ritmo,** to the controversial mambo, and to the cha-cha-cha, the last-known off-shoot of the musical genre created by Miguel Failde.

## The Antonio Arcaño Orchestra

When he created his orchestra in 1937, the flutist Antonio Arcaño Betancourt returned to a purely instrumental format, in order to escape the uncertainties of featuring singers who would either become too popular and then leave or pass away. His orchestra was prestigious from the start: Jesús López on piano; Israel "Cachao" López, a member of the Symphony Orchestra, on double bass; Ulpiano Díaz on the *timbal*; Raúl Valdés and Elizardo Aroche on violin; and, on the *güiro*, Oscar Pelegrín, who was later replaced by Gustavo Tamayo. The brother of Cachao, Orestes López, was the double-bass player of the Symphony Orchestra and could also play cello and piano. In the early 1940s, Arcaño formed a large radio orchestra, La Radiofónica, whose string section was the size of a symphony orchestra's: eight violins, three violas, and two cellos.

> Every day, we would introduce a *danzón*. Orestes López composed about two hundred of them. . . . The López brothers played symphonic music, but since the Concert Association paid them fifteen or twenty pesos per month, they were obliged to play at dances or in the dancing academies. It's the miserable condition of

musicians in symphony orchestras that allowed me to have an orchestra of high quality. And we raised the *danzón* to the rank of a symphony. (Arcaño, Hernández, 1986, p. 55)

From that point on, the cello became part of the best *charangas* orchestras, and Arcaño expanded his violin section with musicians who were members of La Radiofónica, such as Félix Reina, Antonio Sánchez, known as "Musiquita," and Enrique Jorrín. Another innovation took place as well: the introduction of a *tumbadora*, a drum reserved until then for the *conjuntos** of *son*, and this brought new rhythmic and sound possibilities.

## The *Danzón Nuevo Ritmo* and the Mambo*

Arcaño renewed harmonies, melody, timbre, and—what is probably most striking to the layperson—the rhythms, whose modifications were influenced by Orestes López. In the new *danzones*, the introductory section is quite brief and is not repeated. A slow segment follows the introduction, classical in style, and generally dominated by the strings. Then comes a much faster and more syncopated section that Arcaño called mambo. The *danzón* titled *Mambo*, which was composed in 1937 by Orestes López and first performed on Radio Mil Diez, is entirely in this style: The piece goes immediately to the climax of the dance, with syncopated motifs in both the piano and strings, accompanied by the double bass. The *tumbadora* also intervenes in the spaces where the *timbal* traditionally does not play. In 1948, Arcaño defined the secret of the mambo in the magazine *Bohemia*:

The mambo is a type of syncopated *montuno* that possesses the rhythmic flavor, the informality, and the eloquence that typify what is Cuban. The pianist attacks a syncopated solo; the flute listens to it and improvises. The violinist performs rhythmic chords on double strings. The double bass adapts its base rhythm (*tumbao**); the *timbalero* responds with the bell. The *güiro* imitates the sound of the maracas; the *tumbadora* supports the rhythm of the double bass and reinforces the *timbal*. (Giró, 1996)

This style inaugurated a new era, that of both rhythmic and melodic use of the strings. At the same time, a new style of improvisation on the flute was born and would hence be used by all the modern *charangas* orchestras. But the very term *mambo* unleashed a controversy that has never been resolved: Is the *danzón nuevo ritmo* indeed the basis of the musical genre also called *mambo* and later popularized throughout the world by Damaso Pérez Prado, or is this bold assertion largely unsubstantiated, as some detractors would claim?

## Who Invented the Mambo?

To the controversial question of the creation of the mambo, Benny Moré answers, in his composition *Locas por el mambo* (Crazy for the Mambo): "*Un chaparrito con cara de foca.*" Seal's Head was one of the nicknames of Pérez Prado. But in Cuba, not everyone agrees with Benny Moré, beginning with Arcaño and Orestes López, who, on seeing Pérez Prado proclaim himself "the king of the mambo," considered themselves cheated out of the genre's paternity.

Leonardo Acosta asserts that, in reality, the mambo was simply in the air. The 1940s were a period of experimentation by jazz band orchestras, and Pérez Prado began to orchestrate, at the same time as Chico O'Farill, the repertoire of the Casino de la Playa orchestra with the singer Orlando Guerra ("Cascarita"). Then, from 1943 to 1944, he became the orchestra's pianist. With this big band, which included drums, five trumpets, two trombones, and five saxophones, Pérez Prado experimented with concepts different from those of the period. Then he created his own orchestra. But success eluded him, and the criticism of him occasionally took on violent forms; so he left for Mexico City in 1948.

The orchestra that Pérez Prado put together in Mexico City modified to some degree the classic makeup of the jazz band: He kept a single trombone, to signal the changes in rhythm and tempo; he modified the saxophone section, with two altos, one tenor (instead of two) and a baritone; and he increased the number of trumpets to five (Acosta, 1989). The rhythm section included two *tumbadoras* instead of one, *bongó*, and *timbales* fitted with cymbals. When Pérez Prado was asked to define his rhythm, he answered simply: "The basis is syncopation: It's the saxophones that play the syncopations in all the themes; the melody is carried by the trumpets; and the melodic-rhythmic accompaniment is carried by the double bass, combined with the bongos and the *tumbadoras*" (Prado, in Hernández, 1986).

To complete the description, one should also note the systematic use of dissonance in the upper register, as well as a voice to punctuate the music with scat singing. In 1948, Pérez Prado recorded a first mambo, which he described as "classic," *José y Macamé*; then he composed pieces with a rapid tempo: *Mambo #5*; *Mambo, que rico el mambo*; followed by *Mambo #8* and many others that were a huge success. In the early 1950s, this rhythm was all the rage in New York, where it created a frenzy at the Palladium, and Pérez Prado was hailed everywhere as its creator. In 1951, Alejo Carpentier extolled the mambo by noting its extraordinary instrumental, melodic, and harmonic creativity. More recently, the musician and musicologist Radamés Giró asserted that the mambo is in a league of its own—a revolution in Cuban dance music that owes the López brothers only its name (Giró, 1996). In 1982, Enrique Jorrín, somewhat irritated by this dispute, told me:

> The *tres* players of the eastern regions have played since the end of the last century syncopated musical values that spread throughout Cuban music. Orestes López took up the rhythmic cell of these *tres* players and included this musical syllable, able of being infinitely multiplied, in his music. Syncopation is no one's property. Orestes López used it and so did Pérez Prado. Each of them then orchestrated it in his own manner. Pérez Prado did not redo the *danzón*: he simply orchestrated his own version of Cuban syncopation. (Interview, 1982)

## The Cha-cha-cha

Enrique Jorrín is precisely the person to whom is attributed the last-known variant of the classic *danzón*: the cha-cha-cha. The son of a tailor and clarinet player from Pinar del Río, he moved to Havana in 1930, learned to play the violin at about age eleven with a teacher from the district of Atarés, and then entered the Felix-Arpiza municipal conservatory (today called Amadeo-Roldán). He was about sixteen when he played in a professional orchestra for the first time, that of the Contreras brothers, to replace his brother. Then he became a member of Selección del 45. He worked for Arcaño's orchestra until 1946, when he joined the rival *charanga*, the Orquesta América, which had been created in 1942 by Ninón Mondéjar. There, Jorrín experimented, in the last part of his *danzones*, with what would eventually become the cha-cha-cha, a rhythm and dance destined for a long career. A dispute would ensue as to the exact origin of the cha-cha-cha, to the point of provoking the breakup of the orchestra; Jorrín then created his own orchestra in 1954.

The first compositions registered under the name of *mambo chachachá* and recorded in 1953 were *La Engañadora* and, on the record's flip side, *Silver Star*, which already proclaimed: *"Chachachá es un baile sin igual"* (The cha-cha-cha is a dance like no other). However, Jorrín states that the orchestra had already been performing this new style for several years:

> Since 1948, I was playing with the Orquesta América in a big dance hall, the ballrooms of *Prado y Neptuno*, and that is where I started to free up the last part of the *danzón*—the mambo, as Arcaño called it. All the pieces recorded from 1953 on were already known by the public—*El Tunel, La Engañadora, El Alardoso*. I had composed them in 1949. Their broadcast via records and on the radio simply allowed them to be known beyond the dance hall. In the orchestra, we began to modify the rhythmic accent of the syncopated *danzón* by reentering the strong beat on the first beat of the measure and by introducing two sixteenth notes that are resolved with one eighth note: one, two, one-two-three. The cha-cha-cha is danced on the beat; the movement propelled by the *güiro* is parallel to the dancer's steps. The dancers began to emphasize this new beat; the hall was big, and they marked this special cha-cha-cha pattern all together. We could hear their soles rubbing the floor in rhythm, and I named this sound with the onomatopoeia *cha-cha-cha*. (Interview, 1982)

Enrique Jorrín (1926–1987),
composer, violinist, bandleader, and
father of the cha-cha-cha

The cha-cha-chas recorded since 1953 present an instrumental introduction of eight to sixteen measures, followed by the body of the piece, which sets a steady rhythm: "The characteristic of the cha-cha-cha is the beat and the off-beat, not syncopation," insisted Enrique Jorrín. But other musicians, such as the violinist Musiquita, emphasized that the credit for this rhythmic revolution belongs to the *güiro* player Gustavo Tamayo who, one day, displaced the accent by following the dancers' steps; the orchestra, taken by surprise, let loose, and the dancers, delighted, followed in lock-step.

The new genre reintroduced singing, which had been abandoned while the Arcaño orchestra dominated the scene. In the América orchestra, the singing began with a few simple phrases, sung in unison by two or three musicians; the phrases were separated by instrumental measures, so as not to lose the rhythm; then the singers started telling a story. Jorrín, for example, was inspired by two anecdotes, which he made into the story of "La Engañadora," a woman who was a magnificent deceiver and whose body was padded with rubber.

The immense success of the cha-cha-cha revived the popularity of the *charanga* orchestras in the 1950s. Its rhythm is both simple and infectious, and the singing allows composers to compete with other musical genres in seeking inspiration for the lyrics—accounts of great and small events, satire, and picaresque characters. Furthermore, since it was easily combined with other rhythms—*bolero-cha, danzón-cha, canción-cha*—it guaranteed a varied repertoire, an advantage that had previously been enjoyed only by the *son*. All of Cuba dances the cha-cha-cha, which is exported everywhere, in a more or less watered-down form. From that point on, *charanga* orchestras ran the gamut of dance rhythms. Enrique Jorrín was one of the first to break with the strictly established orchestral format by adding three trumpets to his orchestra during a tour in Mexico. The public was appreciative. Back in Cuba, he kept the extra brass instruments. However, the orchestra was criticized unanimously when it amplified the double bass and the violin (interview, Hernández, 1986).

## The Orchestras

A good number of *danzonera* orchestras of previous decades are still active: those of Antonio María Romeu and Cheo Belén Puig; the Chepín-Choven orchestra of Santiago de Cuba, created by the violinist Electo Rosell "Chepín" and the pianist Bernardo Choven; and the Almendra orchestra of Abelardo Valdés, author of the *danzón* of the same name, Melodías del Cuarenta, with the flutist Eloy Martínez and the percussionist Miguel Santa Cruz. This last orchestra produced, in 1953, the Charanga Sensación of Rolando Valdés. In a small town near Camagüey, Florida, Armonías del 48 was created in 1948; in 1959, it became Maravillas de Florida, with a five-key ebony flute, violins, viola, and cello. In spite of its extraordinary quality, this orchestra, which is still active, could never compete with the others, because there is no hope for success outside Cuba—a situation as inevitable in the past as it is today.

The 1950s were marked by nightclubs and cabarets such as Montmartre, the Havana Hilton, and the Tropicana. Segregation remained a problem: There were dance halls reserved for white people; social clubs of black people and of mulattos. But popular nightspots multiplied along the beach of Marianao, known as "the university of music," with its public of dancers and music fans. One of the most prominent flutists of the period was José Fajardo, who was born in the province of Pinar del Río and died in December 2001. It was to Fajardo that Maestro Arcaño turned over the leadership of his orchestra in 1946. In September 1949, José Fajardo founded Fajardo y sus Estrellas with the musical elite, the López brothers, Jesús López, the virtuoso violinist Virgilio Diago, the *timbalero* Ulpiano Díaz, and the percussionist Tata Güines (Federico Arístides Soto). The demand was so strong that Fajardo assembled, under the same name, three orchestras that played on the same evening, and which he assigned according to the prestige of the location; he himself ran from one venue to the next, with his ebony flute, while juggling his schedule (interview, 1987). After the Revolution, he was accused of "musical exploitation" and, though found not guilty, he used a trip to Japan in 1961 as an opportunity to go into exile.

Meanwhile, an orchestra established itself in the capital that combined technical perfection with an inimitable flair, supplanting all others in popularity: the Orquesta Aragón, created in 1939 in Cienfuegos by the double bass player Orestes Aragón. The year 1940 marked the arrival of a very young prodigy of the violin and of orchestration, Rafael Lay, who took over in 1948 when Aragón fell ill. A classical orchestra with cello, the Orquesta Aragón first went to Havana for a specific series of engagements. The RCA-Victor company, which had not contracted with any of the big *charangas* of the period, bet on the newcomers and, in 1953, recorded *El Agua de clavelitos*, then *Tres lindas Cubanas* and *Mentiras criollas*. In 1954, the headlining flutist left. Then appeared Richard Egües, another prodigy, who introduced in his melodic and rhythmic improvisations a new type of dialogue with the dancers. All sorts of new choreography were created, based on his solos. The Aragón orchestra was doubtless the most inventive of all orchestras of the period, with respect to rhythmic combinations (*pacá*, *onda*, etc.). *Pare cochero* triumphed in 1954 and, the following year, the orchestra became truly Havanan, with a regular program on Radio Progreso. In no time at all, those who had been treated with a certain arrogance as "peasants" dethroned all the others. The popularity of the two principal singers, whose voices—with an immediately recognizable timbre—formed, in unison, a perfect trio with the voice of Rafael Lay, surpassed the popularity of the other orchestras. José Antonio Olmos, known as Pepe, and Rafael Bacallao, known as Felo, took with them, around the world, the impressive list of Aragón's hits, which are considered classics following the example of *El Bodeguero*.

Admired in Africa, in Latin America, and in the Caribbean, Aragón's popularity persisted in Cuba even after the Revolution. The accidental death of Rafael Lay in 1982, the departure of Richard Egües in 1984, then the retirement of the singers who were replaced by their sons, and the death in 1997 of the cellist Tomás Valdés certainly changed the makeup of the orchestra, besides it is difficult for a classical *charanga* to adapt to the new sounds in vogue in contemporary music. But the violinists Rafaelito Lay, Celso Valdés, and Dagoberto and Lazarito González are maintaining the tradition.

Among the other classical *charangas* orchestras that have continued since the Revolution, Estrellas Cubanas must be noted. This orchestra was created in 1959 by the violinist Félix Reina, who died in 1998. Reina was the composer of *Angoa* and of *El Niche*, which were *danzones* composed in the days of La Radiófonica of Arcaño; in the 1960s, he composed *Vuela paloma* and the bolero *Si te contara*, with singers of the caliber of Raúl Planas and Raúl (Rolo) Martínez. The Charanga Rubalcaba was founded in 1962 under the name of Charanga Típica de Conciertos by the pianist and musicologist Odilio Urfé and his brother José Esteban; the orchestra is now directed by the pianist Guillermo Rubalcaba. All these orchestras maintain the *danzón* in their repertoire. Dance is once again performed in the tradition by several associations, such as the Círculo Amigos del danzón Miguel Failde Pérez of Matanzas, which transmits to young schoolchildren this unknown heritage. And every year a *danzón* festival takes place, where orchestras and dancers compete.

*Charanga* orchestras that have been modernized, but without any radical change in instrumentation, have continued until recently; these include Original de Manzanillo and Ritmo Oriental, founded in 1958 by the double-bass player and leader Humberto Perera. He emphasized polyrhythms, with his string quintet (four violins and a cello) and flute, linked to a rhythm section of drums as well as traditional instruments. His trump card is a contagious rhythmic pulse, with a rather rapid "oriental (eastern) style" tempo. Ritmo Oriental has also been one of the first Cuban groups to stage genuine choreography, and very young musicians just out of music school have tried out their orchestration skills with this group.

# VI

# Song:
## TROVA, BOLERO, "FEELING"

### From Salon Songs to Popular Songs

In the eighteenth and early nineteenth centuries, the ruling classes asserted their taste for the "salon song," a genre of song that still owed much to the repertoire in fashion in those circles: French romances, German lieder, Italian opera arias, and Neapolitan songs dating back to the Kingdom of the Two Sicilies under Spanish rule. To this musical mix were added various forms of Spanish song (romances, *tiranas*, *polos*, *boleras*), the *tonadillas* of musical theater, and influences from the American continent, because the exchanges between the Yucatan and Cuba grew more frequent after the Ten Year War, with the exile of numerous Cuban nationalists to Mexico.

In 1841 appeared the first *habaneras*, which were songs in verse with piano accompaniment and a rhythm of the Havana quadrille. *El Amor en el baile*, presented for the first time at the Café La Lonja, in the capital's historic center, was published in

103

contemporary Havana newspapers in 1842 (Lapique, in Giró, 1996). This genre created a sensation in Spain, where it is still performed today, as well as in various South American countries. The migrations of French people from Louisiana, the repatriation to Cuba of the families of Spanish soldiers defeated in Mexico and elsewhere, and the constant traffic between Cuba and Spain explain how it came to be that the same song could appear in the repertoire of various countries. Such was the case with *La Paloma*, a habanera composed in the 1860s by the Spanish composer Sebastián Yradier, and claimed by Spain, Mexico, and Cuba. On the island, this type of song diverged slowly from the compound meter of the European model, and became characterized by simple meter before becoming part of the Cuban song repertoire. In 1892 Eduardo Sánchez de Fuentes composed *Tú*, a habanera in 2/4 time, for which Fernán Sánchez later wrote lyrics. But the first pieces titled *canción cubana* remained stamped with melodies in compound meter. Such is the case with *La Bayamesa*, which was dedicated to a young girl from Bayamo; this song was composed in 1852 by Carlos Manuel de Céspedes, the future "father of the nation." The original lyrics eventually took on a symbolic value, because the patriots of Bayamo played a primary role in the insurrection of the Mambis.

## The Beginnings of the Traditional *Trova*

In the late nineteenth century, there appeared in popular circles of the eastern region a type of poetry that was sung, composed, and performed by authors who commented in verse on everything that seemed to them worthy of attention. For them, music was a simple means of expression, a way to spend a few moments of leisure at home, among friends, or at the neighborhood café. Sometimes, they composed for a serenade sung in front of someone's home. Thus was born what would later be called the *vieja trova*, or traditional *trova*, formed in Santiago de Cuba in the last third of the nineteenth century. To a French ear, *trova* or *trovador* might suggest their *trouvères* and *troubadours*, but in Cuba *trovadores* designated these authors-composers-performers who accompanied themselves on the guitar.

### Pepe Sánchez, the Precursor

The precursor of the *trova*, José "Pepe" Sánchez (1856–1918), was born and died in Santiago de Cuba. A mulatto, he first became a tailor; then he rose in the social hierarchy by becoming an investor in copper mines and a representative of a textile firm established in Jamaica. Contemporary accounts celebrate this extraordinary musician, who was entirely self-taught, as a remarkable guitarist with a beautiful baritone voice, gifted with a sense of harmony and composition such that, according to his contemporaries, only the best were able to perform his pieces. His home was frequented by such well-known musicians as Jorge Anckermann (who was to produce many of his compositions on the stage of the Alhambra Theater) and Brindis de Salas, the first internationally famous Cuban violin virtuoso, as well as by the future generals of the army of independence, Antonio and José Maceo, Guillermo Moncada, and Quintín Banderas. Pepe Sánchez gave the song its definitively creolized form, with compositions such as *Rosa no. 1*, known also as *Templadme la lira*, *Cuando escucho tu voz*, *Pura*, *Rosa no. 2*, *Me entristeces mujer*. The first Cuban bolero, *Tristezas*, which was composed in 1883, is also attributed to Pepe Sánchez.

## The Heirs

Pepe Sánchez taught guitar and music to a number of celebrities of the first *trova*: Gumersindo (Sindo) Garay (1867–1968), Rosendo Ruiz Suárez (1885–1983), and Alberto Villalón Morales (1882–1955), all of whom were born in Santiago de Cuba and died in Havana. This core group of the *trova santiaguera* was joined by two other well-known musicians: Manuel Corona Raimundo (1880–1950) and Patricio Ballagas Palacio (1879–1920). Raimundo was born in Caibarién, in the province of Las Villas; he arrived in Havana as a young man with his family, became a tobacco worker, and spent a few years in Santiago, where he performed with the core *trova* group. Palacio was a native of Camagüey, who died in Havana (private archives of Radamés Giró, quoted in Cañizares, 1992).

Like other musical genres born in the eastern province, the *trova* too followed the migrations of its creators west as they sought to improve their economic situation. From the beginning of the twentieth century, the *trovadores* began to gather in Havana. They went from café to restaurant, and they performed in the movie theaters during

Sindo Garay (1877–1968)

reel changes. Thanks to radio, their work was broadcast across the country. In 1906, Edison produced the first cylinders of Sindo Garay. However, a good number of their compositions were lost because most of the artists did not know how to transcribe their music, and only their recorded hits have reached us.

### Characteristics of the Early *Trova*

The guitar has a particular style in the *trova*. Besides the harmonic progression in whole tones or chromatics, in the rhythmic sequences, the *rayado*\* or *rasgueado* technique, achieved by using all fingers like a fan, is especially remarkable; this technique was used a great deal in Spanish popular music and in flamenco music. Of course, songs and serenades can be performed with one voice, but the *trovadores* of the eastern region cultivate the duo, with a particular way of articulating the sec-

Los Compadres

ond voice, in the singing of the first voice as well as in the guitar accompaniment.

Patricio Ballagas brought innovations to this style and
founded a genuine school. He started to compose in 4/4 time
and introduced singing with two juxtaposed voices, in which
the second performs in counterpoint lyrics different from
those of the first. This innovation was taken up by Rosendo
Ruiz in such classics as *Confesión* or *Falso juramento*. It is also
found, with a personalized style, in all great duos that followed. This important second voice gave Francisco Repilado, a
tobacco worker who was both a *trovador* and a clarinetist, his
nickname, Compay Segundo. From 1942 to 1955, he traveled
the world with Lorenzo Hierrezuelo as part of the Los
Compadres duo before putting together his own quartet.

María Teresa Vera (1895–1965)

No theme is excluded
from the popular lyrics
that characterize the *trova*
repertoire: love affairs and
unrequited love go hand
in hand, as do celebrations
of nature, humorous anec-
dotes, and—since many of
the authors were active
participants in the wars of
liberation—the theme of
nationalism as well. The
few titles that follow give a
glimpse of this great variety of themes. From Sindo
Garay we have, among
some three hundred works
in his repertoire, *El Hura-*

*cán y la palma*, *Tardes grises*, *Clave a Maceo*, *Perla marina*, and *Ojos de sirena*. Manuel Corona is the composer of *Santa Cecilia*, *Guitarra mía*, *Aurora* (in response to his composition *Longina*), *Mercedes*, and *Tú y yo*. We credit Rosendo Ruiz with *Junto a un cañaveral*, *Se va el dulcerito*, and *Mares y arenas*. As for Alberto Villalón, he has left us *Está muy lejos*, *Me da miedo quererte*, *Boda negra*, and *Yo reiré cuando tú llores*.

Other, younger composers acquired great fame. Among them were Rafael "Teofilito" Gómez, Miguel Companioni, Manuel Luna, and Eusebio Delfín. Like their elders, these composers created duos, trios, and quartets. Outstanding among them was the voice of a woman, María Teresa Vera, whose duos with Rafael Zequeira, then with Lorenzo Hierrezuelo, left their mark on the history of the *trova*. She performed the compositions of others, in particular those of Manuel Corona, while marking them with her creativity; but her own creations (*Veinte años*, *Cara a cara*, *Esta vez tocó perder*, *Hé perdido contigo*, *Porque me siento triste*) are unforgettable compositions.

## Other Types of Cuban Songs

### The Bolero

Among the compositions of this period are several boleros. This genre is found in its Cuban version as early as *Tristezas* by Pepe Sánchez. The Cuban bolero shares only its name with the Spanish dance. The Spanish bolero is structured in three parts, in a compound 3/4 meter. This dance derived from the *seguidilla* and first appeared in 1780, becoming especially popular in Andalusia. It existed in Cuban salons from the early nineteenth century on. However, the bolero that arose in Santiago in 1883 was a type that was danced by couples, in a simple 2/4 meter. Its melody and guitar accompaniment were marked by the presence of the *cinquillo*. In his dictionary of Cuban music, Helio Orovio quotes an unpublished essay by Vicente González-Rubiera (the *trovador* Guyún) and by the son of Rosendo Ruiz, himself a famous composer, in which the first forms of the Cuban bolero are analyzed: "Two musical sections of sixteen measures each, separated by an instrumental passage performed on the upper guitar notes and called *passacalle*. These boleros can be in a major or minor key or can alternate between major and minor keys" (Orovio, 1992).

The *cinquillo* distinguishes the bolero from other forms of song of the eastern region. Rosendo Ruiz Jr. points out that the eastern bolero had a rather lively tempo at first. The vocal melody reproducing the syncopations of the five basic notes of the *cinquillo*, often combined with the *tresillo*, three syncopated notes of unequal value: |$\frac{4}{4}$ ♩. ♩. ♩ | The quintet of Pepe Sánchez, Los Reyes del Bolero, shows that, in the early twentieth century, depending on the circumstances, a falsetto voice, taken from the lyric opera tradition, was added to the duo of tenor and baritone that was established from the outset.

Little by little, these early forms of the bolero adopted a more fluid melody and rid themselves of the rigidity imposed by the *cinquillo*. The composers adapted already existing poems, and the melodic line then followed the text's own rhythm. Rosendo Ruiz Jr., cites as examples of this evolution two great bolero classics: *Ella y yo*, more often known by its first line, *En el sendero de mi vida triste*, which was set to music in 1916 by the Havanan Oscar Hernández Falcon to lyrics by Urrico Ablanedo; and, in 1921, *¿Y tú qué has hecho?*, renamed by the public in the same fashion, as *En el tronco de un árbol*, which was composed by Eusebio Delfín Figueroa (Rosendo Ruiz Jr., in Giró, 1996).

## Genres Emerging from the Theater:
### *Guaracha*, *Criolla*, and *Guajira*

At the turn of the twentieth century, some of the sung styles that had emerged in burlesque theater in the preceding century then entered the domain of the *canción*.

The *guaracha* retained its essential features: a lively tempo, commentary on any news item, and a dialogue between soloist and choir. The *trovadores* quickly included it in their repertoire, and it became the genre that specialized in humor, in satire and double meanings. Ñico Saquito, with Los Guaracheros de Oriente, and Faustino Oramas ("El Guayabero") have left us many pieces of this type.

The *criolla* and the *guajira*, on the other hand, celebrate the natural beauty of landscapes and of peasant life, as colored in idyllic hues by the city-dweller. The popularity of these styles reached its height during the first years of the Republic, when the white peasant was praised and people of African descent were ostracized. These styles retained the compound meters of the era of Spanish *zarzuelas*, as in the *criolla Mujer bayamesa* of Sindo Garay or such *guajiras* as *Mi estancia* and *La Alborada* of Alberto Villalón, which were recorded in 1919 by Floro Zorilla. Of these two genres, only the *guajira* enjoyed great popularity through the transformation it underwent in its contact with the *son*.

## The Spread of the *Son*

The eastern *son*, first rural and then urban, influenced all eastern *trova* well before it acquired a different form in Havana. The famous Trío Matamoros is the living example of the fact that the lines between *trova*, bolero, and *son* fluctuate. Miguel Matamoros, guitar and first voice; Rafael Cueto, second guitar and third voice; and Siro Rodríguez, second voice and

maracas or *claves*—all three men were already prominent figures in the *trova santiaguera* when they got together in 1925.
Miguel had already performed several times in Santiago theaters; he was thirty-one and, the year before, he had been
hailed in Havana with his first trio. The guitar technique was
no longer limited to the classic *rasgueo*; the constant presence
of small percussion, as well as the habit of hitting the guitar
with the hand to accentuate the polyrhythm, signaled the
influence of the *son*. The trio also composed boleros such as
*Promesa*, which was featured on its very first recording of 1928,
with *El que siembra su maíz*, and which soon was in all the
*vitrolas*, the ancestors of the jukebox. The trio also composed
*bolero-son* pieces, such as *Lágrimas negras* (Black Tears), which
was one of the first of the genre in the original format of the
*trova*.

The appearance of the *son*, which had already upset the
structure of the *danzón*, also introduced a new phase of song.
All kinds of dance orchestras adopted it. The orchestrated
bolero thus modified its structure and came to enjoy large-
scale commercial broadcasts (Loyola Fernández, 1997). The
Puerto Ricans Rafael Hernández, Pedro Flores, and Daniel
Santos are part of this heritage, as is the Mexican Agustín Lara.
Moreover, the tradition of the Mexican bolero, which began in
the Yucatan in the 1920s, constitutes an entirely separate
genre, different from its Cuban counterpart. The *guajira* abandoned what was left of its compound meter and embraced a
2/4 dance rhythm. Other musical genres "of the street," such
as the *pregón*, an ancient song used by wandering street ven-
dors to attract clients, were also mixed with the *son* and traveled around the world. But a great number of these successes
came from the *trovadores*.

## *Trova* and the Show Business Industry

The traditional *trova* will always exist, even if the music industry loses interest in it, in favor of big bands. Singing to guitar accompaniment is part of daily life in Cuba, and this social function, in its simplicity and urgency, is the best guarantee of the permanence of this form of expression. New songs have emerged, and the ancient musical heritage has been transmitted from generation to generation, through family celebrations. Groups of amateurs or professionals have continued to create and produce locally. The tradition of polyphonic song, which is still strong among choral singing groups, maintains this practice; many singers of the Orfeón de Santiago, as well as those from other choral groups, are also anonymous *trovadores*. Furthermore, after the Revolution, the Casa de la Trova of Santiago had no trouble whatsoever in continuing to function.

## The Piano Era

In the 1930s and 1940s, especially in the capital, there was a harmonic and melodic evolution in song. In the large recreational venues, movie theaters, and bars, the piano became the accompanist's instrument of choice.

Once again, popular tunes inspired composers known in the world of concert music, including the pianist / composer Ernesto Lecuona (*Como arrullo de palmas, Siboney, María La O, Se fué*), his sister Ernestina Lecuona (*Ya que te vas, Junto al río*), Gonzalo Roig (*Quiéreme mucho*), Eliseo Grenet (*La Perla de tu boca*), Jaime Prats (*Ausencia*), and Rodrigo Prats (*Une rosa de Francia*). Like Lecuona, other renowned artists of Guanabacoa distinguished themselves in this new style of song. "Bola de Nieve" (Ignacio Jacinto Villa Fernández), who began in a movie theater in his hometown, was—with Ernesto Lecuona and René Touzet—one of the first composers to make use in popular music of innovations by the French composer Claude Debussy. He sometimes sang his own compositions and also provided piano accompaniment for Rita Montaner, a lyric singer who had triumphed, since the 1920s, in all genres—*zarzuela*, opera, and concert music. She also performed "Afro" songs, which were written by Cuban composers to honor their country's African heritage, inspired by the *negrismo* movement, which involved all the arts after the 1920s. *Mamá Inés*, the famous tango congo of Eliseo Grenet, and *El Manisero*, of Moisés Simon, traveled around the world and captivated Paris in 1928. It was also Rita Montaner who gave to a very dark-skinned Bola de Nieve this affectionate nickname (Ball of Snow), which remained with him.

As these artists conveyed a popular influence in another style, performers and composers for the piano flourished from the 1930s to the 1950s. Pedro Junco, who died of tuberculosis at the age of twenty-three, left us unforgettable boleros: *Soy como soy* (I am what I am) and *Nosotros*, which was composed under the shock of an announced death ("Ask me no more questions; it's not for lack of tenderness; I love you with all my soul, and for your own good I bid you farewell"), have become veritable anthems in Cuba. Among the female figures, along with the guitarist Lily Batet and her *Alma de roca*, there also was the pianist Isolina Carillo, who created the lasting work *Dos gardenias*. Right up to the 1940s, the great names of this generation of pianists included: Orlando de la Rosa (*Ya sé que es mentira, Cansancio, Vieja luna*); Juan Bruno Terraza, who lived for a long time in Mexico and who made his career throughout Latin America (*Alma libre, Sentir, Cantar y llorar*); Felo Bergaza (*Si tú me lo dijeras, Por eso tienes la culpa, Seguiré sin soñar*); and Julio Gutiérrez (*Llanto de luna, Involvidable*). Having emerged from a comparatively higher social group than that of the traditional *trova*, these pianists studied music formally and sought formal perfection, which led to sophistication in their styles. Their compositions offered more elaborate melodies, a great rhythmic suppleness, more complex harmonies, and the use of literary metaphor, which for them is virtually systematic. But commercial pressures required the creation of hit records in succession, and poetic creativity occasionally suffered. Along with great talents came a mawkish commercial product, noted for a sentimentalism bordering on the hackneyed, where love could do nothing but suffer the treachery of women—a love drowning in tears, witnessed only by the silence of the night and the glacial indifference of the moon.

It was in the 1940s, in reaction to this threat of artistic sclerosis, that artists came to the fore with renewed interest in guitar accompaniment and imposed a new style of song. They borrowed from English the watchword that translates their manner of musical expression: "feeling," later transcribed phonetically "in the Cuban style" as *filin*.

### The "Feeling" (or *Filin*) Movement

Originally, the "feeling" movement was not a school, but a group of self-taught friends, who, when not unemployed, did any odd job, and would get together for their own pleasure at the home of a group member, Angel Díaz, in the Callejon of Hamel.

How did these musicians define themselves? First, as a new generation, nourished by the traditional poetic song of the early masters of the *trova*, but also on the lookout for all types of music—whether it was the *son* of Ignacio Piñeiro, the blues or jazz of the United States, the classical music of Chopin and Debussy, or the music of Nat King Cole, Glen Miller, or the

Arcaño orchestra:

> The jazz musicians of the period were noted for the frequency and sensitivity of the improvisations they performed on the basic theme, and when we used to listen to one of them begin a phrasing where sensitivity overpowered the technical aspect, we used to say: "What 'feeling'!" And we ended up using this word to characterize various attitudes toward life. . . . Little by little, the term was used for designating our musical language, then a type of song, a style at once harmonic, melodic, and literary. . . . The song of the previous era was a bit weepy, sentimental to the point of being vapid. Our own texts relate to everyday reality, the vitality of young people wanting to find their own path . . . , they grapple with reality, with the necessity to face life. They are lyrical, but with a lyricism that has nothing to do with the morbidity of pain or of solitude. (César Portillo de la Luz, interview, in *Contreras*, 1989, pp. 17–18)

Besides a shared appetite for life, it was the sensitivity of the interpretation and the new guitar harmonies that held this group together: Ñico Rojas recounts how surprised he was when, in the Los Pinos neighborhood, many kilometers from where the original group had met, he met a José Antonio Méndez who, without ever having heard any of them, played the guitar in the same way. The *filin* compositions are legion: *Rosa mustia*, of Angel Díaz, became the group's theme. Among the most important compositions, let us cite: *Quiéreme y verás, Novia mía, Si me comprendieras*, of José Antonio Méndez; *Tú, mi delirio* and *Contigo en la distancia*, of César Portillo de la Luz; *Ahora sé que te quiero* and *Mi ayer* of Ñico Rojas; and *Ya no te puedo amar* and *Hasta mañana vida mía*, of Rosendo Ruiz

Quevedo. We note in these pieces the use of chromatics in the melody and in the chords, as well as the primacy of lyrics over rhythm—characteristics that allow for great freedom of interpretation.

In the early 1950s, their work began to be considered by other musicians: Bebo Valdés dedicated a *danzón* to them, titled *Jóvenes del filin*, orchestrated by the violinist Antonio "Musiquita" Sánchez; and the Conjunto Casino brought them fame by offer-

César Portillo de la Luz (born 1922)

ing bolero adaptations of several of their compositions, in the unforgettable interpretation of Roberto Faz.

After 1959, the great "feeling" voices of Elena Burke and Omara Portuondo continued to be presented in cabarets, and the Pico Blanco, the cabaret of the Hotel Saint-John, became *"el rincón del feeling."* But one evening in 1989, after the show, José Antonio Méndez was run over by a bus; and Elena Burke, the *"Señora Sentimiento"* (the *grande dame* of feeling), now very ill, performs rarely.

The *nueva trova* movement was officially created in 1972; one offshoot of the movement took up an evolving form of the *trova* and *filin* tradition. *La era está pariendo un corazón*, composed by Silvio Rodríguez in 1966, is supposed to mark the birth of this new style—a style that Pablo Milanés, Omar Portuondo, and Sara González (among others) would mark with their personalities.

# VII

# The Son

Though it has become "the very expression of the identity of the Cuban people" (Eli, Gómez, 1989), the *son* is nonetheless present, in various forms and under various names, in all of the western Caribbean, the region of intense maritime exchanges, which includes Cartagena (Colombia), the Yucatan Peninsula (Mexico), Jamaica, the Cayman Islands, Haiti, the Dominican Republic, and Puerto Rico. Even before the expansion of the media, sailors and migrant laborers spread this music, popularizing the vast instrumental, lyrical, and dance features of the Cuban *son*.

For a long time, the appearance of the "first" *son* was dated back to the sixteenth century, on the strength of a document published in 1893 by a musician from Santiago de Cuba, Laureano Fuentes. The *Son de la Ma' Teodora* is said to have been composed by two free black women from Santo Domingo, Teodora and Micaela Ginés. This assertion is highly questionable today. Although this *son* did indeed reach us by oral transmission, its structure is typical of the nineteenth century.

The possibility that this structure should result from a "transculturation" dating as far back as the sixteenth century seems farfetched (Muguercia, 1971).

## An Originally Rural and Already Afro-Cuban Genre

Though the exact date of the appearance of the *son* is uncertain, much more is known about its place of origin. The field investigations conducted in the past twenty years by the musicologist Danilo Orozco prove that the *son* was born about 1860 in the rural enclaves of the eastern mountains: the Sierra Maestra, which frames the southern coast between Cabo Cruz and the port of Santiago de Cuba, bordered in the north by the Río Cauto valley; and the Sierra de Cristal, which stretches farther east, between Mayarí, Guantánamo, and Baracoa. When the musical forms called *son* arrived in the suburban zones of the region in the late nineteenth century, they already bore the Afro-Hispanic mark, both in instrumentation and in song structure.

Many factors explain how this fusion of Spanish and African roots could have taken place in this early, rural phase. The first families that settled in the island's eastern regions were most often of Spanish origin, from Andalusia or the Canary Islands. However, in the eastern region more so than in the western, laborers of African origin, especially Bantu and Dahomeyans, worked in small agricultural enclaves in the mountains and in mining areas, far from the urban centers. The *cimarrones* (runaway slaves) soon found refuge in the mountains. After the collapse of the plantation system during the Ten Year War, the slaves scattered throughout the region; the two wars of liberation in the nineteenth century favored,

in these eastern regions, an even more intense mix than elsewhere among freed slaves, mulattos, and whites, all of whom
were partisan to the national cause. Finally, for reasons both
geographic and sociological, the original family units around
which the *son* was constituted and transmitted were dispersed
among urban and rural areas, though they maintained very
close relations with one another. Furthermore, the term *son*
originally designated a collective celebration, where these
songs and dances were performed. It is therefore plausible that
such activities appeared concomitantly in many locations
where interaction between urban and rural areas and contacts
between whites and people of color were common.

Danilo Orozco gathered into an anthology various examples of old forms of this music, as orally transmitted to the sur-
viving descendants of the old families that constitute the core
transmitters of rural music. The example of the Valera Miranda family, natives of the Cauto River region and the performers in this first anthology, was reissued on a compact disc produced in 1997 by Ocora-Radio France, with more updated
musical pieces.

## The Antecedents of the *Son*

### The *Changüí**

Often considered a simple regional variant of the *son*, the
*changüí* in fact presents specific traits that mark it as an older
genre. The *changüí* developed in the Guantánamo region,
more specifically, as older people describe it, around the coffee
plantations of Yateras, on the mountain (interview with Antonio Cisneros, 1990). Several Guantánamo groups, from the
families that kept these traditions alive, are today involved in

maintaining and revitalizing the *changüí*.

The traditional instrumentation of the *changüí* includes neither the guitar nor the *claves*. Here, the *tres* is the only melodic guide. The bass is provided by a *marímbula*, bigger than the African *sansa*: on the back part of the wooden sounding board, which is shaped like a rectangle or a trapezoid, are arranged three to seven metal strips of various lengths, which the musician, sitting on the sounding board, plucks to make them vibrate. When this instrument is not available, the *botija*\* or *botijuela* is often used; this is a simple jar with a hole in it. The performer blows into the hole and modifies the pitch with the pressure of one hand against the other. The Creole *bongó* (which consists of two small drums, of different sizes, which are attached) is still made in the old way: the drumheads are attached with nails and tuned to a low pitch, unlike the *bongó* used in the *son*, which improvise in a high register. The last particularity of this instrumentation is a metal scraper called a *guayo*,\* which is scratched rhythmically. Originally, musicians simply used a kitchen grater for cassava. The absence of a fixed rhythmic pattern, underscored by the absence of the *claves*, is characteristic of the *changüí*. The *tres* has an essential role, with very segmented musical phrases, and a constant dialogue with the *bongó*. "Here, we call these two instruments the fighters, because they're always discussing! What's more, in the *changüí*, the *bongó* plays not on the beat but on the off-beat, which gives a much less stable rhythm than we find in the *son*" (interview with Cisneros, director of the Changüí de Guantánamo group, 1990).

At certain moments, to announce a new phase of the piece, we hear the plaintive call obtained by the pressure, the friction, and the relaxing of the player's finger on the skin—the glissando.

According to Antonio Cisneros, two types of *changüí* survive today. One is used especially in dance, with a rapid tempo; the other is a sort of oratorical contest in quatrains (which are called *réginas*\* in the eastern region), in which the improvisers trade funny barbs. As for the choreography, it maintains something of its former elegance, with its forward- or backward-sliding steps, its *carríl*, in which the dancers move from one end of the dance floor to the other, and its measured turns, which the female dancers love. Originally, it was the woman who asked her partner to turn her, whenever she felt so inspired. And, in order to avoid soiling her partner's shirt, she always held a handkerchief in the hand, which she laid on his shoulder (interview with Evelia Noble, 1990).

Certain traditional *changüís* have been taken up by dance orchestras. In 1957, Elio Revé, a native of Guantánamo, introduced the *changüí* with his *charanga* orchestra in Havana, in an orchestrated version of *Fiesta en Cecilia*. Later on, certain of his compositions, such as *Changüí campanero* and *Changüí clave*, enjoyed great success. As for *Pastorita tiene guararé*, it was featured in an adaptation by Los Van Van and in several versions outside the island.

### The *Nengón*

The *nengón*, of which several regional variants exist (in the mountain region of the two Sierras, in the valleys of the Cauto and the Toa), presents general characteristics which are close to those of the *changüí*: rhythmic instability, elimination of the *claves*, and the *tres*'s particular manner of segmenting or accentuating the meter. The *tres* is frequently accompanied by the clapping of hands on or off the beat. As for versification, it freely mixes four- and ten-line verses, much in the manner of those found in the rural music of western Cuba, but without a fixed model (Orozco, *Notes*, 1987). One of the curiosities of its instrumentation is the use of a musical bow, the *tumbandera*, also called the *tingotalango*, which assumes the function of a bass. A Bantu origin is attributed to this instrument, and its sound box is a more or less deep hole dug in the ground, which is then covered with a web of palm fibers, to which is attached the sole string. The string itself is attached at the other end to a flexible branch. The vibrations are created either by plucking the string or by striking the fiber web and the string itself with two small pieces of wood (Eli, Gomez, 1989).

### The *Sucu-sucu*

The *sucu-sucu* is a variant that originated on Pine Island, now called the Island of Youth. The island, rich in minerals, was first a hiding-place for freebooters, then a deportation center where the Spaniards built a model penitentiary. Immigrants from the Cayman Islands, from Jamaica, and from the eastern regions of Cuba contributed to the creation of an original instrumentation in Cuban music: accordion and harmonica, sometimes guitar and violin (Linares, 1974), were brought into the classical instrumentation of the eastern *son*. The machete often replaced the metal *guayo*; and we find calypso rhythms cutting through a rhythmic structure similar to the *son*.

### The *Son Montuno*

When it arrived in the suburban zone of Santiago de Cuba, the eastern *son* kept the mark of its rural origins in the name it was given: *son montuno* (*son* of the mountains). According to oral tradition, it was a *tres* player named Nené Manfugas who introduced it at carnival in 1892. Its instrumentation included the *tres*, the *güiro*, and the *bongó*, to which were added, under the influence of the *trova*, a guitar, maracas, and *claves*, marking the syncopated simple rhythm (one-two-three, one-two) which imposed itself as one of the characteristics of the *son*. Nevertheless, the eastern *son* retained a quick tempo from its antecedents, and the *clave* was not as tyrannical as it would later be in the *son* of Havana. The *marímbula* quickly replaced the *botijuela*, on account of its superior harmonic capacities. From then on, the *bongó* was tuned higher, as in all popular urban music, complementing the fringes of superimposed timbres. To this distribution of timbres, Danilo Orozco added the notion of "action fringes," which intervene during the segments operated by the *tres*, in the manner in which the sounds are incorporated in and act upon each other with the orchestral musical syntax (interview, 1988).

The *son montuno* acquired its special character from this superimposition, on the dance, of sound registers and different rhythmic lines within a relatively stable meter, as well as from the structure of the song. This structure was basically marked by the alternation between a recurring element, the refrain sung by the chorus, and the soloist's improvisation, according to forms that have varied in the course of the genre's evolution. An early type of alternation was done line by line; Alejo Carpentier, Lydia Cabrera, and Fernando Ortiz see in it a similarity with the "African sung games" and more generally with group songs. Carpentier even emphasizes that this question-answer structure "had drawn attention of certain authors of the Spanish Golden Age as being an African musical characteristic." In the interludes of their compositions, this is how they had the characters playing blacks sing. The *Son de la Ma' Teodora* is constructed on this model, with its refrain punctuating each of the soloist's sentences: *Rajando la leña está*

Trío Matamoros with the composer Miguel Matamoros (1884–1971)

(She is cutting wood). Another form, sometimes combined
with the first, introduces the eight-syllable quatrain (*régina*),
which permits the soloist to amplify the narrative part of his
song, while alternating with the chorus; the intervention of
the chorus in the refrain (*estribillo*) can go from a single phrase
to an entire verse. The soloist-chorus sequence of contrasting
alternation, which corresponds to the climax of the piece, is
called *montuno*. It is precisely this infinity of possible combinations that constitutes the richness of the eastern *son*; the
Trío Matamoros gives numerous examples of these variations.
In *La Mujer de Antonio*, to each phrase of the soloist comes the
response of the chorus's fixed theme *Camina así* (That's how
she walks). In *El que siembra su maíz*, after a longer exposition
in the form of a *pregón*, the chorus intervenes, at first with two
lines, *El que siembra su maíz/que se coma su pinol*, then punctu-

ating each line of the couplet in quatrains with *¡Sí señor!* and *¡Cómo no!*.

While the *danzón*, grand master of the era, was still a salon dance necessitating the presence of an entire orchestra, the *son* needed only good improvisers, string instruments such as the guitar and the *tres*, and some percussion, for which one could always get by with whatever came to hand. Its tempo and its narrative and communicative aspects, reinforced as they were by the response-oriented structure of the song, made its rhythm extremely contagious. Its structure allowed it to integrate other sound registers and to incorporate all sorts of instruments, at once melodic and percussive, which contributed to its evolution.

### The Arrival of the *Son* in Havana

Opinions vary on how the *son* spread from the eastern region to the capital. In 1909, the government of José Miguel Gómez formed a "permanent army" of Cuban soldiers, sent to garrisons outside their native regions, to prevent them from fraternizing with the population in the event of repressive measures. This principle, for once, served the cause of music. Thus soldiers from the eastern region who were adepts of the *son* arrived in the capital. They mixed at neighborhood parties and played in halls reserved for them. Among them were Sergio Danger on the *tres*, Emiliano Difull on guitar, and Mariano Mena on the *bongó* (Blanco, 1992).

The other version of how the *son* spread takes into account the agricultural migrations within the island, day laborers moving from one region to another following different harvests, and the movement of workers needed for certain construction projects. Radamés Giró cites the example of several of composers who, in Pinar del Río or in Matanzas, recall having composed *sones* in their most rudimentary form: "A tune for three or four words, behind which was repeated a phrase which everyone sang in a chorus while working," said the *tres* player Chico Ibañez, while gathering memories of 1906 (Giró, 1996, p. 222).

One can see how these contradictory factors may have come together. Moreover, the *trovadores* were the first, with the *coros de clave y guaguancó*, to bring the *son* into their repertoire. The capital city became the crucible in which the *son* first stabilized its instrumental format and then evolved to the rhythm of the innovations of orchestras and musicians. From Havana, the son spread in its new form throughout the island and then abroad, thanks to boat crews, to short-wave radio, and to recordings.

The first recordings were made in February 1917 in New York, for Columbia Records, by a group called Cuarteto Oriental; there was no mention of the musicians' names (Díaz Ayala, 1994, p. 324). Jesús Blanco named the musicians of this quartet, organized in Havana in 1916 as the first professional group: Ricardo Martínez (leader and *tres*), Gerardo Martínez (first voice and *claves*), Guillermo Castillo (*botijuela*, then guitar), and Felipe Nery Cabrera (maracas). A few months later, they were joined by Joaquín Velazco on the *bongo,* who was replaced in 1918 by Óscar Sotolongo. That same year, RCA-Victor, always on the lookout for innovations, sent a team to Havana to record a "typical group" in an improvised studio put together at the Hotel Inglaterra: These were the *trovadores* Manuel Corona (guitar and second voice), María Teresa Vera (*claves* and first voice), and "Sinsonte" (third voice and maracas), accompanied by two musicians who announced the golden age of the *son*, Alfredo Boloña on the bongos and Carlos Godínez on the *tres*.

# The Havana *Son*: Sextet and Septet

During this period, when musicians gathered according to needs and contracts to enliven neighborhood parties, the *son* was considered a lower-class type of music. Judicial chronicles of the period are replete with sentences of "the practice of immoral dances with African instruments" (Blanco, 1992, p. 16). Nevertheless, the local bourgeoisie began to be attracted to this new rhythm. In 1916, the nephew of President Mario García Menocal chose musicians from the Los Apaches group, which had emerged from the Paso Franco *coro de guaguancó*, to perform at the Vedado tennis club. This was an exclusive venue reserved for white people, and the musicians, among whom was Carlos Valdés, the father of Carlos "Patato" Valdés, were, of course, asked to use the service entrance!

One band that became famous around 1919–1920 was the Sexteto Habanero, which came out of the Cuarteto Oriental. The sextet, which recorded as early as 1918 with the RCA-Victor label, embodied an early period of the Havana *son*; by first codifying the instrumental format: one guitar (Guillermo Castillo García, leader and second voice), one *tres* (Carlos Godínez), *claves* and first voice (Gerardo Martínez Rivero), one *botija* (Antonio Bacallao), soon replaced by the *marímbula*, the *bongó* (Óscar Sotolongo), and the maracas (Felipe Nery Cabrera). The band's compositions also contributed to giving the *son* its Havanan structure: a musical introduction where the *tres* is dominant; then a first part, a sort of exposition, sung in several voices; then an instrumental passage, which announces the *montuno*, with its structure of soloist-chorus and question-and-answer. The example of *Papá Montero*, composed by Eliseo Grenet in honor of that mythic character of the rumba, gives a glimpse of the similarities and differences with

Singer Benny Moré (1919–1963) and
trumpeter Felix Chapottín (1907–1983)

its eastern antecedent. First there is an exposition in six lines
that departs from the *régina*; then comes the *montuno*, in
which the chorus punctuates each of the soloist's lines with:
"*¡Zumba! Canalla rumbero*" (Drunkard! Rogue of a *rumbero*).
Musical groups of the same type multiplied; among them
there arose in 1923 the Sexteto Boloña, which was named for
its founder, a *bongocero* (*bongó* player) who became a guitarist,
and in 1924, in Matanzas, the Sonora Matancera.

### Early Innovations

The *son* slowly made its way into the higher spheres. In
1923, the Sexteto Habanero was hired for a ball, but on two
conditions: that the musicians wear a stage uniform and that

they replace the *botija* or the *marímbula* with a (supposedly) nobler instrument, the double bass. Gerardo Martínez thus abandoned his *claves* for this instrument and Antonio Bacallao had to leave the orchestra (Blanco, 1992). The *botija* and *marímbula*, which were less expensive than the double bass, were kept in the groups for a while, but soon most sextets adopted the double bass, because of its far superior harmonic possibilities.

The second big innovation that modified the timbre of the orchestra was the introduction of a trumpet in 1927. The first trumpeter of the Sexteto Habanero, Enrique Hernández Urrutia, was replaced a few months later by Félix Chapottín, who later went on to great fame. The singer Abelardo Barroso, who had an impressive career, also started with this band. The Sexteto Habanero, which had become a septet, was at the height of its glory and, beginning in 1925, its recordings became best sellers. At a big music festival in May 1925, the group won the competition for best *son* orchestra, with a composition by its leader, Guillermo Castillo, recorded the following year for Victor—*Tres lindas cubanas*. Soon, all *son* groups included a trumpet to rival the power of the Septeto Habanero. But the true power of the septet derived from the fact that it included at least three composers: Gerardo Martínez (who wrote *Elena la Cumbanchera* and *El Florel*), Carlos Godínez (who wrote *Alza los pies, congo, Desde que comiste el mango,* and *La Diosa*), and Felipe Nery Cabrera (who wrote *Bururú Barará, Marcha abakuá*). Little by little, the public would no longer be satisfied with mere novelties. When the Trío Matamoros seduced the Cuban capital in 1928 and went on to conquer the whole world, in spite of competing orchestras, it was not only because of its vocal and rhythmic richness, but also because of the picaresque and poetic nature of its lyrics.

Another great innovator of the *son*, Ignacio Piñeiro, also made use of this talent.

### Ignacio Piñeiro and the *Septeto Nacional*

Ignacio Piñeiro was born in 1888, in the Jesús María neighborhood: He learned to improvise in the *coros de clave y guaguancó*, while working at the usual odd jobs, as cooper, mason, tobacco worker, and dockworker. In 1926, he was the double-bass player of the Sexteto Occidente, where María Teresa Vera taught him the art of this instrument and where Miguelito García (second voice) stood out by using a *tres* with nine strings.

In December 1926, Ignacio Piñeiro founded the Sexteto Nacional with three great names of the *trova*: Alberto Villalón on guitar, Bienvenido León (second voice), and Juan de la Cruz Hermida (third voice). They were joined by one of the best *bongoceros* of the day, José M. Carriera "El Chino" Incharte, and the *tres* player Francisco Solares. A few months later, the trumpet player Lázaro Herrera joined the band, which came to be known as the Septeto Nacional, which replaced the Septeto Habanero in public favor. Some of the most famous members of the Septeto Habanero, such as the singer Abelardo Barroso and the *bongocero* Agustín Gutierrez, were lured from the Septeto Nacional.

This orchestra ushered in a new stage of the *son*, which lasted up to the mid-1930s. Ignacio Piñeiro's ambition was to broaden the musical and literary possibilities of the genre by employing his talent as an improviser of *décimas* in writing lyrics inspired by a great variety of themes. This diversity is reflected in the titles of many of his works: *Mayeya, no juegues con los santos*; *Esas no son cubanas*; *Suavecito*; *Échale salsita*; *Salomé*; *Entre tinieblas*; *No me perturbes*. Today these works are part of the international repertoire. Ignacio Piñeiro also promoted the evolution of the structure of the *son*. His instrumental introduction combined *tres* and trumpet; the exposition, which was longer, was still sung in many voices. However, in the course of his compositions, the soloist came to the forefront. From the very beginning, the soloist was featured, in alternation with the chorus; the improvisation was developed in the second part, with greater independence from the chorus. The trumpet, which responded to the singing, became the veritable protagonist of the group. The master of the Septeto Nacional himself often said that he made certain innovations of the Trío Matamoros his own by adapting them to the orchestral format. These innovations in thematic exposition and harmonic elegance enabled him to reinforce the lyricism of the song and of the melody without abandoning the highly rhythmic character of the *son*. The singer no longer led the alternation with the chorus, as in the older *son*—whence its name of *guía*—but became a separate personality whose name began to be remembered, as were the names of soloists Alfredo Valdés, Marcelino "Rapindey" Guerra, and Bienvenido Granda.

Ignacio Piñeiro was also one of the first practitioners of a tendency that spread at this time: the combination of the *son* and other dance rhythms. Piñeiro developed the *guajira-son* (*Lejana campiña, Vueltabajera, Alma guajira, Eterna primavera*), the *rumba-son* (*Mi yambú, Sobre una tumba una rumba*), the *son-pregón* (*Échale salsita*), and the *guaracha-son*, in which he took up several compositions of one of the specialists of the genre, Ñico Saquito. The repertoire of *son* orchestras broadened considerably due to this musical cross-fertilization that continued into the 1940s and 1950s.

Sextets and septets proliferated in the 1930s, and the competition was difficult to maintain. With his trumpet player, Lázaro Herrera, Piñeiro in 1931 helped to set up an entirely female orchestra: the Septeto Anacaona, with the five Castro sisters. Then he gave up the leadership of the Septeto Nacional; the group broke up in 1937 but started up again in 1954.

### The Very Strange Story of the *Guajira Guantanamera*

The Cuban musicologist Helio Orovio recounted the story of *Guajira Guantanamera*, whose various versions have gone around the world, a few years after an interview which the journalist Neisa Ramón published in the January 23, 1987, issue of the magazine *Bohemia*. It is a poignant example of the peregrinations of a melody and of how fluctuating are the borders between rhythms. The story begins in Guantánamo with Herminio García Wilson, a musician who was born in 1904

Joseíto Fernández

and who was nicknamed Diablo Wilson because of his skill on the *tres*. At the age of ten, he started working in a bakery. He later said that the bakery workers, to put up with their job, played and sang boleros and *sones* through the night. He made his debut with coworkers in an *estudiantina*.* One day in 1929, the band was to play at a birthday party and while waiting for the guests to arrive, the musicians began to improvise. As a young girl passed by, the singer paid her a gallant compliment. This displeased the beauty and she responded to him with an insult. Stung to the quick, one of the musicians countered: "Who does she think she is, this peasant girl from Guantánamo?" From these words, Diablo Wilson improvised a few measures and a *montuno*, and thus was born the *Guajira Guantanamera*— with an improvised melody and lyrics, with which the singer Felipe Corona gently poked fun at a somewhat uppity peasant girl! That same year the refrain traveled to Havana with the singer and three musicians intent on trying their luck in the capital.

The sequel is better known, since it concerns the singer Joseíto Fernández, who has long been credited with the melody. Joseíto Fernández was born in Havana in 1908. Known in the 1930s as a singer of *danzonete*, he created his own *danzón* orchestra and often shared the stage with Cheo Marquetti, a singer who made his name in various sextets. According to the musicians, it was Marquetti, called the king of the *guajira-son*, who supposedly had the idea to use the eastern melody to pay homage to women from his own territory. Joseíto Fernández then supposedly did likewise. The secret of the *Guantanamera* is that different lyrics have been adapted to a single melody. Joseíto Fernández recounted:

> In 1935, I was with the "typical" orchestra of Alejandro Riveiro at Radio CMCO. The broadcast always began with a classical piece and ended with a little rumba. One day, we decided to change this practice. I adapted a *guajira* that I had composed in 1929, and we turned it into the theme song marking the end of the broadcast. It was the *Guantanamera*, and I sang a differ-

ent ten-line verse every day to the same melody. I also
wrote the lyrics. That's how the *Guantanamera* became
popular. When the orchestra arrived at a ball, everybody asked for it. (Orovio, in *Unión*, 1993)

The second episode in this saga began at Radio CMQ, which
created, in 1939, a broadcast titled *El Suceso del día* (The Events
of the Day), in which Joseíto Fernández and another singer, La
Calandría, commented on the news in *décimas*. In 1941, the
singer recorded, again to the same tune, *Mi biografía*, in which
he talks about his life, and *Guardabarreras*, with critical lyrics
denouncing railroad accidents at crossings that lack guardrails.
Other compositions with the same rythm and melody
followed—such as *Cuento mi vida*, *Amor de madre*, and *Así es el
arte*—which linked together several ten-line verses, without
any instrumental passages to separate them; these compositions resembled an epic narrative, evocative of the Spanish
*romancero*—a type of Cuban epic, to narrate simple little facts!

The story of *Guajira Guantanamera* does not stop there, because the version that traveled around the world is that of the
poem *Versos sencillos* (Simple Lines of Poetry) by José Martí. In
the 1950s, the classical composer Julián Orbón sat at the piano
one evening in the company of friends and adapted the lines
of the Cuban patriot to the tune of *La Guantanamera*. One of
the people present that evening took the sung poem with him
to the United States. The American folksinger Pete Seeger liked
the song well enough to adapt it to his own style. All this happened in the period of protests against the Vietnam War and
the heyday of folk ballads. The tune and the lyrics became
popular and their apotheosis occurred one June evening in
1963 at a concert in New York City's Carnegie Hall. This is how
*La Guantanamera*, improvised one evening at a party in Guantánamo, became known the world over.

## The *Conjuntos* Era

After the Sexteto Habanero and the Septeto Nacional, two orchestras ushered in a new stage in the development of the *son* and brought it closer to its contemporary sound: those of Arsenio Rodríguez and the Conjunto Casino. The great *tres* player, blind since the age of thirteen and nicknamed "El Ciego maravilloso," was originally from Güira de Macurijes, in the province of Matanzas. In 1933, he settled in the capital, where all the orchestras were looking to amplify their acoustic and sound possibilities. To reinforce the counterpoint in the higher register, they were already using two, or even three, trumpets. In the late 1930s, the percussionist Chano Pozo put together the Conjunto Azul orchestra, which played regularly in the studios of Radio RHC-Cadena Azul. He also added his five *tumbadoras* to the lineup. That same year, the Conjunto Casino made its debut with a piano, but without a *tumbadora*, at the summer casino of the Marianao beach. Arsenio Rodríguez took on these innovations and, at the same time, established an instrumental format specific to a new lineup, which would definitively keep the name *conjunto*. Arsenio mastered several instruments, including ritual Bantu drums; he already had to his credit a number of popular compositions in which the oppression of black people and their spiritual strength were a source of permanent inspiration—works such as the famous *son-afro Bruca maniguá* and various pieces in homage to the black neighborhoods of Havana.

In the early 1940s, Arsenio Rodríguez took over the leadership of the Sexteto Bellamar and changed it from top to bottom within a few months. He also created his Conjunto Todas Estrellas: piano, *tres*, double bass, *tumbadora*, *bongó*, three trumpets, and three singers, one of whom also played guitar. Arsenio had a very personal style on the *tres*, percussive and rhythmic at the same times. He also introduced the innovation of creating a sounding block comprised of *tres* and piano and endowed the piano with a rhythmic function in the *tumbaos*, somewhat in the manner of the *danzón nuevo ritmo* of Arcaño, and with improvisations that took up the harmonic progressions that ordinarily would be performed by the *tres* and the guitar. The orchestra became a veritable training ground for the explosive talents of many future *son* stars. Among them were the pianists Lino Frías, known later as the pianist of the Sonora Matancera, Rubén González, nicknamed "El Bonito", and Luis (Lilí) Martínez Griñan, cited as a model by all the current pianists of the Caribbean area, from Eddie Palmieri to Papo Lucca. Among the trumpet players, we should note Alfredo "Chocolate" Armenteros, who was trained in the school of the Septeto Habanero, Rubén Calzado, and Félix Chapottín, whose solos set the style for several decades. Finally, there are voices that will always mark the history of the *son*: those of Marcelino Guerra, who would go on to pursue his career in the United States; René Álvarez; René Scull; and especially the *sonero* par excellence Miguelito Cuní. When Arsenio Rodríguez left to settle in the United States in 1951, it was Chapottín who succeeded him as the head of what became the Conjunto Chapottín y sus Estrellas. At the time, the group still featured Lilí Martínez, who composed and arranged many of the orchestra's famous themes, and the voice of Cuní, reinforced by that of René Álvarez. Next to Ignacio Piñeiro, Arsenio Rodríguez left the richest repertoire of great classics.

The Conjunto Casino developed a style different from that of Arsenio Rodríguez. The repertoire of this orchestra, at first made up exclusively of white musicians, was based on the alternation of boleros, sung by Roberto Espí, and of rapid *guarachas*. Though the *son* had earned a few stripes in high society, it was still considered a plebeian type of music. In 1949, when Carlos "Patato" Valdés joined the orchestra, he became the first black musician to join a lineup of whites. With this percussionist, the *tumbadora* took on another dimension, as melodic as well as rhythmic, in addition to an important technical innovation: for it was Patato who, in 1952, had the idea of installing a system of keys to stretch the skins of his drums, which until then were stretched by being heated with an open flame. Patato spoke about his apprenticeship:

> My father was Carlos Valdés. He played the *tres* in the Los Apaches band, which was the cradle of the Sexteto Habanero and of the Sexteto Boloña, and he composed several of the great hits of the time: *Maldita tímidez, No me desprecies, Los hombres no lloran.* I first learned to play the *tres*, and my father, to initiate me on the drums, made me play on an old stringless banjo on which he had stretched a very fine calfskin. He would say to me: "You must learn to master the sound of this skin, which is as fine as parchment." He also made me a *marímbula*, from an old crate and eighteen springs from old clocks, and with an empty food can, he made me a *güiro* for me to learn how to keep time. I also learned to dance; before, I was a dancer. Then I entered the *comparsas* of the Los Sitios neighborhood, because it's in the street that one learns to play the drums. (interview, 1989)

Carlos "Patato" Valdés entered the Sonora Matancera in 1943 as a *tres* player, and on the death of Valentín Cané, he moved to the *tumbadora*. But he left the band in 1945 in order to develop as a musician. As he put it:

With the Matancera, one always had to play the typical *son*. So I joined the Conjunto Kubavana of Alberto Ruiz, with Armando Peraza on the bongó. It was the most modern orchestra of the time. In 1949, I joined the Conjunto Casino, in the *Casablanca* Cabaret, I was the first black musician to cross the racial line; an orchestra mixing black, white, and mulatto musicians doesn't have the same sound. I showed the white audience that the drum wasn't a savage thing, the drum is like a woman: You must love her, caress her so she'll give you what you want. If you hit the drum hard, you'll get nothing out of it. When I invented the tension system with keys, I was able to tune the *tumbadoras* differently, and I started playing with two drums, to develop the melody. We played differently from Arsenio. I like the bolero style, more delicate, softer than the *son montuno*. I used to listen a lot to the Mexican singers, Toña la Negra, and I began to modify the rhythm of the *tumbadora* in the boleros. I've always liked improvising rhythmic patterns, but above all I like the melody of my drums. If you take the example of the *tres*, Arsenio Rodríguez is the master of rhythm, but Niño Rivera is the king of melody; with his Conjunto Bolero, you get the impression that you're hearing a *danzón*. (interview, 1989)

The new era inaugurated by the *conjuntos* allowed orchestras to play all existing Cuban rhythms, with the single exception of the *danzón*. The arrangements entailed new harmonies and the singers' position became fixed: If each orchestra was immediately identifiable by its sound, it is also true that its popularity was linked to that of the singer. Hence the name of Conjunto Casino is inseparable of the names of Roberto Espí, Agustín Ribot, Orlando Vallejo, and above all Roberto Faz (who created his own group in 1956). In a similar manner,

Bienvenido Granda and then Celia Cruz would assure the success of the Sonora Matancera in the 1950s.

## The Jazz-Band Era

The importance of singing voices did not diminish with the vogue of big bands. Within the limits of this study it is, of course, impossible to include a history of jazz in Cuba or of the contributions Cuban musicians made to U.S. jazz. However, mention should be made of the perennial names Chano Pozo, Machito y sus Afro-Cubanos, and Mario Bauzá, who was a violin, clarinet, and saxophone player before he became a trumpet player.

In Cuba, the 1930s saw a proliferation of jazz bands. Their repertoire was originally made up of U.S. dance rhythms, but gradually they began to play Cuban rhythms and fused them with jazz orchestrations and improvisations. Their audience was that of the big cabarets, and some of them made a career abroad, mostly in the United States. Among the best known, should be noted: the orchestras of Hermanos Castro, created in 1929; René Touzet; Armando Romeu; Hermanos Palau; Casino de la Playa (1937), with the voice of Miguelito Valdés, then of Orlando "Cascarita" Guerra; and the Orquesta Riverside, which reached its zenith in the 1950s with the singer Tito Gómez. This period gave birth to a pantheon of renowned musicians, pianists, saxophonists, trumpet players, trombonists, guitarists, double-bass players, and drummers. Among them, Pedro "Peruchín" Justiz deserves special mention, because he revolutionized the art of the piano; his innovations became part of the popular piano style.

Born in Banes, in eastern Cuba, Pedro Justiz received his initial musical training from his family. His grandfather was director of the municipal brass band of Antilla. The first instrument Peruchin played was the alto saxophone. He learned to play the piano, ostensibly from his mother, though he in fact practically learned by himself. In 1933, he settled in Santiago de Cuba where he worked with the Chepín-Choven orchestra, which had been formed the previous year and was directed by Electo "Chepín" Rosell, a concert violinist and composer, and Bernardo Choven. Pedro Justiz then left for Havana and joined the Casino de la Playa orchestra. In the 1940s, he joined the Armando Romeu orchestra, which brought together in the Tropicana Cabaret some of the era's finest instrumentalists. Finally, in the 1950s, Pedro Justiz became a pianist and arranger at the Riverside.

This was the era of the *descargas*,* which were at first referred to as "Cuban jam sessions." This tradition had existed in Cuba for several years: Musicians would get together and, starting with a given theme, begin to improvise. The Panart label, and then the Gema label, sought to distinguish themselves by adding a commercial dimension to what was initially just a pleasure shared among friends. The musicians who gathered for these recordings gave a sense of their versatility and proved once again the absence of barriers between the different musical genres and formats. In these recordings, we can hear the *tres* of Niño Rivera; the flute of Richard Egües and of José Fajardo; Emilio and Osvaldo Peñalver on tenor and alto saxophone; Tata Güines on the *tumbadora*; Guillermo Barreto on the *timbales* or drums; Israel "Cachao" López on the double bass; the trumpet players Alejandro "El Negro" Vivar, "Chocolate" Armenteros, and Chico O'Farill; and the trombonist Generoso Jiménez. The recordings of this period are marvels. They include instrumental versions of pieces from the popular repertoire, side by side with more straightforward jazz compositions, bringing together instrumentalists who navigate between concert music, *charangas* orchestras, *conjuntos*, and jazz-band lineups, among whom we should mention those of Bebo Valdés, father of the pianist and founder of Irakere, Chucho Valdés.

### The *Banda Gigante* of Benny Moré

Bartolomé Maximiliano Moré is a veritable legend of popular music. Born into a poor peasant family of Santa Isabel de Las Lajas, in the province of Las Villas, he is a descendant, through his mother, of the first king of the *cabildo congo*, a slave of Count Moré. Bartolomé Moré grew up within the aura of ritual music performed by the Casino de los Congos, where he learned the art of drumming. But his peasant ties also made him an improviser of *décimas* and *tonadas*. He rejoined his mother in the region of Camagüey, where she was a laundress, and worked on a sugar plantation. With the local *trovadores*, he perfected an apprenticeship in guitar and *tres*, then participat-

Benny Moré with family members

ed in a local *conjunto* and in a trio where he sang second voice. In 1940, he left for Havana, to try his luck. There he sang in bars, with his guitar, and participated in radio broadcasts with various groups. He owed his breakthrough, in 1944, to Miguel Matamaros, who meanwhile had created a septet, and then a *conjunto* bearing his name. One day Matamoros returned from a tour voiceless, there-

Benny Moré (1919–1963)

fore incapable of honoring a contract for that very day. Siro Rodríguez recommended Bartolo Moré, as he was known, and the singer made his debut with the prestigious band. He made 78-rpm recordings with the band and, in 1945, he took part in a tour of Mexico. When his Mexican contract expired, he decided to stay in Mexico and signed an exclusive contract with RCA-Victor. He quickly acquired the reputation of being able to sing whatever rhythms were fashionable, Cuban or otherwise, and to sing them happily, in his own personal style; among these were not only boleros, *guaracha*, *son*, and mambo, but also *merengue*, *plena*, and *porro*.

He joined the big band of Pérez Prado and, in 1952, he returned to Cuba where he worked mainly with jazz bands.

These included the jazz band of Mariano Mercerón in Santiago de Cuba, which was famous for its *danzónes*, and where he sang alongside two future singing stars, Fernando Álvarez and Pacho Alonso. Then he worked with the jazz band of Bebo Valdés, which had just created the *batanga* rhythm, which was no doubt too complex to have any commercial success at the time. Finally, he worked with the jazz band of Ernesto Duarte, with whom he recorded several albums. But he complained of the racism of the bandleader, who excluded him from performances in cabarets, theaters, private parties, and other chic venues of the period, and he set off in search of musicians who could enable him to achieve his dream to have a band of his own.

On August 3, 1953, Benny Moré presented for the first time his giant lineup on a Radio CMQ program: piano (Ignacio "Cabrerita" Cabrera), double bass (Alberto Limona), *tumbadora* ("Tabaquito"), *bongó* (Clemente "Chicho" Piquero), drums (Rolando Laserie, who would later become a singer), four saxophones (Santiago Peñalver, Miguel Franca, Roberto Barreto, and Virgilio Vixama), three trumpets (Alfredo "Chocolate" Armenteros, Rigoberto Jiménez, and Domingo Corbacho), one trombone (José Miguel), and two additional singers, Fernando Álvarez and Enrique Benítez. Benny Moré did not know how to transcribe music, but he had an extraordinary ear. The experience he had acquired in other jazz bands allowed him to assimilate all the harmonic possibilities offered by those bands, and he dictated to the arrangers (Cabrerita, Peruchín, Generoso Jiménez) the sounds and rhythmic patterns he wanted for them to transcribe. Enrique Benítez remembers:

> When he told the band to stop during rehearsals, something had to be wrong. His ear was a veritable

radar. Nothing escaped him. He would put his hands
on his head, stop singing, turn around, and say: "Stop
. . . One of you is behind . . . Listen to how it should be
done." And with his mouth he would start doing:
"*Cum pá, cum patá, cum pá . . .*" until the musician
played the passage in question to perfection. (Martínez
Rodríguez, 1993)

As varied as the rhythms were, the band maintained great
unity in its arrangements. It exploited all the possibilities of
the brass section, with several voices and in unison. The performance of Benny Moré, the register of his voice, and his
expressiveness are especially noteworthy. In 1954, he had
already acquired his nickname "Bárbaro del ritmo," for the
special way he had of placing the lyrics on the rhythm. In
time, he modified his lineup by increasing to four the number
of singers and trumpets, and periodically replaced the other
instrumentalists (Generoso Jiménez on trombone; Jorge
Varona, future member of Irakere, on trumpet; Jesús López on
*tumbadora*). His thin profile, his baggy pants held up by sus-
penders, his panama hat always on his head, his dancer's elegance, and his expressiveness turned this idol into an icon.
Even after the Cuban Revolution, his popularity remained as
vigorous as before, but he died of cirrhosis of the liver in 1963.
The musicologist Leonardo Acosta has summed up perfectly
the originality and the importance of this singer:

> We don't consider Benny as the *initiator* of some-
> thing new, but rather as a synthesis, as the high point
> of everything that was done in our popular music in
> the fifty years that preceded him: *son, danzón, trova,*
> mambo, *feeling,* rumba, and bolero. I think that this is
> where his true significance rests, and, to succeed in the
> music, he had to be nothing but an exceptional per-

former. . . . He closes and sums up brilliantly an entire era. That's why he won't be a school, why he had no successors, even though we see the mark he left on many current singers. But, in general terms, we can affirm that he was unique and inimitable. (Acosta, in Nasser, 1994)

# VIII

# Music Since
# the Revolution

Following the 1959 Revolution, some orchestras, instrumentalists, and singers left Cuba, because they refused to bend to the conditions of the new regime. The government nationalized the hotels, the cabarets, and the record labels, and closed down some venues of popular entertainment. An era of Cuban music came to an end while another began abroad with the émigré orchestras. The music produced on the island was no longer distributed outside the country. The Latin American and European left of the 1970s later popularized the politically oriented songs of the *nueva trova*. Cuban bands traveled mostly in "friendly" countries. If they appeared at a few musical festivals in France in the 1980s, it was through the initiative of individual towns or pioneers unafraid of braving musical adventures. Not until the commercial boom of the 1990s did foreigners discover that music was still being made in Cuba, even if under difficult and sometimes contradictory conditions.

## The New Context

After 1959, official cultural policies in musical matters were articulated around a few central goals: to safeguard the most authentic cultural roots and national traditions; to promote the movement of amateur musicians and singers in order to discover new talent; to train high-quality professional musicians by providing better musical education; and to create structures allowing for musical experimentation. But the general conditions of shortages faced by Cuban society after 1960, the primacy given to ideological struggle, and the tendency toward bureaucratization had considerable influence on real cultural practices and led to criteria with contradictory consequences.

To highlight the traditional cultural heritage, folk-music groups were formed throughout the island. In Santiago de Cuba, for example, there was the Conjunto Folklórico de Oriente, which in 1975 gave rise to the Conjunto Folklórico Cutumba, and in Havana, the Conjunto Folklórico Nacional. According to Rogelio Martínez Furé, cofounder in 1962 of the latter group: "It's not a question of creating the exotic for tourists by cutting off folklore from its real and living roots, but rather one of presenting our various traditions through the aesthetic prism of creators, in order to reach a universal language" (interview, 1986). In his book *Diálogos imaginarios sobre folklor*, Furé opposes two concepts of folklore—one, a living entity in constant evolution; the other, a fixed museum of tradition. The very insistence with which Furé places these two concepts in opposition would seem to indicate that such a dialogue is not as imaginary as he claims (1979, pp.

257–275). Outside the aesthetic context, many cultural officials consider such traditions to be outdated relics in the era of the "new man."

## The Training of Musicians

All over the island, music schools, regional conservatories, and professional schools opened and provided a very high level of instruction. Each student learned to play several instruments, while also studying composition, harmony, and orchestration, in a program of study focused on classical and contemporary music. Although it was first excluded from these schools, the study of popular music eventually became a field of specialization at the end of the course of study. However, as most young musicians trained in this system confirm, popular music is still considered by their teachers to be of relatively low prestige; in the name of excellence in training, popular music is taken to be a minor art. Many cultural officials consider these types of dance music mere entertainment rather than a genuine creative field; popular music is given neither the financial support nor the opportunities to be broadcast that it deserves. The urgency of economic production (which gives priority to labor) and the prevailing shortages (implying, for example, a lack of funds with which to buy instruments or amplifying equipment) prevent people from questioning the choices that are already made but rarely explained. The Los Van Van orchestra broached this topic in 1989 in *Yo no soy de la Gran Escena*, which was a reference to a television program devoted to opera and classical music, and which plainly denounced what Juan Formell considers a form of discrimination.

For popular music to remain creative, the question of the relationship between musical groups and their audience is essential. And the new status of musicians highlights this necessity. Since the Revolution, musicians have been considered "music workers." After a periodic evaluation, they are classified in two categories and paid a fixed salary, according to their classification, thus they are protected from the laws of the marketplace. In theory, their creative freedom is greater, since competition and emulation among groups no longer depends on trade but rather on the popularity acquired because of public performances or in radio and television broadcasts.

## The Media and Public Concerts

Everyone complains about the system of broadcasting. Leonardo Acosta, a musician and musicologist, has gathered the gist of criticisms aimed at the media in his book *Del tambor al sintetizador* (*From the Drum to the Synthesizer*). Such criticisms have already been echoed in the magazine *El Caimán barbudo*: too little focus on music, dubious choices, absence of directorial creativity (Acosta, 1985). In fact, no audience is satisfied neither the listeners seeking traditional genres, nor the young people crazy for "foreign" music (rock, pop, funk); the only exceptions were the "old folks." The Sierra Maestra band, which started to perform in 1976 with the original *son* sound, is an exception (interview, Juan de Marcos González, 1988).

The only remaining options were public performances. However, during the 1970s, most popular venues shut down for economic reasons (food, drink, electricity, amplification), and also because these gatherings where young people got a bit too worked up turned into riots. Thus carnivals became the only true space for popular entertainment, where one could have a direct sense of the intensity of ties between musicians and their audience. On a daily basis, dance bands could be found in dance halls or on the porches of *circulos sociales*, which were types of neighborhood houses. State-run companies managed contracts, according to a system that has been criticized for its bureaucratic ponderousness. Again because of the difficult economic situation, these venues grew steadily rarer until they too disappeared. Musicians also performed in the cabarets in big hotels, to which Cubans have access, thanks to the tickets distributed by their trade unions; however, the shows given there are not necessarily musically up-to-date. The Tropicana, where prestigious musicians are featured, is the tourist showcase; its spectacular revues are Cuban, of course, but they are based on U. S. shows.

Musical activity is in fact concentrated in the annual festivals of bolero, cha-cha-cha, *danzón, son,* and even *habanera,* or in competitions and celebrations of particular composers or performers. But these exceptional events, without ties to daily musical involvement, risk lapsing into the conventional, according to Leonardo Acosta, who calls for the deep study of the ancient heritage in schools "in order to develop new musical forms that maintain the essence of our roots while incorporating new elements that help define our contemporaneousness" (Acosta, 1985).

## The Might of the Dollar and Its Effects

With the legalization of the dollar in 1993, the setting up of joint venture companies and tourism, a market for Cuban bands and records has developed outside the island. The taste foreign audiences have for the most traditional forms of music has revived a sector that never ceased to exist, but had remained marginalized due to lack of exposure. Forgotten treasures from the 1920s to the 1950s are being reissued today on a large scale. Musicians who had retired long ago are reap-

pearing up front on the international stage—Francisco Repilado ("Compay Segundo"), the Vieja Trova Santiaguera, and
the singers and musicians featured on the three albums released by the British label World Circuit: The Afro-Cuban All-
Stars; Son de Cuba, with the *Buenavista Social Club* album, winner of the Grammy Award in the United States in 1998; and
Ruben González, who thus recorded, at the age of seventy-
seven, his first solo album. A great number of Cuban orchestras have been recording with foreign labels, from the most
traditional groups (such as the excellent Conjunto Los Naranjos, created in Cienfuegos in 1926, the Septeto Santiaguero,
the Estudiantina Invasora, and the Cuarteto Patria) to the
most "modern." For the foreign professional who are scouting
for musical talent in Havana, also turn their quest toward the
island's interior.

However, this boom should not obscure the fact that compact disks and hi-fi equipment, as well as the new clubs that
opened thanks to tourism, are accessible only to Cubans with
dollars in sufficient quantities. In the capital city, the Salon
Rosado Benny Moré at *La Tropical,* which reopened in 1986, is
one of the few places where Cuban currency is accepted. It
welcomes the "grandparents' balls" (*baile de los abuelos*) to
great acclaim, with orchestras such as the Conjunto Chapottín, the Septeto Habanero, the Septeto Nacional, and the Charanga Rubalcaba, which keep alive the repertoire of the "gold-
en age." It is also the "dance test" where all the orchestras can
evaluate their popularity with the younger generation.

Indeed, even though poorly broadcast, all forms of musical
expression remain alive in Cuba. Musicians' wages permitted
traditional orchestras to stay afloat, for better or worse, and
the national musical heritage has also been passed down outside official venues. Performances within family and among

friends continued: A guitar, a bottle, a footstool, and a spoon are often enough to start a party, and there is always someone to sing songs and boleros. The Cubans' memory of this repertoire astonishes the foreign visitor. Music has never become simply a consumer product; it has remained a collective practice and a form of social identity.

In the period after the Revolution, young people's musical aspirations were expressed in a thirst for new sounds and modern style, reflected in their passionate interest in such groups as the Beatles, Genesis, and Pink Floyd. Inspired by these bands, Síntesis emerged in 1976. Recent years have seen the appearance of a large number of rock groups and rap groups. However, since the late 1960s, some composers have sought to restore the ties between the young people and their Cuban roots by reasserting, under new conditions, the trends already present in previous musical history: the fusion with other contemporary musical forms, the impact of dance, and the communicative function of lyrics. We shall now turn our interest specifically to the various components of this trend.

## Musical Evolution

### The ICAIC Group for Sound Experimentation

Paradoxically, the movie industry may well be the domain that best integrated for a while the double perspective of past and future. At first some documentaries were dedicated to a few great names and orchestras, such as Benny Moré (*¡Que bueno canta Usted!* of Sergio Giral), Ignacio Piñeiro, the orchestra of Arcaño (*Rompiendo la rutina* of Oscar Valdés), the Conjunto Folklórico Nacional, the Trio Matamoros (Luis Felipe Bernaza) and Juan Formell (*A ver que sale* of Oscar Valdés)—and to such musical genres as the rumba, the *punto*, the *conga*, the *tonadas* of Trinidad, and Abakuá music (Acosta, 1985).

Along with the work of these filmmakers, we see the creation in 1969—spearheaded by the ICAIC (the Cuban Institute of Cinematographic Art and Industry)—of the Grupo de experimentación sonora, directed by Leo Brouwer, an internationally famous composer and guitarist. Leo Brouwer set himself various objectives: to develop music for cinema; to promote politically and socially oriented song, with the pioneers of what would become the official movement of the *nueva trova*—Pablo Milanés, Silvio Rodríguez, Noel Nicola, Martin Rojas, Eduardo Ramos, and Vicente Feliu; to safeguard the most authentic roots of popular music while working to renew it; and to study contemporary techniques of composition and production, such as electroacoustics and recording techniques. Officially founded in 1972, on the initiative of the Communist Youth Movement, the *nueva trova* imposed for a decade an indisputable musical tyranny, through politically oriented songs that were promoted at the expense of other forms of musical expression. Nevertheless the musical achievements of this group would be decisive for the experimental trends of the young Cuban musical expression of the 1970s and the 1980s, represented by such diverse bands as Irakere, Afro-Cuba, Algo Nuevo, and by the pianist Emiliano Salvador.

**Instrumental Music**

In 1959, the Quinteto instrumental de música moderna was set up, with Frank Emilio Flynn on the piano, Papito Hernández—then Orlando "Cachaíto" López—on double bass, Guillermo Barreto on drums, Tata Güines on the *tumbadora*, and Gustavo Tamayo on the *güiro*. After setting up the Los Amigos band, they followed the tradition of the *descargas* of the previous decade, while also playing mostly in the National

Symphony Orchestra. The Orquesta Cubana de Música Moderna appeared in 1967, thanks to the initiative of Guillermo Barreto, with a selection of the best young instrumentalists of the time: From this group emerged the founding nucleus of the future band Irakere.

The brilliant composer and pianist Gonzalo Rubalcaba also was a member of this group. With his first band, Proyecto, he examined the creative possibilities of jazz not found elsewhere. The Jazz Plaza Festival of Havana regularly features an impressive number of native jazz bands, which sometimes appear with artists from the United States. But this music generally attracts only an informed audience. Inspired by the contemporary creative quality of jazz, Gonzalo Rubalcaba evolved toward what certain musicians call "the music of the twenty-first century." He remains profoundly Cuban, while speaking a universal language. When he is accompanied by his Cuban quartet (Felipe Cabrera on bass, Julio Barreto on drums, and Reynaldo Melián on trumpet), his personality explodes in the performance, much as it does in the harmonic and rhythmic creativity.

### Juan Formell and Los Van Van: Innovation and Social Commentary

In the realm of dance music, some new Afro-Cuban rhythms appeared in the first decade after the Revolution. Musical elements from the African heritage merged with the exaltation of struggles for independence in Africa. Enrique Bonné formed a giant orchestra, made up entirely of drums and percussion instruments. Pedro Izquierdo (Pello el Afrokán) added brass to it and launched the *mozambique*, which links eastern *conga* and *tumba francesa* to the rhythms of Havana. The orchestra of Pacho Alonso inaugurated the *pilón*, whose

Los Van Van

dance imitates the grinding of food in a mortar. However, none of these rhythms lasted very long.

It was not until 1969 and the creation of Los Van Van, under the leadership of Juan Formell, that such experimentation in sound was systematized in dance music. The son of a musician, Juan Formell belongs to the rock'n'roll generation—as a young man, he played electric guitar while listening to Elvis Presley hits. In 1965 to 1966, he presented a few of his compositions to Elena Burke, the "Señora Sentimiento"—queen of *feeling* and song. Elena Burke recorded four of his songs, and Juan Formell's was made in musical circles. Then, at the end of 1967, he joined the orchestra of Elio Revé, where he remained until he formed his own band in late 1969.

Elio Revé, a percussionist and native of Guantánamo who died in an accident in the summer of 1997, was called "the father of the *soneros*" and had always been a discoverer of young talent. Beginning in 1956, he led a *charanga* orchestra in Havana with which he popularized the eastern *changüí*, by modernizing it. Nourished on the *tumba francesa*, on ritual drumming, on *son* and on rumba, Revé insisted on poly-rhythms. However, the limitations of the *charanga* orchestra held him back musically, and Formell made changes that would prove decisive for the band's future. With Formell, the electric bass guitar and the metal flute made their official entries into the *charanga*. In Santa Clara, however, the excellent Aliamen orchestra (1964) had already adopted these novelties, but this innovation had remained completely ignored by audiences from the capital. After the departure of Juan Formell, the orchestra of Elio Revé continued to evolve: The flute disappeared, but the originality of the musical format dubbed *charangón* (piano, *tres*, bass guitar, violins, three trombones, *bongó*, *tumbadora*, *batá*, *timbal*, *guayo*, and *campana*), along with a dance-oriented repertoire, assured the group's great popularity.

In December 1969, Formell decided to form his own orchestra. The national political campaign to reach a goal of ten million tons of sugar cane was in high gear, and he chose the name Van Van, anticipating the success of the political campaign as well as that of the band ("It'll work out!"). His goal was simple: He wanted to make people dance by sheer strength of a captivating rhythm and incantation, with a line-up that featured neither virtuosos nor brilliant soloists. He incorporated into the basics of the *son* rhythmic elements he borrowed from the music of other countries. He looked for new sounds and called the style he created *songo*. Today, according to Juan Formell, no one invents new rhythms; people only combine already existing ones: *son*, *merengue*, reggae, *ranchera, shake*, pop, funk. The *songo* is a variant of the *son*, within modern musical parameters. It can evolve in its components, but not in its general concept: "True innovation lies in the way of writing music for orchestration" (interview, 1986).

Formell retains the *güiro*, because he considers its permanent presence to be indispensable to the band's rhythmic cohesion. He uses violins in a rhythmic rather than a melodic way, "to bring them closer to the old *rayado* of the guitar." The cello of the old days has disappeared, and the flute often makes up a harmonic block with the bass. In 1980, the orchestra incorporated trombones, which are used for supporting the violins; then it incorporated keyboards, which reinforce the sounds of the different instruments without replacing them. In 1990, it was the saxophone's turn to make its entry. Percussion also evolved. Alongside the *tumbadoras*, the *paila* became the drums; the percussionist Changüito (José Luis Quintana) used his knowledge of drums and ritual rhythms. By transposing the rhythmic patterns, he achieved his *breaks* in a different manner—in high, not low register, on the strong beat. Samuel Formell, his successor in 1994, basically has continued along the same line (interviews 1986, 1988, 1990).

The success of Los Van Van is due also to the song lyrics. They tell about happenings, great and small, that animate people on the island, with sometimes contradicting commentaries between soloist and chorus. They also note society's failures, not aggressively, but with light-hearted irony; for example, they say *No es fácil* (Life isn't easy) instead of "Life is tough."

The depiction of situations and characters in these lyrics can be seen as an extension of the former narrative tradition. These may include a variety of situations touching Cubans'

Los Van Van

personal lives, such as the shortage of water, the unexpected birth of triplets, the television set that breaks down in the middle of a baseball game; and the overpopulation of Havana. They also include a number of political and social themes, such as the tendency of Havanans to have contempt for "invaders," known also by their nickname "Palestinians"—that is to say, inhabitants of the eastern provinces who come to the capital to seek their fortunes; the tendency to mimic the fashions from "developed" countries, from the choice of pets to the production of "designer breads" that are extravagant in the Cuban context; and, more generally, the tendency to favor appearances; a certain concern about the young, who are demanding and unaccustomed to making efforts; negligence of employees who don't care about the interminable lines of customers and are sometimes thoroughly unpleasant; certain abuses by those employees who exploit the system, from the butcher who retails meat according to the charms of his female clients to the bureaucrat who is able to seduce young beauties thanks to his car; and more recently, the uncertainty of what will become of a society turned on by the dollar and the frenzy of business. Nothing escapes the chronicle told in these lyrics. On the love theme, the lyrics reflect the general contradictions: themes of great tenderness and poetry appear next to a very male-oriented view of women's faults (their jealousy and their mania for butting into everything) and of women's qualities (the sensual beauty that fires up men's blood). Finally, the success of Los Van Van has been bolstered by the group's ability to find charismatic singers to perform these all-encompassing lyrics: Pedro Calvo, the very young Mario Rivera, and Roberto Fernández have contributed to the special relationship that the orchestra has had with its audiences.

In the 1970s, Los Van Van had foreign emulators, who adapted some of the orchestra's compositions, as evidenced in *La Candela* by Tipica 73 in New York. In Cuba itself, the orchestra's instrumental innovations inspired Manuel Simonet, a young pianist and composer born in the province of Camagüey. The leader of Maravillas de Florida since 1987, he left for Havana in 1993 and set up Manolito y su Trabuco. To the traditional *charanga* (violin, cello, flute, piano, *tumbadora*, and *güiro*), he added bass guitar and keyboards, as Los Van Van had done; drums and timbales were placed side by side; and two trumpets were added to two trombones. Well armed with a traditional as well as contemporary repertoire, this lineup includes three singers, two of whom are true *soneros*—El Gallo and the former singer of Aliamen, El Indio.

## Tradition in Modernity:
## Son 14 and Adalberto Álvarez

Camagüey is also the birthplace of pianist and composer Adalberto Álvarez. More than two hundred of his themes have been adapted in Cuba and throughout the world. His mother was a *trova* singer and a member of the city's professional choir; his father directed Avance Juveníl, a *conjunto* that shared the stage with Havana orchestras in the 1950s, such as Benny Moré, Chapottín, and Riverside. At the age of nine, Adalberto Álvarez was accompanying these great musicians on the *güiro* and the *claves*. Although he wanted to become a pilot, he enrolled in the regional conservatory; then assumed the leadership of his father's band, joined the Escuela nacional de arte of Havana, but left it again to apply his knowledge to popular music. His composi-

tions gained the attention of Joseíto González, who was the pianist and artistic director of Rumbavana, an orchestra that was also developing a new style of performing the *son*. However, because they remained isolated in their province, Adalberto Álvarez and his orchestra remained unknown in the capital. He and some of his musicians then moved to Santiago de Cuba, and Son 14 was formed on November 11, 1978.

Adalberto Álvarez

Adalberto introduced a trombone alongside the trumpets, while maintaining the *tres* tradition. He used both piano and keyboards, reinforced the use of the bell (*cencerro*), and gave a special place to the sequence of improvisation that breaks the monotony of the opening theme. Today he explains that these two latter elements are linked to the influence of the salsa from the 1970s; writing that he had discovered salsa while listening to Venezuelan radio broadcasts. Son 14 signed a contract to play in Caracas, where the audience went wild over the great *sonero* with the raucous voice, lead singer Eduardo "Tiburón" Morales.

Adalberto's compositions go to the very sources of the *son* and the *trova*. The lyrical introductions are sung in two voices; then the rhythm accelerates, perfectly adapted to the agility of dance in this period and to its eastern roots. The pianist also adapts boleros and traditional *sones* by modernizing the arrangements and maintaining the rhythmic freedom of the ever-present *bongó*. The earlier recordings already contained compositions of a slower tempo that prefigure the later style. For these recordings, the orchestra was bolstered by the pianist Frank Fernández, a soloist of the Symphony Orchestra, and by the *tres* of Pancho Amat; both musicians improvised splendid duos.

In 1981, Tiburón was joined by Félix Valoy, a singer whose voice has a perfect timbre and a wide range; Félix Valoy followed Adalberto Álvarez and half his musicians when, at the end of 1983, he decided to try his luck in Havana: The group Adalberto Álvarez y su Son played in Havana for the first time on February 25, 1984; meanwhile, in Santiago, Son 14 was reorganized, though it maintained the same musical concept and spirit. In its sound, as in its arrangements, the Havana orchestra has a more noticeable *salsera* profile than the other

Cuban bands of the period. Adalberto molds the *son*, giving it a streamlined elegance, without excessive virtuosity. Using lyrics with romantic or picaresque themes, without vulgarity, he has earned the nickname *Caballero del son* (the gentleman of the *son*). The recruitment in 1997 of the singer Aramís, one of the best voices of Cuba today, breathed new life into the orchestra. Adalberto has been the reference point of the young, who remain attached to the *son* without excessive complexity. One such example is that of the pianist Juan Carlos Alfonso, who, after acquiring his skills in the Elio Revé orchestra, set up Dan Den while searching for these new sounds.

### The Irakere Orchestra: All-Out Fusion and Virtuosity

The orchestra named Irakere (a Yoruba word meaning "forest") belongs to the outermost bounds between classical music, popular music, and jazz and has left its mark on the musical experimentation of the younger generation. In the early 1960s, the pianist Jesús "Chucho" Valdés, together with the guitarist Carlos Emilio Morales, the drummer Enrique Pla, and the percussionist Oscar Valdés, set up the band known as Jesus Valdés y su Combo. They joined the Orquesta cubana de música moderna in 1967, while they also continued to perform together, first as a quintet, then as a sextet, with the double-bass player Carlos del Puerto and the saxophone player Paquito de Rivera.

From there was born, in 1973, the orchestra that would outdo all others and, for a few years, would strip Los Van Van of its supremacy. Irakere at first caused a sensation by adding to dance music the *batá* drums; and the group worked under the direction of Oscar Valdés to create a fusion of Afro-Cuban

Poster of Irakere, founded 1973 in Havana

rhythms and percussion with contemporary sounds. The drums are reinforced by the *tumbadoras*; the guitar and bass are electric, played alongside the piano, the flute, and the keyboards. From the very beginning Irakere has had one of the most brilliant brass sections in history (trumpets, saxophones, and trombone). Whether on brass or percussion, all the Irakere musicians are virtuosos. But what the young people really liked best were the electronic effects of the first dance record, with *Bacalao con pan* and *Xiomara*. Over the years, the band has remained in the avant-garde of innovation, working not only to unify synthetic with natural sounds, but also to mix programmed rhythms with traditional percussion. The general concept is applied freely to dance as well as to instrumental music, Afro-jazz, and contemporary music, with some high points, such as in *Misa negra*; rhythms with Yoruba instruments and language, are fused with jazz, as in *Tierra en trance* and *Mr Blue*, an "Irakerian" vision of Duke Ellington. "Irakere is a style," Chucho Valdés keeps repeating. This style allowed the orchestra to obtain a visa to record with CBS in the United States in 1978, and also earned it a Grammy Award in 1979.

Chucho Valdés is a giant, measuring 6 foot 6 inches in height, whose hand has no trouble spanning twelve notes. He and Gonzalito Rubalcaba are considered to be among the best jazz pianists in the world. As Chucho Valdés states:

> My father was one of the greatest Cuban musicians, Bebo Valdés; in 1952, he created the *batanga* rhythm, which went nowhere until I revived his idea and brought it up to date with the use of the *batá* drums. Bebo knew popular music very well; at the same time, he was a great jazz musician, an accomplished pianist. He always told me that, to be a pianist, one should be familiar with all types of music, not just our Cuban music: this [the Cuban music] represents our roots, but we can enrich them if we know classical music, which gives an irreplaceable technique, or the improvisations and harmonies of jazz. Fusion is universalization. Historically, all music was formed this way, by enriching itself through outside influences. You must listen to everything, so you can then define yourself as a composer, and that's the most difficult thing. (interview, 1988)

There is no doubt that this ability is precisely what has allowed the Irakere orchestra to survive all the defections and breakups. For the young musicians who chose the path of fusion after them faced great difficulties freeing themselves from Irakere's influence.

## Two Experimental Groups:
## Opus 13 and Afro-Cuba

From the mid-1970s, the young generation of professional musicians who were trained in music schools tried to enter the musical scene. In 1977 Afro-Cuba was formed, under the leadership of the saxophone player Fernando Acosta. The music of Afro-Cuba covers all experimental areas, from traditional rhythms to jazz flavors that no longer owe anything to "Cubop," with amazing rhythm and brass sections. The true passion of these musicians—almost all of whom are arrangers—is jazz and its manifold possibilities of expression. Two years later Opus 13 was organized, "the work of a collective of thirteen musicians," according to its director, the violinist Joaquín Betancourt. He had worked for a few months with Los Van Van; afterward he went on a yearlong cultural mission to Angola. Back in Cuba, he got together with his former classmates from music school and founded the group Opus 13. Joaquín Betancourt explains:

> Our ambition was simple: to make popular music of a level as high as concert music. Our theoretical and practical training was strictly classical, but to express ourselves by creating popular music was a spiritual necessity, even if Bach and Mozart were coming out of all our pores; for us, nothing was incompatible. Afro-Cuba had the same ambition, and most of the young musicians coming out of the schools have this ability. Our two orchestras had succeeded in establishing a different style in what we now call Latin-jazz, but we all ended up having to pull back. The media and the program directors didn't want to understand; for them, it

was a question of choosing between playing concert music and making people dance. So we made some concessions: We got closer to dance and, at the same time, to Irakere. It's hard to tread such ground. As of 1982, we created two separate repertoires—one for the concert hall and one for the dance hall and we also developed choreography. (Interview, 1997)

Afro-Cuba evolved toward concert-oriented instrumentation with the use of synthesizers, an innovation introduced by the ICAIC Experimental Sound Group and by Leo Brouwer. It accompanied Silvio Rodríguez on his grand tours during the 1980s. Opus 13 split up in 1991, but it had been a true school, where stars such as Miguel Angá Díaz first honed their collective skills. One part of the orchestra then became Paulito y su Elite, now renamed Paulito FG. For his part, Joaquín Betancourt continued with Banda JB, which eventually broke up; he then devoted himself to composing and arranging.

### The Turning Point: 1982–1983

In late 1983, Oscar D'Leon and his orchestra, the Venezuelan idols of international salsa, were invited to the Varadero festival. For a long time, this charismatic singer had been using the Cuban musical repertoire of the 1920s to the 1950s, and he remains today one of the most faithful promoters of the *son*, the cha-cha-cha, and the *guaracha*. According to those who attended the festival, the visit of Oscar D'Leon and his orchestra had the effect of an electroshock. Never before had an orchestra attracted such a crowd. The young people, who are always extremely interested in what comes from abroad, again fell in love with the classics they discovered at that performance, in arrangements and sounds perceived as new, fresh, and adapted to international sounds and tastes. The singer's ability to improvise and his choreography, with the white double bass he used at the time, unleashed great enthusiasm. And when he declared, "If I hadn't been born Venezuelan, I'd have liked to be Cuban," the response was delirious.

Once again popular music was broadcast on radio and television and a change was perceptible, even in the musicians' way of doing things. Until that point, most dance bands had been using a rapid tempo, in tune with the complexity of the percussion and the experimental aspects of the music; couples moved to choreography that had emerged from the *baile casino*, with innumerable *vueltas* and successive twirling. In 1982, Los Van Van launched a new rhythm they named *conga-son*, which became a great success: This rhythm is evident in *El Baile del buey cansado* (The Dance of the Tired Ox). People danced separately to a slow and measured rhythm. According to Joaquín Betancourt, this style had a dual influence. From then on, the orchestras' tempo became *freneticía*, a phenomenon that would become more pronounced with the popularity of the salsa ballad abroad—while the habit of dancing separately would be adopted by the young. In the mid-1980s appeared the *despelote*, in which the Revé orchestra excels. During the *montuno* section of the dance, women perform vigorous, sexually suggestive movements of the waist and hips. In 1983, with the great success of Los Van Van, *Por encima del nivel (Sandunguera)*, this new style became firmly established.

## Second Turning Point (1987–1988): NG La Banda

The year 1987 marked a turning point or rather a logical consequence of the Cuban musical boom. Since 1985, a workshop of young musicians and singers from various orchestras sought to define a new type of popular music around a recording project. The main person of the group was José Luis Cortes, a brilliant flutist and talented composer. A native of Santa Clara, he began his professional career with Los Van Van before joining Irakere in 1980. Several albums with evocative titles emerged from this phase: in 1985, *Santa Clara Fusión, Siglo I ANE* (First Century before our Era), with original compositions celebrating ritual music, Africa, and the *danzón*; in 1986, *Siglo II NE* (Second Century of our Era) and *Abriendo del ciclo*; in 1987, *A través del ciclo*, two all-star albums that brought together all the musicians who supported the project. Then came a series of albums that concentrated on creating a distinct musical personality. This high discographic productivity aroused jealousy at a time when it was not easy to produce a record in Cuba. The leaders of other orchestras blamed this unilateral action for breaking the cohesion of their groups. The musicians had to make a choice; in 1988, the group NG La Banda, the New Generation, was formed, with almost the entire brass section of Irakere.

Musically, the group followed in the footsteps of Irakere. José Luis Cortés composed and arranged several of the band's dance hits, and never renounced the seven years he spent with Irakere. At first, his rhythm section included a piano, a keyboard, a bass, drums, a *tumbadora*, a *bongó*, two trumpets, and one—then two—alto and tenor saxophones, not counting the trombone and, of course, the flute. The orchestra's aim has been the aim of the entire younger generation: to use all the complexity of harmonies and sounds of contemporary classical music to develop and modernize fundamental genres of popular music.

"Our contemporary music is entirely urban," explains José Luis Cortés, "so we must keep the essence of the *son* from the heart of the mountains, *monte adentro*, and we must transform it because we live in the heart of the city, *monte afuera"* (interview, 1989).

The musical achievement of his group rose to challenge: No limits seemed to exist for the growing complexity of the rhythmic sequences or the power of the brass instruments nicknamed *"los metales del terror!"* To familiarize the dancers with the music as soon as the piece begins, José Luis Cortés quickly moves to the *montuno* (the improvisational, climatic section), thus modifying the musical structure (interview, *Gaceta de Cuba*, 1996). He also features two singers, each with a very different style—Issac Delgado, for the most melodic romantic pieces, and Tony Calá, a true vocal phenomenon who gives everything he's got.

During the carnivals in the summer of 1989, NG La Banda enjoyed a stunning success with young people. Then arose the controversy that continues to this day: The official gatekeepers of culture took umbrage at lyrics they deemed to be, at best, without value, and at the vulgarity of sexual gestures accompanying some pieces. NG La Banda was telling the chronicle of Cuba, but in a way different from Los Van Van, that is, by confronting head-on certain troublesome subjects. Their early lyrics offer unrestricted praise for the color black, for the culture of neighborhoods considered marginal (*Los sitios entero*, *La Expresiva*), and demand respect for their systems of worship and divinities (*Santa Palabra*)—though racism, officially, is said to no longer exist and religious practice is still considered to be obscurantist. More generally, NG La Banda targets everything smacking of hypocrisy or of any variance between revolutionary discourse and reality. It does not wave the flag of revolt, but proclaims its wish that young people may be and may live as they see fit. These themes are reflected in the following refrain, from 1989–1990, addressed to the group's detractors: "Impossible to mask / The sun with just one finger / The truth is the truth / Stop making those faces at me."

Somebody once called Cortés a *tosco* (a hick, rough-hewn) and the nickname stuck. These controversial, critical lyrics are just one part of NG La Banda's repertoire, but they are the most popular. The controversy became more venomous in 1993, on the subject of the satire on *picadillo de soja*, a vegetable blend that, at the height of Cuba's food shortages, came to replace meat. Rumor had it that the substance was the cause of an epidemic of blindness whose very existence the government first denied. Eventually they had to admit that there was a vitamin deficiency. A similar scandal occurred a year later, when the legalization of the dollar made some young women chase after foreigners: *La Bruja* (The Witch) and its concise refrain ("Get on your broom and leave") are addressed to those who abandon their Cuban fiancés out of venality. But the Union of Cuban Women saw in the song an attack on the honor of women in general.

Despite an avalanche of criticism, many young Cubans still idolized the band. Through its unabashed use of street language common among certain strata of the population, its codes and key words borrowed from African languages, NG La Banda joins a tradition that has always existed, but clashes with the educational image of a Revolution that preferred to erase all the social baggage of the past. Thus the band became the instrument of revealing a social phenomenon that represents, at the very least, a true malaise.

**Fusion, Rap, and Salsa:**
**A Music at the Crossroads**

From then on, some young groups rushed into what seemed

to them the path of guaranteed popular success. What started as a mere trend, now became a systematic pursuit. Religious themes became obligatory. Since rap music is the internationally recognized expression of "ghettos" marginalized by their respective societies, NG La Banda adapted spoken words to a Cuban rhythm. This approach has become the rule, completely changing the articulation between soloist and chorus. The *montuno* section has since been filled with these chanted (i.e., "rapped") words, which go together with the sexual motions of the dancers.

A new step was taken by the Charanga Habanera, which had been banned from the stage for six months, at the end of 1997, for alleged eccentric behavior in bad taste during a televised performance at the Youth Festival. In fact, the crisis had been brewing for a long time, because compared to the group's leader, David Calzado, José Luis Cortés appears very mild mannered. A violinist and former arranger with the Ritmo Oriental Orquesta, David Calzado started playing with his own band, Charanga Habanera, in 1988 at the Monte Carlo Casino on a five-year contract. At the time, the Charanga Habanera was an orchestra with violins and flute and played all the old standards. In early 1992, the first change occurred with the introduction of keyboards, two trumpets, and one saxophone. Then Calzado eliminated the violins, but kept the name Charanga Habanera. Beginning in 1993, the band caused an outburst of mass hysteria among Cuban teenagers. The spectacle of musicians swapping instruments, dancing, and performing gymnastic feats while continuing to play became a sensation. The band targeted its audience and built its popularity, with large doses of double meanings and coded expressions, around two basic themes: money and sex. "Papping" they hailed pleasure at all cost, and cast the responsibility for their cynicism on the architects of a society the young did not choose. Undeniably, the music makes one dance; however, it repeats itself from disk to disk, as do the lyrics. Thus began the era of "bidding wars" among new bands, in which each tries to outdo all the others (Manolín El Médico de la Salsa, Bamboleo).

The controversy surrounding populism and bad taste partly masks a real problem. Cuba has a large number of highly qualified musicians who seek a place and are torn between their training at the schools that have forged very similar musical ideas in them, their audience, and the tendencies of the outside market. In the 1990s everybody began to speak of "Cuban salsa", a term discredited on the island for many years in the past. Only a tiny portion of today's popular music actually fits the category of what is called "international salsa." Certain bands, such as Yumurí y sus Hermanos, which once hesitated between these sounds and fusion, now return to the roots of the *son*. But among Cuban bands, the polyrhythmy of percussion remains dominant. And the often aggressive fusion—in which keyboards overpower the acoustic piano—responds to the young musicians' need to go back to everything they have learned and imagined musically. Their audience finds in this an echo of its own preoccupations and a space within which to define a personal identity. This approach sometimes seems tedious to a foreign audience not always able to grasp the orchestral complexity in its totality.

The orchestras that have adopted this type of fusion are today at a crossroads. The very breakup of Irakere is emblematic. The percussionist Miguel Angá Díaz chose a solo career, allowing him to play on demand without locking him into a specific style. The flutist Orlando "Maraca" Valle formed Otra Visíon, an instrumental jazz band, that went back to dance music. Oscar Valdés created Diákara, a band that follows the Afro-jazz trend by renewing ties with the early work done by Irakere, minus any commercial compromises. In early 1997, some of the young musicians of Irakere got together with others to set up Habana Ensemble. The group is led by the saxophone player César López, who is joined by two trumpets, drums, *tumbadora*, piano, bass, guitar, and small percussion instruments. Their aim is to renew ties with a more melodic line; an ambition well served by the voice of Leo Vera, with adaptations of international themes, while the group also offers, in the same evening, an instrumental jazz repertoire.

Another trend seeks to combine Cuban fusion with the sounds of international salsa. Two examples of this are Paulito FG and Issac Delgado. Paulito FG, formerly Paulito y su Elite, first emerged from the final years of Opus 13. Issac Delgado, who comes from NG La Banda, was also a member of the band Proyecto de Gonzalo Rubalcaba. In 1992, Issac decided to form his own band, and Gonzalo Rubalcaba helped him with recording his first album, *Dando la hora*, which received the EGREM Award. In 1993, *Con ganas* was released, featuring the inevitable hit song on a religious theme, *Vengo con iré*. Various salsa bands of New York and Puerto Rico have adapted the themes of these two albums. Issac Delgado's band split up at the end of 1994. Its drummer, Giraldo Piloto—also a former member of NG La Banda—formed Klimax, while Issac Delgado followed the path that would bring him closer to international salsa. Since then, he has been recording for the RMM label of New York. The singer is convinced that his rhythm section (drums, *paila*, and *tumbadora*) and the experience of his music director, Joaquín Betancourt, will keep him from becoming flat and dry. He also has confidence in the international dimension of the themes he develops: women, love, and the problems couples face. One notes in his music an expression of a driving ambition to penetrate the international market and to gain recognition outside Cuba.

Giraldo Piloto, an excellent jazz composer, also writes love themes treated with humor, a smiling sensuality, and eroticism ("Tie up your hair, it's falling on my face"), without excessive literary ambition, but also without vulgarity. He is the son of Giraldo Piloto, one of the two composers of the duo Piloto y Vera from the 1950s. He is also a nephew of Guillermo Barreto, the great percussionist whom we have often quoted in this book. Giraldo Piloto is perhaps one of the most gifted arrangers of his generation.

Klimax is the band musicians like and which must be seen onstage. It is constantly involved in musical research. From concert to concert, we note their innovations—in harmonies, in the relationships between the various sections, and in the way vocal parts fit into the orchestration. But the very people who claim to be hard-line followers of Klimax also add that few people can manage to dance to such complex music! According to Giraldo Piloto, however, such a claim is not completely true. He smiles about this, as he does about everything, and answers that, even if one does not understand, one can still listen and feel. This young drummer believes in his vision: beauty in the melodic line and complexity of harmonies. He believes most of all in the future of a music that is entirely in transition—music that, at the crossroads between tradition and unrestricted innovation, is seeking its path toward universality.

# By Way of a Provisional Epilogue:
## *BUENA VISTA SOCIAL CLUB* OR *TIMBA CUBANA?*

### Salsa or *Timba?*

Since 1997, most musicians working with new sounds no longer define their compositions as *salsa* but as *timba*. This is not simply an argument about words. Salsa, which was established in New York City after the blockade of Cuba, has a specific history—one that began long before the music was given that name. From the outset, *salsa cubana* developed from the expressed will of the Caribbean communities—especially of their Puerto Rican constituency—in a situation of social marginalization. The music that thus developed was an affirmation of certain specific cultural values. The evolution of the music then came to be that of all music standardized by com-

Pepín Vaillant (1929–2001) played with
major orchestras in Paris in the 1950s
and returned to Cuba in 1963. Until his
death he was a role model for younger
musicians such as Anibal Avila from the
Afro-Cuban All Stars.

mercialization, and a good portion of what is sold today under the label of *salsa* no longer has much in common with what was produced in the 1970s and in the early 1980s. In the face of this history, the younger Cuban generation distinguishes itself by affirming its own identity.

Originally, *timba* designated the marginalized neighborhoods of large cities. *Timba* and *timbero* are expressions that appear frequently in the context of the rumba, exclamations with which, in the lyrics of the *guaguancó* or the *columbia*, one called out to the drummers, to encourage them—in a sense, to give them a kind of warm-up. By re-adopting the term *timba*, musicians of the new generation are insisting on the determinant role of percussion in the complex fusion of their orchestrations. At the same time as they recognize the value of their academic training, they are rehabilitating the "school of the street," underscoring the importance of a tradition rooted in African culture, and recognizing the value of popular knowledge and creativity.

At the end of 1997, Juan Formell, the music director of Los Van Van, put together the Dream Team Cuba-Timba Cubana. His intention was to gather onstage representatives of the various innovative generations, in order to prove the existence and the quality of musical development since the Revolution. Besides the most visible orchestra leaders—Juan Formell, Adalberto Álvarez, José Luis Cortés, Paulito FG, Issac Delgado, and Manolín, "el médico de la salsa"—this gigantic big band reunited singers and musicians who emerged from each group. The press sometimes criticized the choice of participants, not to question the legitimacy of those present, but to express regret for those who were absent, such as the pianist Manolito Simonet, leader of Manolito y su Trabuco, or other excellent bands from the island's interior. In early 1998, the Dream Team Cuba appeared before more than ten thousand spectators, and a few months later, on the anniversary of the independence of the former colony, the Sociedad General de Autores y Editores de España (SGAE) organized the same show in Havana, in front of the Capitole—this time with the participation of Spanish artists.

Clearly, there was another intention behind Juan Formell's initiative: to attempt to counter the fashion—apparently irresistible abroad—of Cuban musical expression from before the Revolution performed in the old style. Since roughly 1994, the European public, with France and Spain at the forefront, has been enthusiastic about the eastern *trova*, and Francisco Repilado (Compay Segundo) and the Vieja Trova Santiaguera have enjoyed new triumphs.

Nick Gold, director of the World Circuit label established in London, took an interest in the project conceived in the late 1980s by Juan de Marcos González, a *tres* player and former

The Afro-Cuban All Stars

leader of the band Sierra Maestra. This band has fought tire-lessly since 1976 to rehabilitate the *son* in Cuba. The idea behind Juan de Marcos González's project was to pay homage to the authentic roots of Cuban music by bringing together, around a repertoire of the 1940s and 1950s, instrumentalists and great voices of the past who would be joined by younger musicians: the soul and proficiency of the past joined with the technical skills and know-how of today. At the time, no one in Cuba supported this project, which was considered destined to fail. But in 1996, World Circuit decided to produce it. How, from the initial project of Afro Cuban All Stars with the CD *A toda Cuba le gusta*, did they move to a triple production—with *Buena Vista Social Club*, then *Introducing . . . Rubén González*, and, especially, how did they get from there to the "Buena Vista phenomenon"? By way of an answer, one can only spec-ulate, but the records are selling by the millions: *Buena Vista Social Club* won a Grammy Award in 1998, and at the Berlin Womex in 1999, Nick Gold and Juan de Marcos González were given the newly created Womex Award "for the excellence of their work in the service of world music."

## *Buena Vista Social Club:* A CD, a Film, and an Edifying Story

In March 1996, Nick Gold was in Havana for a recording at the EGREM studios, of the scheduled production with Juan de Marcos Gonzáles, as well as an album produced by Ry Cooder. He had planned to bring together guitarists from Cuba and Africa, including Ali Farka Touré of Mali, for this occasion. However, the Africans were unable to obtain travel visas to Cuba, and Ry Cooder decided at a moment's notice to make the recording with Cuban musicians suggested by Juan de Marcos González, *Buena Vista Social Club*. Two years later, Ry Cooder returned to produce the first solo recording of Ibrahim Ferrer, one of the veteran singers. This is when Wim Wenders filmed part of his documentary, which he completed in Amsterdam and in New York City's Carnegie Hall.

The name of the film refers to the title of a *danzón* composed in 1940 by Orestes López as a tribute to the club in Buena Vista, a neighborhood on the outskirts of Havana. These clubs existed in almost all neighborhoods and welcomed famous bands. On weekends, blacks and mulattos would go to these clubs to dance; well-to-do whites, as a requirement of segregation, frequented the fashionable casinos and nightclubs.

### The Singers

The life and personality of the musicians on the album are interesting in that they reflect the musical life before the Revolution—as one sees, for example, in the economic difficulties of the *trovadores*. All of these musicians, whether instrumentalists or singers, did their job with talent, but no more and no less than did many others in this period of musical profusion. In the Cuban context described in the previous chapter, these musicians had been out of the limelight for a long time, and most people who had known them in the years before the Revolution thought they were dead.

The senior musician was Máximo Francisco Repilado Muñoz, who is known by the name **Compay Segundo**, a reference to the second voice that had always been his singing specialty. Born November 18, 1907, in Siboney in the eastern part of the island, he followed his family to Santiago de Cuba, the nearby big city. As did his brothers, he played the *tres* and the guitar, and he began composing at the age of fourteen. Of course, he knew the other *trovadores* of the period, such as Rafael Cueto and Sindo Garay. He sang and played with various local groups, duos, trios, *estudiantinas*, and along with his brother, he was a member of the sextet Los Seis Ases of the El Tivolí district. Around 1924 he got the idea to amplify the possibilities for the sounds and harmonics of his instrument by creating a hybrid of the *tres* and the guitar, a type of *cuatro*, which he called *armónico*, a guitar tuned to the octave, to which he added a seventh string in the middle.

In Santiago, he also learned to play the clarinet from Enrique Bueno, leader of the municipal band of which he became a member. It was with this musical group that Compay Segundo traveled to Havana in 1929. Five years later Ñico Saquito, the famous composer of *guarachas*, suggested that he join the quintet Los Cuban Stars with his armónico to give another performance in the capital. There he met Evelio Machín, a member of the Cuarteto Hatuey, with Lorenzo Hierrezuelo and Marcelino Guerra. In 1938 they left together for Mexico, where Compay Segundo acted in two films, *Tierra brava* (Brave Earth) and *Mexico lindo* (Pretty Mexico). On his return, he joined the Conjunto Matamoros, this time as a clarinetist, and remained with the group for fourteen years. In a similar manner, from 1949 to 1955, he joined with Lorenzo Hierrezuelo to form the duo Los Compadres, which would travel throughout the world. This duo was extremely popular in Latin America, and when they separated, Compay Segundo set up his own group, in response to an invitation to the Dominican Republic. After the Revolution of 1959, there was a period of relative inactivity, with the exception of a few performances in the cabarets that were still open and an invitation from the Smithsonian Institution in Washington for the Festival of Traditional Cultures of America.

Not until the 1990s did Compay Segundo y Sus Muchachos (Compay Segundo and His Boys) return to the stage, first in France and Spain, and then elsewhere in Europe, the United States, and even Japan. On the island of Cuba, however, during this same period, Compay Segundo was unknown. A Cuban journalist reported in the magazine *Salsa Cubana* that, during a performance of the group in a Havana club in 1997, there were only two people in the audience, he himself and an English friend whom he had invited.

**Ibrahim Ferrer**, born February 20, 1927, is a native of San Luis, in the eastern province. At the age of twelve, after the death of his mother, he earned a living doing odd jobs and singing in the streets of Santiago. In 1940, he and a cousin formed an amateur group that performed at private parties in his neighborhood. Then he sang with local bands, such as le Conjunto Wilson, the Conjunto Sorpresa, and Maravilla Beltrán. He became famous with the band Chepín-Choven, conducted by the pianist Bernardo Choven and the violinist Electo "Chepín" Rosell, the composer of a great success performed by Ibrahim Ferrer, *El Planatal de Bartolo*.

In 1953, he joined the band of the famous singer Pacho Alonso, which was established in Havana in 1959, and in 1962 he went on a European tour with this group. But the Cuban missile crisis blocked their travel to Western Europe and the United States. When Pacho Alonso left the band, later called Los Bocucos, in 1967, Ibrahim Ferrer remained as a solo singer beside Carlos Querol Montalvo and Roberto Correa as director. Although they were excellent, Los Bocucos met the same fate as almost everyone who continued to cultivate the *son* and the *guaracha*. They traveled only to "sister countries" in Eastern Europe and were exposed to frequent bureaucratic harassment. Undoubtedly, this is what made Ibrahim Ferrer decide to retire in the early 1980s and to resume his odd jobs. Alongside Pacho Alonso, a great bolero specialist, he performed mostly *sones*. Ibrahim Ferrer was known for his talents as an improviser and for his voice, but he remained mostly in the shadow of the master. After the Revolution came the blockade, internal as well as external. Not until they were awarded a Grammy did the state label EGREM produce a recording from recent archives that gave the public the opportunity to discover *sones*, *guarachas*, *guajiras*, *pilones*, and *boleros* performed by Ibrahim Ferrer and Los Bocucos. In the film *Buena Vista Social Club*, one can clearly perceive the charisma emanating from this singer. With modesty and simplicity, he recounts the old problems, his deep belief in the Regla de Ocha-Ifá, his special affection for Babalú Ayé represented in the features of the beggar Saint Lazarus of the Catholic Church. Ibrahim Ferrer's delight, at the age of seventy-two, in recording his first solo CD, produced by Ry Cooder, did not change his humility; nor has there been any dampening of his pleasure in finally singing boleros and his own compositions, such as *De camino a la vereda*.

**Manuel Puntillita Licea Lamot** was born in Holguín on January 4, 1927, and died December 4, 2000. He learned music in a children's band in his hometown, where he played the cymbals. His father, who was a tailor, played the timani; his uncles played the saxophone, trumpet, and drums. Fascinated by the jazz band Los Hermanos Áviles, he decided to become a drummer and first worked with the Tentación band, then with the Hermanos Coallo band. With Orquesta Licea, made up of musicians from his family, he left for Camagüey. During the feast of Saint John, where the music groups played live on the radio, all the singers had lost their voice, and so someone who had never before sung professionally did so on the broadcast: It was such a success that the trumpet player Julio Cueva hired him for his jazz band, and he made his debut in Havana in 1945. The band did a live broadcast from Radio Mil Diez, and that is where he got his nickname, Puntillita. In performing *El Son de la puntillita*, by the composer from Matanzas, Félix Cárdenas, Manuel Licea improvised quatrains and ten-line stanzas. These improvisations were such a success that, from then on, he was called nothing but Puntillita. In 1948, he signed a contract with Radio Cadena Suaritos; then he worked with various prestigious groups, such as the Orquesta Romeu at the Sans Souci Cabaret and the Adolfo Guzmán band, at the Montmartre Cabaret. Comfortable with Cuban rhythms, he had the ability to improvise, an accurate and sensitive style, and a remarkably accurate voice—the hallmarks of the great performers of *son*, *guaracha*, and boleros.

The only woman in the group was **Omara Portuondo**, who was born in Havana on October 29, 1930, in the Cayo Hueso district. She had first been a dancer, like her sister Haydee, but both had been equally passionate about singing. Since their childhood, they had been listening incessantly to the voices of Ella Fitzgerald and Sarah Vaughan. They joined the group that would carry the *feeling* movement, and it was during a presentation for Radio Mil Diez that Omara Portuondo was given a nickname that would remain with her, *la novia del filin* (the fiancée of *feeling*). In 1952, she and her sister, Haydee, formed a femenal vocal quartet with Elena Burke and Moraima Secada. The group Las D'Aida was directed by the pianist Aida Diestro, who surprised the artistic world with her musicianship, her creativity, and her "swing." After the Revolution, Omara's career continued, first with the renewal of the quartet, and then, from 1967, as a soloist.

A great interpreter of feeling, *son*, and bolero, Omara always remained, along with Elena Burke, among the favorites of Cuban audiences, working in cabarets and the big hotels and representing Cuba at innumerable festivals throughout the world. Her duets in the film and on CD—with Compay Segundo and, above all, with Ibrahim Ferrer—constitute the pinnacle of tenderness, delicacy, and lyricism.

**Eliades Ochoa**, who was born in 1946, symbolizes the link between singers and instrumentalists, between two generations and between the *trova*, *guaracha*, and *son*. This musician is considered one of the finest interpreters of rural music from the east, the region of which he is a native. He never parts with his wide-brimmed hat, typical of the farmers of this region. He also crafted his own particular instrument—an eight-string guitar, of which the fourth string, in D, and the fifth string, in G, are doubled by a string tuned to the higher octave. As a child, he began to play the guitar—as many did—on the street corners of Santiago; then he started a trio before participating, for nine years, in a cultural and political radio program dedicated to rural life. From the 1970s, he was a famous artist of the Casa de la Trova of Santiago. In 1978, as guitarist and principal singer, he became the leader of the Cuarteto Patria, a group founded in 1939 by Pancho Cobas.

His group was a little less marginalized than others during what was a difficult period for popular music; it performed during festivals and undertook many tours abroad, although Eliades Ochoa himself said he hated such long trips because he missed his native province. He owes his success partly to his status as a government official for cultural affairs, but mostly to his work of renewing the repertoire and to the authenticity of the rural music of the east, in all its diversity.

### The Instrumentalists

The public's preference, without any doubt, is for **Rubén González**. He was born on May 26, 1919, in Santa Clara. He studied classical music and, in 1934, he graduated from the Cienfuegos Conservatory. Because of pressure from his family, he started studying medicine. Finally, in 1941, he decided to settle in Havana as a pianist. He became a notable figure in the big bands of the 1940s and 1950s, since he preceded Lilí Martínez in the Conjunto of Arsenio Rodríguez, with whom he recorded his first album in 1943. He worked in Panama and Mexico, and spent a few years in Buenos Aires, Argentina. On his return to Cuba, he appeared with the Hermanos Castro band; then he performed with the band of the guitarist Senén Suárez at the great Tropicana cabaret. He joined the Orquesta América, which he then quit in 1957 in order to settle in Venezuela for four years. Almost everywhere one hears that, with the passing of Lilí Martinez and Pedro Justíz Peruchín, Rubén González is the last survivor of a generation of trend-setting pianists. Such a claim would fail to recognize that **José "Pepecito" Reyes** also was part of that generation. Born in 1918 in Santiago de Cuba, José Reyes, like Rubén González, had a classical training in music. He worked in the *conjuntos* (Arsenio Rodríguez, Gloria Matancera, Conjunto Modelo) and in *charanga* groups (Fajardo y sus Estrellas; Pancho el Bravo, nickname of the flutist Alberto Cruz). But not a single celebrity has gone to look for him in his native province, where he still resides, and he remains almost unknown to European audiences.

Each of these pianists has his own recognizable style: Rubén González is known for the delicate harmonies of his improvisation, which are marked by his great knowledge of the *danzón*. He joined Enrique Jorrín's band in 1961, and that is where he remained. When the great violinist died in 1987, Rubén González briefly led the group, but the administrative responsibilities weighed heavily on him, and he retired.

In 1981, under the supervision of Enrique Jorrín, Rubén González had participated in a recording, at EGREM Studios, of the Estrellas de Areito, which has been distributed in Europe since 1999. Unfortunately, many of the musicians on these albums have departed: the trumpet players Félix Chapottín and Jorge Varona; the *tres* player, Niño Rivera; the violinists Enrique Jorrín and Elio Valdés; the singers Miguelito Cuní and Tito Gómez, who passed away in October 2000. On the other hand, Tata Güines, who plays the *tumbadora*, is very much alive, as are several of his companions who appear on the album or in the film *Buena Vista Social Club*. The trumpet player **Manuel "Guajiro" Mirabal**, who was born in 1932 in Melena del Sur, was one of the founders of the Conjunto Rumbavana in 1956. In 1960, he joined the Orquesta Riverside and, from 1967, he worked regularly in the great Tropicana big band, in the Orquesta Cubana de Música moderna, and in the ICRT (Cuban Radio-Television Institute) band. Like all the others, Manuel Mirabal is as comfortable playing popular music as he is with jazz or with classical music, and the style of his solos is praised to the heavens by the great personalities of the world of salsa, such as Oscar D'León and Cheo Feliciano.

*Timbales* player **Amadito Valdés**, born February 14, 1946, in the Los Sitios district of Havana, also had a brilliant career. His father, a famous clarinetist and saxophone player, and the percussionist Walfredo de Los Reyes were his first teachers. He received his formal training at the Alejandro García Caturla conservatory. He enjoys widespread unanimous praise for the precision, sobriety, and purity of his style of playing the *timbales*, but he plays the drums equally well and he can be heard on innumerable recordings of popular music, jazz, or classical music. He also worked well with the National Symphony Orchestra and the big bands in the prestigious cabarets. Since 1971, he has accompanied the female vocal quartet Las D'Aida, which was formed in 1952 by the pianist and composer Aida Diestro and is now led by Teresa García Caturla. Recently Amadito Valdés also has participated in the new group that accompanies **Orlando "Cachaito" López Vergara**, his partner on double bass.

Orlando López Vergara was born on February 2, 1933, in Havana, the son of Orestes López and the nephew of Israel "Cachao" López, two important musicians in the Antonio Arcaño band, who were also figureheads of the *descargas* in the 1950s. Cachaito wanted to be a violinist, but the family tradition had already decided otherwise. His father brought him to the rehearsals of the Philharmonic Orchestra in 1946–1947, as well as to the Arcaño's radio broadcasts. Cachaito made his debut first with the *charanga* band of his aunt Coralia López, who composed, among other works, the famous *danzón Isaura*, then with the band of Pedro Calvo, the father of Los Van Van's singer. Next he joined Arcaño's group and then, in 1954, the Orquesta Riverside. In 1960, he became a member of the National Symphony Orchestra, while still performing in jazz sessions at the Las Vegas Cabaret with Frank Emilio Flynn, Chocolate Armenteros, and many others. "We used to meet in the Havana 1900 cabaret, which became the Club Cubano de Jazz, or in the Club Las Vegas," recalls Cachaito, "and we would improvise together until dawn." Cachaito also played with the Quinteto Instrumental and then the Orquesta Cubana de Música Moderna.

Finally, the instrumentalist **Barbarito Alberto Torres Delgado** should be noted. Born in Matanzas in 1956, he is a veritable virtuoso of the twelve-stringed Cuban lute. For many years, he accompanied Celina González in the group Campo Alegre, since the lute traditionally has been indispensable in the performance of rural music from the west and the central area of the island. He also played an important role in concert music, through his collaboration with the guitarist/composer Leo Brouwer.

## The Breaking Cuban Wave . . . and the New Debate between the Old and the Modern

The incredible success of Wim Wenders' film, undoubtedly linked to the rapid increase in tourism, and the prestige enjoyed by Ry Cooder among those who until then had been unfamiliar with Cuban rhythms, brought this music out of the closed circle of initiates who had nurtured it. From that point on, there was a noticeable increase in the tendency of the market to rush toward the musical treasures that had been piling up in the archives of the EGREM and the Cuban radio stations. The number of Cuban bands that performed abroad from 1996 to 2000 is comparable to the number in the 1950s.

Prestigious representatives of the *charanga* tradition, such as the Orquesta Aragón, which had never stopped performing in Cuba and a few Latin American countries, suddenly were in greater demand in Europe and the United States than they had been in thirty years—which is only right. Ritmo Oriental, one of the innovative *charanga* bands, got together again and recorded an album in 2000. Yet despite everything, the music groups that are most prominent abroad are those whose instrumentation and rhythms most closely resemble those seen and heard in the film *Buena Vista Social Club*—those which the public, partial to musicians and singers who are already retired, loosely consider *son*. This tendency has triggered a rather violent debate in Cuba. No one questions either the beauty of the music or the audience's fascination with the actors' passion for their art. Each of the film's images bursts with their emotions, and the emotion of Ibrahim Ferrer, at the end of his Carnegie Hall concert—in the incredulous, almost painful, expression on his face—speaks for itself. In point of fact, the criticism on the island is directed entirely toward different aspects.

First of all, Cubans were offended by the fact that the film presents Ry Cooder as the great "rediscoverer" of a chapter buried in history, without even the slightest explanation of the fate of traditional music after 1959: not a word about the blockade of Cuba, not a word about the fact that all the musical and cultural roots together with the old repertoire were jealously kept by the people, not a word about the other kinds of music that, in claiming to draw their inspiration from the old rhythms, use the instruments and means that musical training after the Revolution made available to them. "Modernism," a key word among young Cubans, is not mentioned at any time in the film, while any member of the younger generation could have explained what they owe musically to the tradition and what they were breaking away from.

One could rightly object to those criticisms, countering that movie directors are free to show whatever they wish, how ever they wish. The fact remains nonetheless that movie audiences found the ubiquitous presence of Ry Cooder and his son irritating, and they even found the sound of the "Hawaiian" guitar regrettable, as it fills the silences that were so important to the balance of the original music.

## The Myth of the Golden Age

Besides this understandable sensitivity, the essential criticism deals with the fact that the one-sided vision conveyed by the film confines Cuban music within the myth of the "golden age" of the 1950s, in a supposed purity of the past against which the innovations of recent years can only be considered a deviation. This marginalization into a type of "exotic ghetto," removed from the current reality, presents the advantage of satisfying the "retro" nostalgia of foreigners who find these octogenarians and nonagenarians, so natural and full of energy, to be "extraordinarily moving" and who even find the dilapidated apartment buildings of Havana "so marvelously picturesque." Is this just another version of that "weary sensibility, eager for new stimulation" of which Emilio Grenet spoke back in 1939?

In fact, this golden age was never so golden as people would like to believe. In his interviews, Rubén González recalls—as do all the musicians of his generation who have not been afflicted with amnesia—the open racism that ruled during that period, and he readily recounts the following anecdote: On several occasions, when he was recommended as pianist to a big band leader for the Tropicana Cabaret or for some other prestigious club, the response was, "Don't you have anyone a little lighter?"

This tremendous gap between reality and its reconstruction in people's imagination is precisely what has led certain critics to raise the issue of cultural imperialism. Many musicians have resented this musical boom for the performers of the old-style music—as a negation of forty years of their own work, as a negation of their struggle to keep their musical heritage while at the same time renewing it, and finally as a desire to deny the existence of a musical life in Cuba after the Revolution, even a denial of the Revolution itself. For though they might not all be fans of Fidel Castro—that is far from being the case —they are very well aware of what they owe to the Revolution, even if they criticize it, sometimes openly. Moreover, they generally consider themselves as representatives not of a political system, but rather of a Cuba that exists and that, like any other country, wants to be recognized for its true value. The Dream Team-Timba Cubana is a means of facing up to the fact, of asserting that at least one of the "conquests" of the Revolution, musical training, did not collapse with the "socialism of the sister countries." This explains how Juan Formell, one of the first innovators, should put himself on the front line, and how Adalberto Álvarez—who, three years earlier, had been criticizing the new generation, saying that it was losing its traditional roots and was destroying the *son*—should then become part of the project.

## The Vise of the International Market

This self-affirmation doubles as an attempt to protest against the recent trend in the international market—which can be clearly seen in the management of concert tours—to ignore, even to intentionally exclude, new forms of musical expression. Europe, where new types of Cuban fusion music were a novelty that aroused curiosity, had been welcoming *timba* bands right up until around 1997. However, since then, concert organizers have essentially been counting on the "grandpas" who can assure them a full house, while abandoning the other bands or proposing to them contracts for ridiculous, even humiliating, fees. Only the groups with an established reputation, such as Los Van Van and a few others, have managed to play the game well. But in Cuba everyone depends on the dollar, and thus they depend on tours abroad, since performances at tourist venues on the island are, with rare exception, paid in local currency. For the majority of young *timba* musicians, this decline in demand means that they are not living as well as in previous years, even though they are better off than their fellow citizens. In Cuba, as elsewhere, everyone wants to live well, but everyone is not necessarily ready to simply adapt to the whims of the marketplace.

This explains why the musicians are caught in a vise. Their demand, to approach the twenty-first century with a music that reflects their high level of training while adapting to their era and to a young audience, is perfectly justified. But the workings of the market pressure them into playing music with the greatest international appeal—though it may not be very successful in their homeland—such as traditional genres in the style of the 1950s, or else to turn their back on what is specifically Cuban and to play instead a type of commercialized salsa which has become standardized in the United States and in Latin American markets since the mid-1980s. In this domain, as in others, Cubans are experiencing globalization. Moreover, many of the leading groups of the early 1990s have since broken up, since the necessity of going on tour prevailed over musical convictions, more so for the instrumentalists than for the band leaders. But nothing is easier in Cuba than replacing one musician with another who is just as good. It is certainly rather sad to see young musicians, classical and popular, confine their talents to a narrow traditional band performing the inevitable *Son de la Loma, Lágrimas negras*, and *Guantanamera*. Even in Cuba, in bars, restaurants, and hotels, this is how the musicians justify their salary in pesos, hoping for tips in dollars that nonetheless are often few and far between. These musicians hope that, for the rest of the world, this kind of small musical format will be perceived as more profitable, and that therefore it will be easier to get contracts. But the competition is strong, and such a solution is partly a solution of despair for the inland musicians blockaded into their province by the cultural hegemony of Havana, which the official tourist orientation has only served to reinforce.

Furthermore, the youth of Havana plays all sorts of "foreign" music, as can be seen in the growing number of hip-hop groups, despite the rarity of the necessary material—such as synthesizers, turntables, and records. There have always been rock groups; now they are almost prosperous and respected, with their own broadcasts on the State radio stations. Thanks to the initiative of a French manager, the cross-over between techno music and Cuban-ness has occurred with the group Sin Palabras (Without Words), which grafts onto techno music—played by flesh-and-blood musicians with a noticeable presence of Cuban percussion—Yoruba songs performed by an excellent young singer trained at the Conjunto Folklórico Nacional in Havana and a young back-up singer, no less talented, who also can sing solo. This type of music may or may not be appreciated, and the experiment may or may not last, but it at least deserves mention.

From this brief glimpse at the musical boom in Cuba, one can see that the various types of urban music can appeal to a

young audience without necessarily contradicting the musical
expression of Cuban roots, at least not in their current version.
The *timba*, for example, has an aggressive sound, while following the rules of "free-style" dancing, where the dancers'
bodies come close without touching, in explicit sexual gestures—which the observer may find fascinating or vulgar.
Again, in the case of dance, the glaring gap exists between the
situation inside and outside the island. In Europe, dance
schools are flourishing and are attended by a mostly young
public, that is discovering the pleasure of dancing with a partner. For the more enthusiastic dancers, it is a question of learn-
ing more complicated—even acrobatic—moves. Of these, the
famous Rueda de Casino is considered the *non plus ultra* of
popular dance, while it originally appeared as a piece of staged
choreography in well-known cabarets. When one questions
the men and women who frequent salsa clubs in France, they
say they judge the music by a single criterion: whether or not
they can dance to it. This new outlook has various consequences. Most notably, it unquestionably eliminates orchestrations that might be considered too complex or rhythms
that might be considered too fast. Most of these dancers pre-
fer salsa discothèques to concerts, since for them the dancing
is the essential part of the show, and few of these dancers even
know the name of the band to whose music they are dancing.

## A Musical Effervescence
## as Complex and Contradictory
## as the Political Situation

In Cuba, the media have adapted to the dominant trend.
Favoring tourism means that they broadcast, next to traditional music, popular international entertainment, from Ricky

Martin to the Spice Girls (or their equivalent), with a brief appearance by Julio and Enrique Iglesias, who also have devoted fans among Cubans. Radio Taino, the forward-looking radio station created with the wave of tourism in 1994–1995, also broadcast some telephone interviews with Cuban performers on tour abroad and promoted CDs that tourists could buy, in special shops, using dollars. The State radio stations, such as Radio Rebelde and even Radio Taino—and this is one of their positive aspects—offer special programs commenting on the historical background of the music being broadcast, especially for traditional music, whereas for decades the veteran Eduardo Rosillo was practically the only one to take on this role at Radio Progresso. So, finally, radio opened up, though half-heartedly, to other types of music.

Many new groups have arisen, from the latest generations of formally trained musicians, who are trying to make their own place in the sun. Chispa y Los Complices, for example, following the general trend among young people from capital cities of this region of Latin America, mix English and Spanish in the title of their album, *New pa'que vea*, and reflect the enormous attraction of the United States. The pioneers of the *timba* are still very much present and are favorites among young Cubans. The Charanga Habanera got together again after almost all the musicians had broken away from the bandleader, David Calzado, to create La Charanga For Ever, a group that continues in the same style. When they perform outside Cuba, these bands often play a repertoire different from what would assure their success on the island—which underscores just how much the taste of their native audience diverges from that of audiences abroad. La Charanga For Ever also staged a tribute to the great names of *charanga* bands of the past, showing, on this occasion, that they are able to actually sing without rapping—an ability that certain purist detractors had often doubted. These musicians are causing traditional song and instrumental playing to evolve progressively toward a type of *timba* interpretation, in modifying the bass lines and the articulation of the percussion instruments between themselves and with the brass. This also shows that they have not broken away from their traditional roots, that the *timba* is simply their transposition, in another musical era, accentuated by different harmonic concepts and a different technology.

As for José Luis Cortés and NG La Banda, they benefited from this to highlight a large part of their repertoire—some of it already recorded, some not yet recorded; very little of this repertoire actually had been broadcast in Cuba itself. The music was composed of extraordinary instrumental and vocal parts, in a style that was different from what their unsuspecting audiences had associated with them. It was an opportunity to show the excellence of the performers and the creativity of the compositions. But El Tosco is also in a perfect position to "make up" a merengue that sounds exactly like one belonging to a licensed band in Santo Domingo, or a salsa ballad in the style of Miami. This provocative nose thumbing at the international market denounces—by way of caricature—a standardization that would have music depart from the paths of creativity to become nothing more than the reproduction of musical recipes.

According to the Cuban musicians, the young audiences on the island also have an ear for styles other than pure *timba*. This explains how, after eight years of hard work, Manolito y su Trabuco finally became well established among the favorites of 1998–1999. This fine group, whose instrumentation and compositions did not correspond to the norms of the mid-1990s, had difficulty in making a place for itself. But the

pianist and music director Manolito Simonet was able to preserve picaresque texts that were rooted in everyday life, to
strike a balance between various forms of expression, and—
without totally succumbing to the rap trend—to create very
meaningful refrains that enabled all audiences to express
themselves through dance, as they saw fit. Recently there have
been modifications, such as the use of the "baby bass," state-
of-the-art violin amplification, and the recruitment of a very
talented new drummer. Thus the rhythmic efficiencies and the
harmonic potential were strengthened, and there was also
some very promising new vocal work.

Juan de Marcos González also found a new audience. With
the album *A toda Cuba le gusta*, he paid tribute to the great
musicians of the 1950s. Besides the performers in *Buena Vista
Social Club*, three other celebrities of song were present: Raúl
Planas, who was born in Camajuani in 1933 and worked with
la Sonora Matancera, the Conjunto Chapottín, and Rumbavana; Pio Leyva, who was born in Morón in 1917 and was in
the bands of Bebo Valdés, Hermanos Castro, Benny Moré, and
Noro Morales; and Félix Valoy, who was born in Holguín in
1944, a *sonero* who collaborated with Conjunto Chapottín, the
Orquesta Revé, and both of Adalberto Álvarez's groups, Son 14
and Adalberto y su Son. Also on the album were representatives of the younger generations, seasoned musicians: José
Antonio "Maceo" Rodríguez, whose magical voice has been
associated with the Sierra Maestra group since 1980, singing
alongside Alberto Virgilio Valdés and Luis Bergaza; the percussionists Miguel "Angá" Díaz (Opus 13 and Irakere) and Carlito
González (Cubanismo); as well as the trombone player Javier
Zalba (Irakere). The second album by the Afro-Cuban All-Stars
broadened the musical perspective and presented a wider variety of musical genres and types of performance from the twen-

tieth century. The principle of mixing the generations is pre-served: the pianist Frank Emilio Flynn with Lino Borges, Pedrito Calvo, and Teresa García Caturla, whose voice replaced that of Omara Portuondo—who, after recording a superb solo album went on tour with her own band—perform beside younger singers, such as Leo Vera and Dennys Martínez, as well as with instrumentalists such as the flutists Orlando "Maraca" Valle and Joaquín Oliveros and the pianist David Álfaro. Thus their goal—to evolve toward a contemporary and urban sound—seems to have been attained, thanks to the complex, fairly creative arrangements and to a variety of com-pletely refreshing rhythms.

While the groups mentioned up to now feature many jazz musicians, jazz as a musical genre still attracts only restricted audiences. Yet many young musicians have made it their favorite mode of expression. I would like to mention at least three bands (may the others forgive me!) representative of the exceptional creativity of the jazz scene, in very different styles.

The composer and multi-instrumentalist Carlos Maza was born in Chile under the dictatorship and settled in Cuba. He has recorded six albums since 1993, relating his own story. He draws from the roots of the various cultures he was immersed in—Caribbean and Andean, but also European classical and contemporary music—transposing them in orchestrations of amazing audacity, whose sophistication never imposes itself at the expense of the melody. He manages to bring together, in an unusual way, instruments and sound landscapes that peo-ple would normally think were poles apart. The same spiritu-ality turned into music can be found in the compositions of the pianist Omar Sosa, from Camagüey, but this time it is anchored in his quest for mother Africa, which has remained in the mind of the whole diaspora. In the elaborate and sophisticated musical language of today's reality, Omar Sosa renders a message of humanity inspired by ancestral deities. He brings about a dialogue between the voices and instruments from Africa, Moroccan Gnawa, and the African traditions of Brazil, Venezuela, Ecuador, or Cuba, along with the spoken word of the black ghettos in the United States—closer to dub poetry than to media-covered rap music. In both cases, even though it is a necessary component, the extraordinary virtuosity of each musician never goes against the collective spirit of the music. The same can be said of the bass player Felipe Cabrera, who has recorded two albums under his own name since 1999, after fifteen years spent as a member of the Gonzalo Rubalcaba's quartet. Originating from the *rumbero* district of Cayo Hueso, he was one of the first bassoon players in Cuba's national symphonic orchestra, before he chose the double bass as his favorite instrument. In his compositions, inspired by various trends, the echo of Africa prevails, but the Afro-Cuban styles are "deconstructed" and recomposed in an ensemble where jazz harmonies meet with an orchestral writing nourished by contemporary art music.

There remains the question of the "forefathers." Irakere continues its work, but after some great changes in the band, Chucho Valdés has been devoting himself much more to jazz and often one of his sons replaces him in Irakere. His solo recordings on piano show the extent of his virtuosity, his touch, and the richness of his inspiration. As leader of a quartet (with drums, bass, and *tumbadora*), backed up by a flute and voices in a few numbers, he made, under the Blue Note label, three superb albums: *Belé Belé en la Habana, Bryumba Palo Congo*—with a transposition of ritual music into jazz— and *Live at the Village Vanguard*.

But the favorites of Cubans of all generations are the musicians of Los Van Van, who have always tried to innovate, avoiding repetition from one album to the next. On December 4, 1999, Los Van Van celebrated their thirtieth anniversary. A month before, under a U.S. label belonging to the Time Warner Company, *Llegó Van Van . . . Van Van Is here* was released; this was a CD that showed the vitality of Cuban music and the creativity of Juan Formell and other composers: picaresque texts, catchy rhythms, and above all new musical ideas in the manner of merging rhythms and sounds. One of the first results of such a contract with a major record company was the Grammy Award, which the group received for "the best salsa production" of 1999, officially awarded on February 23, 2000, in Los Angeles. The oldest musicians of the band, already retired, would certainly be delighted with this kind of official recognition for excellence in the unfailing work of several decades, and perhaps they might also regret that such recognition should have come so late. As for the audiences, they had long recognized the group's merits. Still, in late 1999, the anti-Castro lobby in Miami was trying—though unsuccessfully—to prohibit access to a concert by Los Van Van, whom they denounced as myrmidons of Fidel Castro.

It is becoming clear that the call for reconciliation between Cubans on the island and those outside, which is even transmitted through the music, is in fact being heard. For music, no matter where it originates, has neither borders nor color, as long as it is good music and comes from the heart—and this, without question, is true of the vast majority of Cuban musical expressions.

# Bibliography

**WORKS CITED**

Acosta Sánchez, Leonardo. *Del tambor al sintetizador*. Havana: Letras Cubanas, 1983.

———. "Reajustes, aclaraciones y criterios sobre Damaso Pérez Prado," in Havana: *Bohemia*, 29 September 1989.

———. *Elige tu, que canto yo*. Havana: Letras Cubanas, 1993.

———. *Descarga cubana: el jazz en Cuba 1900–1950*. Havana: Unión, 2000.

Alén, Olavo. *La Música de las sociedades de tumba francesa en Cuba*. Havana: Casa de las Américas, 1986.

Alén Rodríguez, Olavo. *De lo afrocubano a la salsa*. Havana: Artex, 1994.

Blanco, Jesús. *80 años del son y soneros en el Caribe 1909–1989*. Caracas: Fondo Editorial Tropykos, 1992.

Brandily, Monique. *Introduction aux musiques africaine*. Arles: Cité de la musique/Actes Sud, 1997.

Brouwer, Leo. *La Música, lo Cubano y la innovacion*, 2nd ed. Havana: Letras Cubanas, 1982. Corrected and enlarged, 1989.

Cabrera, Lydia. *El Monte*. 1954. 5th ed, Miami, 1983.

———. *La Sociedad secreta abakuá*. C & R, 1959. Rev. ed., Miami, 1970.

———. *Reglas de congo; Palo Monte Mayombe*. Miami: Peninsula Printing Inc., 1979.

Cañizares, Dulcila. *La Trova tradicional cubana*. Havana: Letras Cubanas, 1992.

Carpentier, Alejo. *La Música en Cuba*, 1945. 3rd ed., Havana: Letras Cubanas, 1988.

Charroppin, Miké, and Verger Dominique. "Entretien avec Gaudiosa Yoya Venet Danger." *Geo* 213 (Nov. 1996): 110.

Chatelain, Daniel. *"La Tumba francesa." Percussions* 45 (May–June 1996): 39–48; 46 (June–July 1996): 21–31.

Contreras, Félix. *Porque tienen filin*. Santiago de Cuba: Oriente, 1989.

De León, Carmela. *Sindo Garay: Memorias de un trovador*. Havana: Letras Cubanas, 1990.

Depestre, Leonardo. *Cuatro músicos de una villa*. Havana: Letras Cubanas, 1990.

Díaz Ayala, Cristobal. *Cuba canta y baila. Discografía de la música cubana, 1898–1925*. San Juan, Puerto Rico: Fundación Musicalia, 1994.

———. *Música cubana. Del areito a la nueva trova*. San Juan, Puerto Rico, 1981.

Duharte Jiménez, Rafael. *El Negro en la sociedad colonial*. Santiago de Cuba: Oriente, 1988.

Eli Rodríguez, Victoria, and Zoila Gómez García. . . . *haciendo música cubana*. Havana: Pueblo y Educación, 1989.

Évora, Tony. *Orígenes de la música cubana. Los amores de las cuerdas y el tambor*. Madrid: Allianza Editorial, 1997.

Farto, Miguel Martín. *La Parrandas remedianas*.Havana: Letras Cubanas, 1988.

Feijoo, Samuel. *El Son cubano: poesía general*. Havana: Letras Cubanas, 1986.

Fowler, Victor. "Los Van Van de aqui a mil anos." *El Caimán barbudo* 22/248. Havana, July 1988.

Galán, Natalio. *Cuba y sus Sones*. Valencia: Pre-Textos, 1983.

Giró, Radamés, ed. *Panorama de la música popular cubana*. Santiago de Cali: Letras Cubanas/Faculdad de Humanidades, 1996.

———. *Leo Brouwer y la guitarra en Cuba*. Havana: Letras Cubanas, 1986.

———. "Todo lo que Usted quiso saber sobre el mambo . . . ." In Giró 1996, pp. 231–44.

Grenet, Emilio. *Música popular cubana*. Havana: Secretaría de Agricultura, 1939.

Guanche, Jesús. *Procesos etnoculturales de Cuba*. Havana: Letras Cubanas, 1983.

Guanche, Jesús, and Dennis Moreno. *Caidije*. Santiago de Cuba: Oriente, 1988.

Guerra, Ramiro. *Manuel de historia de Cuba, desde su descubrimiento hasta 1868*, 1938, 4th ed. Havana: Editorial de Ciencias sociales, 1971.

Hernández, Erena. *La Música en persona*. Havana: Letras Cubanas, 1986.

Hernández Balaguer, Pablo. *Los Villancicos, cantadas y pastorelas de Esteban Salas*. Havana: Letras Cubanas, 1986.

Instituto de Ciencias Históricas (ed.). *La Esclavitud en Cuba*. Havana: Academia, 1986.

*Instrumentos de la Música folklórico-popular de Cuba*. 2 vols. Havana: Havana Ciencias Sociales, 1997.

Lapique, Zoila. "Aportes franco-haitianos a la contradanza cubana: mitos y realidades." In Giró 1996, pp. 153–72.

Lapique Becali, Zoila. *Música colonial cubana en las publicaciones periodicas (1812–1902)*, vol. 1. Havana: Letras Cubanas, 1979.

León, Argeliers. *Del canto y el tiempo*. Havana: Instituto cubano del libro, 1974.

———. *Ensayo sobre la influencia africana en la música de Cuba*. Havana, 1959.

Le Riverend Brusone, Julio J. "La Habana (biografía de una provincia)." *El Siglo XX*, Havana, 1960.

Leymarie, Isabelle. *Cuban Fire*. Paris: Outre Mesure, 1997.

Linares, María Teresa. "La décima y el punto en el folklor de Cuba." *Música* 31. Havana: Casa de las Américas, 1972.

———. *La Música popular*. Havana: Instituto cubano del libro, 1970.

———. *La Música y el pueblo*. Havana: Editorial Pueblo y Educación, 1974.

———. "La tonada campesina y la música cubana." *Nuestro Tiempo* 4 (17), Havana, 1957.

———. "El sucu-sucu: un caso en el área del Caribe." *Música* 44. Havana: Casa de las Américas, 1972.

Loyola Fernández, José. *En ritmo de bolero*. Havana: Unión, 1997.

Martínez Furé, Rogelio. *Diálogos imaginarios sobre folklor*. Havana:

Arte y Literatura, 1979.

Martínez Rodríguez, Raúl. *Benny Moré*. Havana: Letras Cubanas, 1993.

Mauleón, Rebeca. *Salsa Guidebook for Piano and Ensemble*. Petaluma, Calif.: Sher Music Co., 1993.

Millet, José, and Rafael Brea. *Grupos folklóricos de Santiago de Cuba*. Santiago de Cuba: Oriente, 1989.

Millet, José, Rafael Brea, and Manuel Ruiz Vila. *Barrio, comparsa y carnaval santiaguero*. Santo Domingo: Casa del Caribe (Santiago de Cuba)/Universitaria-UASD, 1997.

Moliner Castañeda, Israel, and Gladys Gutiérrez Rodríguez. "La rumba." *Del Caribe* 9/87, 40–47. Santiago de Cuba, 1987.

Moreno, Dennis. *Un tambor arará*. Havana: Ciencias Sociales, 1988. 2nd ed., 1994.

Moreno Fraginals, Manuel. *El Ingenio*. Havana: Ciencias Sociales, 1978.

Muguercia, Alberto. "Teodora Ginés ¿mito o realidad histórica?." *Revista de la Biblioteca Nacional José Martí* 62 (3) (September–December): 53–85. Havana, 1971.

Nasser, Emilio Amin Egeraige. *Benny Moré*. 1985. 2nd ed. Havana: Unión, 1994.

Orovio, Helio. *Diccionario de la música cubana*. 2nd ed. Havana: Letras Cubanas, 1992.

———. *Música por el Caribe*. Santiago de Cuba: Oriente, 1994.

———. "*La Guantanamera* en tres tiempos." *Unión* 15. Havana, 1993.

Orozco González, Danilo. "El son: ¿ritmo, baile o reflejo de la personalidad cultural cubana?" *Santiago* 33 (March 1979): 87–113. Santiago de Cuba.

———. Notas discográficas. *Antología integral del son*, vol. 1, 1987, EGREM, LD–286 and 287.

———. Notas discográficas. *Changüi y cumbancha ¡Ahora sí!*, EGREM, LD 274.

Orta Ruiz, Jesús [Indio Naborí], *Décima y folklor*. Havana: Unión, 1980.

Ortiz, Fernando. *Contrapunteo cubano del tabaco y el azucar.* Barcelona: Ariel, 1973.

———. *La "Clave" xilofónica de la música cubana. Ensayo etnográfico.* Havana, 1935.

———. *La Africanía de la música folklórica de Cuba.* 2nd ed., 1950. Rev. ed. Havana: Editora universitaria, 1965.

———. *Los Instrumentos de la Música Afrocubana,* vols. 1–3. Havana: Dirección de Cultura del Ministerio de Educación, 1952. Vol. 4, Havana: Cárdenas y Cia, 1954. Vol. 5, Havana: Cárdenas y Cia, 1955.

———. "La transculturación blanca de los tambores de los Negros." 1952. *Estudios etnosociológicos.* Havana: Ciencias Sociales, 1991, pp. 176–201.

———. "La [antigua] fiesta afrocubana del día de Reyes." *Ensayos etnográficos.* Havana: Ciencias Sociales, 1984, pp. 41–78.

———. *Los Bailes y el teatro de los Negros en el folklor de Cuba.*1951. 2nd ed. Havana: Letras Cubanas, 1981.

———. "Los cabildos afrocubanos," 1921. Repr. in *Ensayos etnográficos.* Havana: Ciencias Sociales, 1984, pp. 11–14.

———. *Los Negros curros.* Havana: Ciencias Sociales, 1986.

———. *Los Negros esclavos.* Havana: Ciencias Sociales, 1987.

———. "Los viejos carnavales habaneros." 1954. Repr. in *Estudios etnosociológicos.* Havana: Ciencias Sociales, 1991, pp. 202–21.

Padilla Pérez, Maybell, "Los cabildos afrocubanos: génesis." *Anales del Caribe* 14–15. Havana: Centro de Estudios del Caribe/ Casa de las Américas, 1995.

Pichardo, Esteban. *Diccionario provincial casi razonado de voces y frases cubanas.* Matanzas, 1836. Reissue of 4th ed. (1875). Havana: Ciencias Sociales, 1985.

Ramos, Zobeyda. "Complejo genérico del punto." *Música popular tradicional* 3. Havana: CIDMUC, 1987.

Rodríguez, Ezéquiel. *El Danzonete, su autor y sus intérpretes. Cincuentenario de su creación.* Havana, 1979.

———. *Iconografía del danzón.* Havana, 1967.

Rosemain, Jacueline. *La Musique dans la société antillaise 1635–*

*1902. Martinique Guadeloupe.* Paris: L'Harmattan, 1986.

Roy, Maya. "Sur une musique de Los Van Van." *Cuba, Trente ans de révolution,* série "Monde." Autrement, no. 35. Paris, January 1989.

Torres-Cuevas, Eduardo, and Eusebio Reyes Fernández. *Esclavitud y sociedad.* Havana: Ciencias Sociales, 1986.

Valdés, Carmen. *La música que nos rodea.* Havana: Arte y Literatura, 1984.

Vinueza, María Elena. *Presencia arará en la musica folklórica de Matanzas.* Havana: Casa de las Américas, 1988.

Yacou, Alain. "Los refugiados franceses de Saint-Domingue en la región occidental de la isla de Cuba." *Del Caribe* 23. Santiago de Cuba, 1994.

# Discography

All recordings available from descarga.com

## ANTHOLOGIES/COMPILATIONS

*100 Canciones Cubanas del Milenio*: 4-CD Set with 104 Page Book by Cristobal Díaz Ayala, Alma Latina ALCD700, 1999

*40 Years of Cuban Music: La Isla Del Son*, 2-CD Set, Milan/BMG 35868, 1999;

*Antología Integral del Son*: Familia Valera Miranda, 2-CD Set, Virgin España 8485622, 1999

*Bolero De Cuba*, Milan/BMG 35894, 2000;

*Cuba on Fire*: 4-CD Set, Tropicana 9800, 1999

*Cuba Caribe*, Hemisphere/EMI 98649, 1999

*Cuba Now*, Hemisphere/EMI 93156, 1998

*Cuba: I Am Time* — 4-CD Set, Blue Jackel 5010, 1997

*¡Cuba Sí! Pure Cuban Flavor*, Rhino 75733, 1999

*Cubamania! All Salsa, All Dance, All Night*, Global Disc/Platinum 9564, 1999

*Cuban Big Bands* 1940–1942, Harlequin 063, re-issued 1995

*Cuban Danzoneras (1932–1946)*, Harlequin 065, 1998

*Cuban Music: All Original Cuban Studio Sessions:* 5-CD Box Set, Sono 9074, 2001;

*Cuban Revolución Jazz*, 2-CD Set, Milan/BMG 35880, 1999

*Dancing with the Ennemy* — Cuba Classics 2, Luaka Bop / 26580-2, 1991

*De Cuba Son*, Edenways 2014, 2000

Descarga Special Package, Package Set, No. 4, *Cuban Roots–Son And Spice* (15-CDs)

*Early Cuban Danzón Orchestras (1916–1920)*, Harlequin 131, 1999

*Encuentro De Charangas*, 2-CD Set, Musisoft 7395, 1958; re-issued 1999

*Encuentro De Soneros, 2-CD Set*, Musisoft 7374, 1958, re-issued 1999

*Guaguancó. El ritmo propio*, Better Music MSCD 7202, 1998

*Havana Cuba, ca. 1957: Rhythms and Songs for the Orishas*, Smithsonian Folkways 40489, Released 1957; re-issued 2001

*Homenaje a Benny Moré*, Caribe Productions 9564, 1999

*Inolvidables duos latinos*, Caney 902, 1996

*Jazz caliente: the hottest licks of Cuban jazz*, Max 2222, 1999

*La Flor Oculta de la Música Cubana*, Vol. 1, Eurotropical 2721, 2001

*La Isla de la Música*, 2-CD Set, Universal 40126, 1998

*La Música de la Onda de la Alegría: Grandes éxitos de los 50*, Envidia 5002, 1999

*La Ruta del Son*, 2-CD Set, Eurotropical 1922, 2001

*Las Leyendas de la Música cubana* (Bolero-Danzón-Cha Cha Chá-Guaracha Son), 4-CD Boxed Set, Tumi TMG BOX1, 1998

*Los Caminos del Son*, Vol. 1, Promusic PR01, 1999

*Los Caminos del Son*, Vol. 2, Promusic PR02, 1999

*Matanzas Cuba, ca. 1957: Afro-Cuban Sacred Music from the Countryside*, Smithsonian Folkways 40490, 1957, re-issued 2001

*Official Retrospective of Cuban Music:* 4-CD Set, Tonga 9303, 1999

*Putumayo Presents: Cuba*, Putumayo 149, 1999

*Recorrido musical por Cuba*, AF 8024

*Sacred Rhythms of Cuban Santería/Ritmos sagrados de la Santería Cubana*, Smithsonian Folkways 40419, 1995

*Salsa: La música que se fuma*, 3-CD Boxed Set, Sonido 65X3, 1994

*Soneros de Cuba*, Envidia 7030, 2001

*Tabaco & Ron*, vol. 2, Tumi 087, 1999

*The Cuban Dánzon: Before there was jazz 1906–1929*, Arhoolie 7032, 1999

*Trinidad de Cuba*, AZUL Productions AZL 101, 2000

*The Essence of Cuban Music: Tumbao Cuban Classics*, Tumbao CTC-101, 1999

*The Rough Guide to Cuban son* (Enhanced CD w/Data Track), World Music Network 1046, 2000

## RITUAL MUSIC

Abbilona Tambor Yoruba (Complete 8-CD Package Set), Caribe Productions, 1999: *Oyá* (9551), *Obatalá* (9545), *Yemayá* (9548), *Aggayú* (9549), *Changó* (9550), *Orisha Oko, Oddua, Ibeyis, Olokun y Otros* (9552), *Eleguá, Ogún y Ochosi* (9546), *Ochún* (9547)

Celina y Reutilio (with Gina Martín), *Fiesta Santera*, Suaritos 110 and 123

Grupo Afrocuba De Matanzas, *Raices Africanas/African Roots*, Shanachie 66009, 1998

Grupo Oba-Ilú, *Santería: Song for the Orishas*, Soul Jazz Records, CD38, 1999

Lázaro Ros, *Orisha Ayé*, 6-CD Package Set (Changó, Ogún, Ochun, Yemayá, Obatalá, Oyá), Unicornio 6005-10, 2001

Lázaro Ros & Olorun, *Songs for Eleguá*, Ashé 2001, 1996

Merceditas Valdés y los tambores batá de Jesús Pérez, ASPIC 55512, 1996

Merceditas Valdés, *Afro-Cuban*, Tumi Cuban Classics vol. 2, Tumi 0050, 1995

Papo Angarica, *¡Fundamento Yoruba!* Egrem CD 0253, 1998

## RUMBA AND COMPARSA

Carlos "Patato" Valdés, *Patato y Totico*, Mediterraneo MDC-10065, re-issued 1992

Celeste Mendoza y Los Papines, *El Reino de la Rumba*, Egrem 0236, 1997

Clave y Guaguancó with Celeste Mendoza & Changuito, *Noche de la Rumba*, Tumi 085, 1999

Grupo Afro-Cubano de Alberto Zayas "El melodioso," *El yambú de los barrios*, Tumbao 708, 1955, re-issued 2001

Los Muñequitos de Matanzas, *Guaguancó Matancero (1956–1963)*, Tumbao 707, re-issued 2001

Los Muñequitos de Matanzas, *Live in New York*, Qbadisc 9026), 1998

Los Muñequitos de Matanzas, *Oyelos de nuevo*, Qbadisc 9013,

1970, re-issued 1994

Los Muñequitos de Matanzas, *Rumba abierta*, WS Latino 4205, 1958, re-issued 1999

Los Papines, *33 aniversario: Encuentro de tambores*, Oré Cuma Discos 1996001, 1997

Pello el Afrokán, *Pello el Afrokán y su ritmo Mozambique*, BIS 114, 1996

*Rapsodia rumbera*, Egrem CD 0121, 1995

Yoruba Andabo, *El callejón de los rumberos*, Agave Music 22103

## FROM THE DANZÓN TO THE CHA-CHA-CHA

Antonio María Romeu y su orquesta, *Boca linda*, 1931, Tumbao 076, re-issued 1996

Antonio María Romeu (with Barbarito Diez) 1937–1940, *El mago de las teclas*, Tumbao TCD 067, 1995

Arcaño y sus Maravillas, *El melao*, Better Music MSCD 7053, 1999

Arcaño y sus Maravillas, Fondo de archivo sonoro del ICRT, 1947, Bárbaro 220

Arcaño y sus Maravillas, *Danzón Mambo* 1944–1951, Tumbao 29, re-issued 1993

Cheo Belén Puig y su orquesta, *20 grandes éxitos en danzones*, Kubaney 231

Cheo Belén Puig (with Alfredito Valdés and Alberto Aroche), *Me han dicho que me quieres* (1937–1940), Tumbao 078, re-issued 1996

Enrique Jorrín y su orquesta, *Danzón Cha Cha Chá*, Vol. 1, BMG/Tropical Series 24540, 1995

Israel "Cachao" López, *Superdanzones*, Egrem 0225, 1961; re-issued 1997

Israel "Cachao" López, *Cachao y su Típica: Canta Contrabajo, Vol. 2*, Duher 1611

José Fajardo y sus Estrellas, *Cuba*, Tico 1018, re-issued 1996

Orquesta Almendra de Abelardo Valdés (1946–1955), *Mi escorpión*, Tumbao 065, re-issued 1995

Orquesta América de Ninón Mondejar, *Silver Star*, Tumbao TCD 100, 1954, re-issued 2000

Orquesta América del 55, *Los Marcianos*, Tumbao TCD-103, 1956, re-issued 2001

Orquesta América y Orquesta Aragón, *Mano a mano*, Egrem 50, 1993

Orquesta Aragón, *Danzones de ayer y de hoy*, Discuba 532

Orquesta Aragón, *Los Aragones en la Onda de la Alegría*, Bárbaro 250, re-issued 1998

Orquesta Aragón, *That Cuban Cha Cha Cha*, BMG/Tropical Series 2446, 1956, re-issued 1992

Orquesta Aragón, *The Heart of Havana*, vol. 1, BMG/Tropical Series 3204, 1958, re-issued 1992

Orquesta Estrellas Cubanas, *¡A bailar chachachá Muchachos!* Vedisco/Velvet 5100, re-issued 1995

Orquesta Melodías del 40 (1956), *Montuno favorito*, Tumbao 098, 1999

Orquesta Sensación con Abelardo Barroso, *Cumbancha en chá*, Better Music MSCD 7054, 1999

Paulina Álvarez with Orquesta Antonio María Romeu, *Rompiendo la rutina*, Better Music MSCD 7044, 1998

Paulina Álvarez y Joseíto Fernández, *La Dama y el Caballero*, Cubanacan 1709, 1998;

Pototo y Filomeno with Orquesta Melodías del 40, *¡Tremenda pareja!* Better Music MSCD 7214, 1999

## SONG, BOLERO, FEELING

Antonio Machín, *Tributo al bolero cubano*, Caney CCD 803, 1996

Benny Moré, *El Benny romántico*, Sony 82889, 1998

Bola de Nieve, *Show de Bola de Nieve* (Rare recordings from the ICRT), Discmedi 055, 1995

Bola de Nieve, *Bola de Nieve con su piano* (1930s Cuban folklore music), Montilla/Orfeon 13094

Carlos Puebla y sus Tradicionales, *De Cuba traigo un cantar*, Egrem

217, 1996

Carlos Puebla y sus Tradicionales (Carlos Puebla, Santiago Martínez, Pedro Sosa), *La Bodeguita del Medio*, Milestone 9209, 1957;
re-issued 1993

Celeste Mendoza, *Boleros con aché*, Better Music MSCD-7203, 1998

César Pérez Portillo de la Luz, La música de César Portillo de la
Luz, Virgin España 850820

Elena Burke, *A solas contigo* (Fondos sonoros del ICRT), Bárbaro
247, 1995

Elena Burke, *Boleros exclusivos*, Better Music MSCD-72002, 1997

Freddy, *Ella cantaba boleros*, Better Music MSCD-7201, 1998

José Antonio Méndez, *Sentimiento*, Discmedi 231

Lino Borges, *La voz romántica de Lino Borges*, BIS118, re-issued
1996

Olga Guillot, *El arte de cantar*, Cubanacan 1711, re-issued 1998

Omara Portuondo, Moraima Secada, Elena Burke, *Amigas*, Egrem
0165, 1996

Rita Montaner, *Función de gala con Rita Montaner*, ARO 118

Rita Montaner (1928–1929), *La Única*, Alma Latina 004, 1995

Rolando Laserie, *Mentiras tuyas*, Blue Moon ALCD-059, 2001

Rolando Laserie (1957), *15 grandes éxitos*, Disco Hit 1512

Trío La Rosa, *Esto sí que está gracioso*, Tumbao 105, 2001

**NUEVA TROVA**

Leyanis López, *Como la mariposa*, Lusafrica 56725262812, 1999

Liuba María Hevia, *Coloreando la esperanza*, BIS 197, 1999

Liuba María Hevia, *Del verso a la mar*, Eurotropical 19, 1999

Pablo Milanés, *Live from New York City*, 2-CD Set, MB Prosound,
60912, 2000

Pablo Milanés, *Los Días de gloria*, Universal 543627, 2000

Pablo Milanés, *Serie Millenium: 21 éxitos*, 2-CD set, Universal
153569, 1999

Pablo Milanés, *Vengo naciendo*, Universal 40179, 1999

Pablo Milanés, *Despertar*, Universal 140041, 1997

Pablo Milanés, *Plegaria*, Spartacus 22141, 1995

Pablo Milanés, *Buenos Días América*, Universal 40090

Pablo Milanés Yo me quedo, Spartacus 22133

Pablo Milanés, *Cancionero*, World Pacific 80596, 1993

Pablo Milanés, *Amo a esta isla*, Universal 40087, 1981, re-issued 1997

Pablo Milanés, *Filin 1*, Universal 40088, 1981, re-issued 1997

Pablo Milanés, *No me pidas*, Universal 40082, 1977, re-issued 1997

Pablo Milanés, *Versos sencillos de José Martí*, Universal 40080, 1973, re-issued 1997

Pedro Luis Ferrer, *Pedro Luis Ferrer*, Havana Caliente 83188, 1999

Silvio Rodriguez & Pablo Milanés, *En vivo en Argentina*, Ojalá 30418, 2000

Silvio Rodríguez & Rey Guerra, *Mariposas*, Ojalá 0021, 2000

Silvio Rodríguez, *Canciones urgentes — Los grandes éxitos*, Luaka Bop 9 26480-2, 1991

Silvio Rodríguez, *Descartes*, Fonomusic 8070, 1998

Silvio Rodríguez, *Domínguez*, Fonomusic 8070, 1996

Silvio Rodríguez, *Rodríguez*, Fonomusic 8026, 1995

Silvio Rodríguez, *Silvio*, Fonomusic 8001, 1992

Silvio Rodríguez, *Tríptico*, 3 Vol., Fonomusic 8035-8037, 1992

Silvio Rodríguez, *Al final de este viaje*, 1968/1970, Fonomusic 8031, 1991

Silvio Rodríguez, *Causas y azares*, Fonomusic 3050, 1991

Silvio Rodríguez, *Cuando digo futuro*, Fonomusic 8030, 1991

Silvio Rodríguez, *Rabo de nube*, Fonomusic 8033, 1991

Silvio Rodríguez, *Te doy una canción*, Fonomusic 8029, 1991

Silvio Rodríguez, *Unicornio*, Fonomusic 8034, 1991

Silvio Rodríguez, *Oh Melancolia*, Fonomusic 3030, 1988

## VIEJA TROVA AND EARLY SON
## FROM THE EASTERN REGION

Celina y Reutilio, *A Santa Bárbara*, Suaritos 103

Celina y Reutilio, *Rezos y Cantos guajiros*, Ansonia 1392

Celina y Reutilio, *Antología cubana*, Teca 4009, re-issued 1996

Celina y Reutilio, *Cantos de Cuba*, BIS 106, re-issued 1997

Celina y Reutilio, *Santeros y otros*, Spanoramic 121, re-issued 1998

Compay Segundo y su Grupo (1956–1957), *Balcón de Santiago*, Tumbao 093

*Compay Segundo y Los Compadres*, Edenways, 2000

Duo Los Compadres (Lorenzo. Hierrezuelo and Francisco Repilado), 1949–1951, *Cantando en llano*, Tumbao 061

Guillermo Portabales, *15 grandes éxitos*, Disco Hit 1808, re-issued 1999

Guillermo Portabales, *Sones cubanos con Los Guaracheros de Oriente*, Disco Hit 1872, re-issued 1998

Guillermo Portabales, *Viva Portabales y sus guitarras*, Disco Hit 1862, re-issued 1999

Los Compadres, *Legends of Cuban Music*, NC 5026, 2001

Los Compadres (1949–1955), *Sentimiento guajiro*, Tumbao 095, re-issued 1999

Los Compadres, *Antología cubana*, Teca 4006, 2000

Los Compadres, *Época de oro del Duo Los compadres*, Next Music/Musisoft 9070, 2000

Los Guaracheros de Oriente, *Antología cubana*, Teca 4003, 2000

María Teresa Vera, *Éxitos originales*, Kubaney 0229

María Teresa Vera, *The Cuban Legend*, Edenways 2006, 1999

María Teresa Vera with Rafael Zequeira (1916–1924), *El legendario duo de la Trova cubana*, Tumbao 090, re-issued 1998

Ñico Saquito y sus Guaracheros de Oriente, *Adios Compay Gato* (1954–1955), Tumbao 705

Ñico Saquito y sus Guaracheros de Oriente (1946–1951), *Alborada*, Tumbao 094, re-issued 1998

Trío Matamoros y Guaracheros de Oriente, *30 éxitos*, 2-CD Set,

Orfeon 11 971, 1996

Trío Matamoros, *The legendary Trío Matamoros* 1928–1937, Tumbao 016, 1992

Trío Matamoros, *Trío Matamoros* 1928–1939, Harlequin 40

Trío Matamoros, *Trío Matamoros*, Ansonia 1282

Vieja Trova Santiaguera, *Pura Trova: The Best of Vieja Trova Santiaguera* & *Live and rare Tracks:* 2-CD Set with 91-page Book, Nubenegra/Intuition 1105, 2001

## FROM THE QUARTET TO THE BIG BAND

Anselmo Sacasas & his Orquesta (1942–1944), Harlequin 77, re-issued 1997

Antonio Machín (1933–1934), Harlequin 58, re-issued 1997

Antonio Machín, *Cuarteto Machín* 1934–1935, Harlequin 104, re-issued 1998

Antonio Machín, *Angelitos negros*, Better Music MSCD 7042, 1998

Armando Orefiche y sus Havana Cuban Boys (1955), *Nostalgia cubana*, Tumbao 099, re-issued 2000

Armando Orefiche 1951–1961, Harlequin 111, re-issued 1998

Arsenio Rodríguez y su Conjunto (with Miguelito Cuní, Felix Chapottín…), *Clásicas de un sonero*, Seeco 9352, re-issued 1998

*Arsenio Rodríguez y su Conjunto*, Edenways 2002, re-issued 2000

Arsenio Rodríguez y su Conjunto, *Legendary Sessions* 1947–1953, Tumbao 017, re-issued 1992

Bebo Valdés, *Ritmando Cha Cha Chá*: Cuban Classics IX, WS Latino 4211, re-issued 2000

Bebo Valdés, *Mucho sabor*, Palladium PCD 5123, re-issued 1989

Bebo Valdés & his Havana all Stars, *Descarga caliente*, Caney 512, re-issued 1996

Benny Moré, *30 éxitos*: 2-CD Set, Orfeon 13781, 2000

Benny Moré, *Grandes éxitos del Bárbaro del Ritmo*: 2-CD Set, Envidia 7016, 2000

Benny Moré, *Legend of the Century*, Sony 83213, 1999

Benny Moré, *Mucho corazón*, Egrem CD 342, 2000

Benny Moré, *Benny Moré en vivo*, Bárbaro 214, re-issued 1995

Benny Moré, *Grandes éxitos*, BMG 69913, 1999

Benny Moré, *Cuban originals*, BMG 69935, 1999

Benny Moré, *40 temas originales*, 2-CD Set, BMG Latin 72826, 2001

Benny Moré, *En vivo/Live Recordings*, Max 722298, 2000

Benny Moré con la Orquesta de Pérez Prado, *Rompiendo el coco*, Better Music MSCD 7051, 1999

Benny Moré (1955–1957), *The most from Benny Moré*, BMG Tropical Series 2445, re-issued 1990

Carlos Embale, *Rumbas, Sones, Boleros cubanos*, Virgin España 850825, 2000

Carlos Embale, *Que bueno canta Embale*, Egrem CD 0102

Celeste Mendoza, *La voz de Celeste Mendoza, La Guapachosa*, Seeco 9217, 1959, re-issued 1998

Celeste Mendoza, *Que me castigue Dios y otros éxitos*, Orfeon 16153, 2000

Celia Cruz & Sonora Matancera, *At the Beginning*, Universal 160 505, 2001

Celia Cruz con la Sonora Matancera en los estudios CMQ, 1950-1953, Tumbao 091, re-issued 1998

Celia Cruz, *Las muchas Celias*, Cubanacan 1710, re-issued 1998

Cheo Marquetti, *El Rey del ritmo*, Virgin España 850819, 1957, re-issued 2000

Cheo Marquetti, *Región Matancera*, Tumbao 107, re-issued 2001

Chano Pozo with Dizzy Gillespie & His Orchestra, *The Real Birth of Cubop* 1948, Tumbao 102, 1948, re-issued 2001

Chano Pozo, *El tambor de Cuba*: 3-CD Box Set with 143-page Book, Tumbao 305, 2001

Chapottín, *Musicalidad en sepia: Cuní con Chapottín y sus Estrellas*, Maype 110

*Chapottín y sus Estrellas*, Antilla 594

Chapottín y sus Estrellas, *Sabor Tropical*, Antilla 107, re-issued 1993

Conjunto Casino (1941–1955), *Legends of Cuban Music*, NC 5025, 2001

Conjunto Casino, *Via Cuba*, BMG/Tropical Series 25516, 1998

Conjunto Casino, *En Cumbancha*, Fondos sonoros del ICRT, Bárbaro 249, re-issued 1999

Conjunto Casino, *Conjunto Casino con Faz, Ribot y Espí*, 2 Vol., Mediterraneo 10046/10140

Conjunto Casino, *Los campeones del ritmo*, Maype 113

Conjunto Kubavana (1944–1947) & Conjunto Casino (1947–1948), with Carlos "Patato" Valdés, *Rumba en el patio*, Tumbao 34, re-issued 1994

Conjunto Matamoros with Benny Moré, Tumbao 20, 1992

Cuarteto Caney (1936–1939), Harlequin 075, 1996

Cuarteto Machín, vol. 1 1930–1932, Harlequin 24, re-issued 1992

Cuarteto Machín, vol. 2 1932–1933, Harlequin 32, re-issued 1994

Cuarteto Machín, vol. 3 1934–1935, Harlequin 104, re-issued 1998

Félix Chapottín y su Conjunto, *La Guarapachanga*, Better Music MSCD 7057, 1999

Ibrahim Ferrer con Chepín y su Orquesta Oriental, *Mi Oriente*, Tumbao 704, 1960, re-issued 1999

Julio Cuevas y su Orquesta (1943–1945) with "Cascarita" and "Puntillita", Tumbao 032, 1994

Laito Suredo y la Sonora Matancera, *¡Puro Cañonazo!* Seeco 9359, re-issued 1998

Machito and His Afro-Cubans, *Asia Minor*, Tico 1029, released 1956; re-issued 1999

Machito and His Afro-Cubans, *Machito Inspired*: Music Inspired by Ernest Hemingway's "The Sun Also Rises", Tico 1045, released 1957, re-issued 1999

Machito and His Afro-Cubans (1945–1947), *Guampampiro*, Tumbao 089, re-issued 1997

Machito and His Afro-Cubans, *Kenya*, Roulette/Capitol 22668, 1957, re-issued 1999

Machito and His Afro-Cubans, *Si-Si, No-No*, Tico 1033, 1956, re-issued 1999

Manuel Licea "Puntillita", *Homenaje* (1927–2000), Tumi 102, 2001

Mariano Mercerón y sus Muchachos Pimienta (1940–1946), *Yo tengo un tumbao*, Tumbao 064, 1995

Merceditas Valdés, *Un aché para Cuba*, Bárbaro 235

Miguelito Valdés, *Cuban Originals*, BMG 72784, 2000

Miguelito Valdés, *Algo Nuevo: Mambo and Rumba Sessions* (1949), Tumbao 104, re-issued 2001

Miguelito Valdés, *Mambo Dance Session: Historical 1949 Recordings*, Caribe Classics 1050, re-issued 1994

Miguelito Valdés with the Orquesta Casino de la Playa, Harlequin 39, re-issued 1994

Olga Guillot con la Orquesta Hermanos Castro, Caney 802, 1995

Omara Portuondo (under the direction of Julio Gutierrez & His Orchestra), *Magia Negra*, Velvet/Vedisco 5178, 1958

Orlando Guerra "Cascarita," *Carnaval, Trinidad y Hermano*, vol. 1, Fondo sonoro de archivo del ICRT, Bárbaro 215, re-issued 1995

Orlando Guerra Cascarita, *Carnaval, Trinidad y Hermano*, vol. 2 1949–1950: Fondo Sonoro de Archivo del ICRT, Barbaro 216, re-issued 1998

Orquesta Casino de la Playa, Harlequin 051, re-issued 1995

Orquesta Chepín-Choven (Collección de Diamante), DC Productions 9213

Orquesta Hermanos Palau 1939–1941, *La ola marina*, Tumbao 035, re-issued 1994

Orquesta Melodías del 40, *Me voy pa' Morón*, Antilla 05

Orquesta Melodías del 40, *Montuno favorito*, Tumbao 098, 1956, re-issued 2000

Orquesta Riverside, *Bailemos con la Riverside*, Seeco 9088, re-issued 2000

Orquesta Riverside with Tito Gómez, *Cha-Hua-Hua*, Better Music MSCD 7222, 2000

Orquesta Riverside, *One Night in Havana*, Columbia River 170011, 1999

Orquesta Riverside, *Otra descarga*, Bárbaro 244

Pacho Alonso, *Rico Pilón*, BIS 041, 1991

Pacho Alonso, *Una noche en El Sheherazada*, Discuba 521, re-issued 2000

Pacho Alonso, *A bailar con Pacho Alonso*, Discuba 560, re-issued 2000

Pérez Prado and his orchestra, *Cuban originals*, BMG 70046, 1999

Pérez Prado and his orchestra, *The Mambo King vol. 3: Savoy Mambo*, BMG Tropical Series 38032, 1951, re-issued 1996

Pérez Prado and his orchestra, *40 temas originales*, 2-CD Set, BMG Latin 72840, 2001

Peruchín, *The Incendiary Piano of Peruchín*! Plus Orquesta Nuevo Ritmo de Cuba: The Heart of Cuba, GNP 2264, 1999

Pio Leyva, *Sonero* (Cuba Classics III), WS Latino 4206, re-issued 1999

René Álvarez y su Conjunto Los Astros (1948–1950), *Yumbale*, Tumbao 062, re-issued 1995

Roberto Faz, *Saludos a Roberto Faz* (1960), Seeco 9198, re-issued 1998

Roberto Faz, *En Vivo en la Television Cubana* (1965), Barbaro 221, re-issued 1999

Senén Suárez y su Conjunto del Tropicana Night-Club (1952–1953), *Guaguancó Callejero*, Tumbao 048, re-issued 1994

Septeto Nacional Ignacio Piñeiro, *Sones de mi Habana*, WS Latino 4085, 1957, re-issued 1998

Septeto Nacional Ignacio Piñeiro (with Carlos Embale), *Sones cubanos*, Seeco 9278

*Septeto Nacional Ignacio Piñeiro 1928-1930*, Tumbao 019

Septeto Nacional de Ignacio Piñeiro, *El son de altura*, Better Music MSCD 7031, 1998

Septeto y Conjunto Matamoros, *Camarón y mamoncillo*, Tumbao 044, re-issued 1994

Septeto y Conjunto La Gloria Matancera, *Vengo arrollando* (1937–1949), Tumbao 066, re-issued 1995

Sexteto Boloña, *Echale candela* (1926), Tumbao 060, re-issued 1995

Sexteto Habanero, *Sexteto Y Septeto Habanero, Las Raíces del Son* por Senén Suárez, *Grabaciones Completas 1925–1931*, 4-CD Boxed Set with Complete Discography and Book, Tumbao 300), 1998

Sexteto Nacional de Ignacio Piñeiro 1927–1928, *Cubaneo*, Tumbao 097, re-issued 2000

Sonora Matancera, *Live on the Radio 1952–1958*, Harlequin 79, re-issued 1996

Sonora Matancera, *Sonora Vol. IV: Grabado en vivo, La Habana-Cuba 1949–58*, Sonora 004, re-issued 1996

Sonora Matancera 1942–1999, *75 años*, 5-CD Better Music MSCD 7062–7066, 2000

Tito Gómez with Orquesta Riverside, *En vivo*, Bárbaro 224, 1952, re-issued 1996

Tito Gómez con La Orquesta Riverside, Seeco 9076, released 1952, re-issued 1998

Vicentico Valdés, *Mi diario musical*, Seeco 3002

Vicentico Valdés, *Los aretes de la luna*, Better Music, MSCD 7033, 1998

## DESCARGAS

Afro Cuban Jazz Project, *Descarga Uno*, Circular Moves 7003, 1999

Bebo Valdés with Havana Stars, *Descarga caliente*, Caney 512

Cachao y su Conjunto, *Descarga*, Maype 168

Cachao y su Ritmo caliente, *From Havana to New York*, Caney 501, 1994

Frank Emilio & Guillermo Barreto, *Algo Bueno*, Caney 515, 1959, re-issued 1999

Israel "Cachao" López, *Descargas Cubanas: Cuban Jam Session Vol. II*

CD (Panart 1A501-00411), re-issued 1987

Israel "Cachao" López, Descargas: Cuban Jam Sessions, Egrem

0169, 1957, re-issued 1997
Israel "Cachao" López, *Jam Session with Feeling*, Maype 122
Israel "Cachao" López, *Monte adentro*, Blue Moon 2056, 1957, re-issued 2000
Peruchín, *¡La Descarga!* Nuevos Medios 65 611, re-issued 1995
Peruchín, *Peruchineando con Peruchin*, Montmartre Records SY03, re-issued 1995

## TRADITIONAL MUSIC AFTER THE CUBAN REVOLUTION
Afro Cuban All Stars, *Distinto, Diferente*, Nonesuch 79501, 1999
Afro Cuban All Stars, *A toda Cuba le gusta*, Nonesuch 79476, 1997
Afro-Cuban All Stars presents Félix Baloy, *Baila mi son*, Tumi 100, 2000
Alfredo Rodríguez, *Cuba linda*, Hannibal/Rykodisc 1399, 1996
All Stars de La Rumba Cubana, *La rumba soy yo*, BIS 193, 2001
Banda municipal de Santiago de Cuba, Buda 92724, 1999
Barbarito Torres, *Havana Café*, Havana Caliente 83183, 1999;
Boniatillo Eduardo A. López, *A Boniatillo limpio...*, Envidia 7025, 2001
*Buena Vista Social Club*, Nonesuch 79478, 1997
Carlos "Patato" Valdés y Changuito, *The Legend Of Cuban Percussion—The Best of Ritmo y Candela*, Six Degrees 1027, 2000
Carmen Flores, *Babalú*, Ahi-Nama Records 1029, 2000
*Casa De La Trova De Baracoa*, BIS 234), 2001
*Casa de la Trova de Santiago de Cuba*, Corason 120, 1994
*Casa de la Trova*, Erato 3984-25751-2, 1999
Celina González y Reutilio Jr, *Añoranza de Cuba: Sol y Son*, Fuentes 11045, 1999
Celina González with Frank Fernández and Adalberto Álvarez, Egrem 0159, 1995
Celina González, *Alborada guajira*, Egrem 0238, 1997
Changüí de Guantánamo, *Bongó de monte*, Egrem, 0356, 1999
Changuito, *A Master's Approach To Timbales*, Book and CD Package, Manhattan Music 0111B, 1998

Charanga Rubalcaba (Guillermo Rubalcaba), *El Danzón de la Reina Isabel*, Eurotropical 901526, 2000

Charanga Rubalcaba, *Por eso yo soy Cubano*, Eurotropical 0010, 1998

Compay Segundo, *Calle Salud*, Nonesuch 79578, 1999

Compay Segundo, *Lo Mejor De La Vida*, Nonesuch 79517, 1998

Conjunto Casino, *Montuno en Neptuno #960*, RealRhythm 59907, 2001

Conjunto Chapottín y sus Estrellas, *Seguimos Aquí...¡ Chappottineando!*, Envidia 7010, 2000

Conjunto Los Naranjos, *La tradición no se olvida*, Eurotropical 00123, 2000

Conjunto Los Naranjos, *Mi Son tiene piel morena*, Eurotropical EUCD-13, 1998

El Muso y su Gran Sonora, *3 Caras Del Son* — with Cándido Fabré & Tiburón, Tumi 081, 1999

Eliades Ochoa y El Cuarteto Patria, *Sublime Ilusion*, Higher Octave 47494, 1999

Eliades Ochoa y El Cuarteto Patria, *Tribute to the Cuarteto Patria*, Higher Octave 49640, 2000

"El Nene" Pedro Lugo Martínez con Las Estrellas de Areito, *Cuidao con el perro: Un homenaje a Faustino Oramas "El Guayabero,"* Egrem, 2000

"El Nene" Pedro Lugo Martínez Con Las Estrellas de Areito, *Me voy contigo*, Promusic 0016, 2001

El Son Entero, *La Cumbancha*, Playasound 65220, 1999

Estrellas de Areíto, Cuban All-Stars produced by Rubén González, Edenways, 1981, re-issued 1999

Estrellas Areíto, *Los Heroes*, 2-CD Set, Nonesuch 79551, 1979, re-issued 1999

Estudiantina Invasora, *Tírame la pelota María*, Egrem 429, 2000

Familia Valera Miranda, *A Cutiño*, Naive 6886, 1999

Familia Valera Miranda, *Antología integral del son*, 2-CD Set, Virgin España 8485622, 1999

Familia Valera Miranda, *Cuba*, Ocora 570602, 1997

Familia Valera Miranda, *Music from the Oriente de Cuba: the Son*, Nimbus 5421, 1994

Generoso Jiménez and his Orchestra, *El trombón majadero*, Bembé 2017, 1965, re-issued 1997

Generoso Jiménez and his Orchestra, *Generoso, Que bueno toca Usted*, Termidor 89756, 2001

German Obregón y Palma Real, *Fiesta campesina*, Envidia 7031, 2001

Grupo Changüí and Estrellas Campesinas, Traditional Crossroads 4290, 1998

Grupo Sierra Maestra, *Sierra Maestra*, Edenways 2008, 2000;

Grupo Sierra Maestra, *Grandes éxitos*, Artex 26, 1991

Grupo Sierra Maestra, *Tibiri Tabara*, Nonesuch 79497, 1998

Grupo Vocal Desandann, *Descendants*, Bembé 2022, 1999

Habana Ensemble, *Mambomania: A Tribute To Pérez Prado*, Latin World 00004, 1999

Ibrahim Ferrer, *Buena Vista Social Club presents*,

Ibrahim Ferrer with Los Bocucos, *Tierra caliente*, Egrem 0308, 1998

Isabel Becker, *La Profunda*, AZUL Productions 102, 2000

Jovenes Clasicos del Son, *Fruta Bomba*, Tumi 084, 1999

Laíto y su Sonora, *Ahora comienzo a vivir*, Eurotropical EUCD-14, re-issued 1998

Laíto Jr. y Laíto Sr, *Siempre juntos*, Ahi-Nama Records 1033, 2001

Laíto Jr with La Sonora sonora, *¡Sarandonga!*, Ahi-Nama 1025, 2000

Las Nuevas Estrellas de Areito, Egrem 456, Released 2001

Los Guanches, *The corpse went dancing rumba*, Corason 128, 1996

Los Jubilados, *¡Oyeme Cachita!* Corason 152, 2000

Los Jubilados, *No tiene teleraña*, Corason, 2001

Los Papines, *Papines en descarga*, Orfeon 16181, 2001

Machito and His Afro-Cubans, *Soul of Machito*, Cotique 1019, 1971, re-issued 1999

Miguelito Valdés with Machito and His Orchestra, *Reunión*, Tico

1098, 1963, re-issued 1999

Ñico Saquito with Eliades Ochoa, *Al bate*, Egrem 0379, 2000

Omara Portuando con Adalberto Álvarez, *Roots of Buena Vista*, Egrem 163, 1984, re-issued 2000

Omara Portuondo, *Buena Vista Social Club Presents Omara Portuondo*, Nonesuch 79603, 2000

Omara Portuondo, *Veinte Años*, Edenways 2016

Omara Portuondo, *Oro musical*, Max 2186, 1999

Omara Portuondo, *Palabras*, Nubenegra/Intuition 3186, 1996

Omara Portuondo (1973–1997), *Dos gardenias*, Tumi 105

Orquesta América with Chucho Valdés & Felix Reina, *Danzón*, Tumi 005, 1997

Orquesta América, *Sabor Profundo*, RealRhythm 50102, 2001

Orquesta Anacaona, *Lo que tú esparabas*, Lusafrica 362292, 2000

Orquesta Aragón, *En Route*, Lusafrica 362582, 2001

Orquesta Aragón, *La Charanga Eterna*, Lusafrica 362112, 1999;

Orquesta Estrellas Cubanas, *Pa' bailar*, Envidia 7035, 2001

*Orquesta Estrellas Cubanas*, Vitral 4850, 1989

Orquesta Estrellas Cubanas, *A bailar chachachá, muchachos*, Vedisco/Velvet 5100, re-issued 1995

Orquesta Maravilla De Florida, *Levantate y baila*, Caribe Productions 9466, 1996

Orquesta Maravilla De Florida, *50 y más Maravillas*, Last Call 3046132, 1999

Orquesta Maravilla De Florida, *Vieja, pero se mantiene*, Envidia 7012, 2000

Orquesta Melodías Del 40, *Sonando a Melodías*, Envidia 7020, Released 2000

Orquesta Original De Manzanillo, *Se formó el tirijala*, Envidia 6031, 1998

Orquesta Original De Manzanillo, *Puros*, Qbadisc 9003, 1992

Orquesta Ritmo Oriental, *Historia de la Ritmo*, 2 vols., Qbadisc 9007–9008, 1993

Orquesta Ritmo Oriental, *Orquesta Ritmo Oriental*, Bárbaro 233, 1995

Orquesta Ritmo Oriental, *El Ritmo de la Ritmo*, Egrem 0108, 1995

Pancho Amat y El Cabildo del Son, *De San Antonio a Maisí*, Resistencia 104, 2001

Pedro Depestre, *Son Charangas y pasiones*, Latin World 00011, 1999

Quinteto Son de la Loma, *Santiago en el corazón*, NRD 0525, reissued 1999

Raúl Planas, *Te invito un momento*, Egrem 0072, 1995

René Álvarez y su Conjunto, *Guaguancó en el solar*, Tumbao 703, 1999

Richard Egües y su Orquesta, *Richard Egües & Friends: Cuban Sessions*, Latin World 00005, 1999

Richard Egües y su Orquesta, *Havana Club*, Timbo 1101, 1986

Roberto Faz, *Roberto Faz*, Seyer 1122, re-issued 1996

Rolo Martínez, *Para bailar mi Son*, Ahi-Nama Records 1020, 1998

Rubén González, *Chanchullo*, Nonesuch 79503, 2000

Rubén González, *Indestructible*, Egrem 0275, 1997

Rubén González, *Introducing... Rubén González*, Nonesuch 79477, 1997

Septeto Habanero, *Celebrando sus 80 años*, Lusafrica 362302, 2000

Septeto Santiaguero, *La Pulidora*, Nubenegra/Intuition 3266, 1999

Septeto Son La Clave, *Ñaña Rube*, Sonoramico 010, 2001

Soneros De Verdad, *A Buena Vista: Barrio De La Habana*, Narada 10263, 2001

Tanda De Guaracheros, *Guarachas en La Habana*, Envidia 7027, 2001

Tipico Oriental, *Eterna Melodía*, Caribe Productions 9559, 1998

Todos Estrellas, *Trova Santiaguera*, Egrem 0307, 1998

Union Sanluisera, *Charanga*, Playasound 65205, 1998

Universales del Son, *Guateque en Yateras: Changüí*, Envidia 7033, 2001

Vocal Sampling, *Live in Berlin*, Ashé 2008, 1998

## DANCE MUSIC AND JAZZ AFTER THE REVOLUTION

Adalberto Álvarez y su Son, *En Vivo*, Caribe Productions 9503, 1997

Adalberto Álvarez y su Son, *Jugando con Candela*, Havana Caliente 83184, 1999

Adalberto Álvarez y su Son, *A bailar el toca toca*, Caribe Productions 9467, 1996

*Adalberto Álvarez y su Son*, Sony/POW 86563, 1993

Adalberto Álvarez y su Son, *La salsa caliente*, Sonido 3006 620, 1990

Adalberto Álvarez y su Son, *Locos por el son*, Caribe Productions 9502, 1999

Angel Bonné, *Circunstancias*, Egrem 0269, 1998;

Angel Bonné, *Pa' decir lo que siento*, Mojito, 1998

Aramis Galindo, *Esto tiene cohimbre*, Cuba Chevere 06-608, 2001

Asere, *Cuban soul*, Circular Moves 7004, 2000

Azucar Negra, *Andar andando*, BIS 215, 2000

Bakuleyé, *El Fiebre del Ula Ula*, Ahi-Nama Records 1019, 1998

Bakuleyé, *Timbantón*, Cuba Chevere 03-0600, 2000

Bamboleo, *Te gusto o te caigo bien*, Ahi-Nama Records 1024, 1996

Bamboleo, *Ya no hace falta*, ahi-Nama 1024, 1999

Bamboleo, ¡*Niño! Qué bueno está*, Ahi-Nama 1027, 2000

Bebo Valdés, *El Arte del Sabor*: Bebo Valdés en trío con Cachao y Patato, Blue Note 35193, 2001

Bobby Carcassés, *Afrojazz*, RMD 82236, re-issued 1998

Bobby Carcassés, *Jazz Timbero*, Tumi 068, 1998

Calixto Oviedo, *La Recompensa*, Egrem 407, 2001

Cándido Fabré, *Son de Cuba*, Tumi 057, 1996

Cándido Fabré, *Todo Cuba baila con Cándido Fabré*, Max 2141, 1998

Cándido Fabré, *La Habana quiere guarachar contigo*, Tumi 097, 2000

Carlos Maza, *Fidelidad*, Universal, 2002

Carlos Maza, *Mariposa*, Lautaro 0001, 1995

Carlos Maza, *Nostalgia*, Owl Records 079 832339 2, 1995

César Pedroso, *De la Timba a Pogolotti*, Timba Productions 15871, 2001

Chispa y los Cómplices, *New Pa' que vea*, Cuba Chevere 000014, 1999

Chucho Valdés & Irakere, *Unforgetable boleros*, Velas 2005, 2000

Conjunto Rumbavana, *Orquesta Rumbavana*, Mambo Express 10203, 1999

Cuarto Espacio, *Reencuentro*, Ashé 2004, 1993

Cubanismo, *¡Mucho gusto!* Hannibal 1461, 2001

Dan Den, *Dale al que no te dió*, Egrem 57, 1993

Dan Den, *Viejo Lázaro*, Qbadisc 9009, 1993

Dan Den, *Mi cuerpo*, Nueva Fania 106, 1996

Dan Den, *Salsa en Ataré*, Candela/Tumi 42852882/069, 1998

Dan Den, *Mecánica guapa*, Nueva Fania 114, 1999

David Calzado y su Charanga Habanera, *Chan Chan Charanga*, Ciocan HMC2601, 2001

David Calzado y su Charanga Habanera, *El baile del azucar*, Rosita 208, 2001

David Calzado y su Charanga Habanera, *En concierto*, Rosita 209, 2001

David Calzado y su Charanga Habanera, *El Charanguero mayor*, JMI 001, 2000

David Calzado y su Charanga Habanera, *Me sube la fiebre/Love fever*, Milan/BMG 35754, 1993

David Calzado y su Charanga Habanera, *Tremendo delirio*, Universal 40068

Elio Revé y su Charangón, 2 vols., Caribe Productions 9440 & 9441, 1994

Elio Revé Jr, *Changüí en la casa de Nora*, Tumi096, 2000

Emiliano Salvador, *Pianissimo: La leyenda del Jazz Cubano*, Unicornio 9003, 2000

Emiliano Salvador, *Ayer y hoy*, Qbadisc 9011, 1994

Emiliano Salvador, *Emiliano Salvador* (1978 and 1981), Virgin

España 850824

Emiliano Salvador, *Nueva visión*, Qbadisc 9018, 1979

Felipe Cabrera, *Made in Ánimas*, Unicornio 9001, 1999

Felipe Cabrera, *Evidence from El Cayo*, Win Win, 2001

Frank Emilio Flynn, *Ancestral Reflections/Reflejos Ancestrales*, Blue Note 98918, 1999

Gema y Pável, *Cosas de broma*, Nubenegra/Intuition 3181, 1996

Gonzalo Rubalcaba, *Messidor's Finest*, vol. 3, Messidor 15844, 1997

Gonzalo Rubalcaba, *The Best of Gonzalo Rubalcaba*, Milan/BMG 35816, 1997

Gonzalo Rubalcaba, *Supernova*, Blue Note 31172, 2001

Gonzalo Rubalcaba/Charlie Haden, *Nocturne*, Verve/Poly. 013611, 2001

Gonzalo Rubalcaba, *Inner Voyage*, Blue Note 99241, 1999;

Gonzalo Rubalcaba, *Gonzalo Rubalcaba*, Max 213, 1998

Gonzalo Rubalcaba, *Antiguo*, Blue Note 37717, 1998

Irakere, *Grandes momentos de Irakere*, Milan/BMG 35778, 1991

Irakere, *The Best of Irakere,* Columbia/Sony 57719, 1994

Irakere, *Misa negra*, Messidor 15972, 1987

Irakere, *Calzada del Cerro*, Vitral 4053, 1989

Irakere, *Bailando así-Desde Cuba con ritmo*, Fonomusic 3043

Irakere, *Live at Ronnie Scott's* 1991, World Pacific 80598

Irakere, *Indestructible*, Sony/POW 83558, 1994

Irakere, *Afrocubanismo Live!* Bembé 2012, 1996

Irakere, *Babalu Ayé*, Bembé 2020, 1998

Irakere, *Yemayá*, Blue Note 98239, 1998

Issac Delgado & Adalberto Álvarez, *El Chévere de la Salsa/ El Caballero del son*, Milan/BMG 35749, 1994

Issac Delgado y su Grupo, *La Fórmula*, Ahi-Nama Records 1030, 2000

Issac Delgado y su Grupo, *Los grandes éxitos de Issac Delgado*, RMM 84077, 2000

Issac Delgado y su Grupo, *Rareties*, RMD 82276

Jesús Alemany, ¡*Cubanismo*! Featuring Alfredo Rodríguez, Hannibal/Rykodisc 1390, 1996

Jesús Rubalcaba, *Estoy aquí*, Envidia 7019, 2000

Jesús "Chucho" Valdés solo, *Live in New York*, Blue Note 93456, 2001

Jesús "Chucho" Valdés, *Live at the Village Vanguard*, Blue Note 20730, 2000

Jesús "Chucho" Valdés, *Belé Belé en La Habana*, Blue Note 23082, 1998

Jesús "Chucho" Valdés, *Chucho Valdés live*, RMM 82251, 1998

Jesús "Chucho" Valdés, *Solo piano*, Blue Note 80597, 1993

Jesús "Chucho" Valdés, *Pianissimo*, Mojito 12020, 1994

Jesús "Chucho" Valdés, *Lo Mejor de la Timba cubana: Antología y Evolución de la música cubana*, vol. 1, Egrem 243, re-issued 1997

José Luis Cortés, *Latin Fever*, Caribe Productions 9513, 1997 José Luis Cortés y NG La Banda, *Baila Conmigo*, Promusic 0015, 2001

José Luis Cortés y NG La Banda, *The best of NG La Banda*, Hemisphere/EMI 21391, 1999

José Luis Cortés y NG La Banda, *Toda Cuba baila con...NG La Banda*, Max 2086, 1998

José Luis Cortés y NG La Banda, *Veneno*, Metro Blue 93985, 1998

José Luis Cortés y NG La Banda, *En cuerpo y alma*, 2-CD Set, Caribe Productions 9489, 1997

José Luis Cortés y NG La Banda, *Nuestro hombre en La Habana*, Caribe Productions 9471, 1996

José Luis Cortés y NG La Banda, *La cachimba*, Caribe Productions 9470, 1996

José Luis Cortés y NG La Banda, *En directo desde el patio de mi casa*, Caribe Productions 9462, 1996

José Luis Cortés y NG La Banda, *De NG La Banda para Curaçao*, Caribe Productions 9456

José Luis Cortés y NG La Banda, *La bruja*, Caribe Productions 9436, 1995

José Luis Cortés y NG La Banda, *Simplemente lo mejor de...NG La Banda*, Caribe Productions 9435, 1994

José Luis Cortés y NG La Banda, *Llegó NG Camará*, Artex 072, 1993

José Luis Cortés y NG La Banda, *Echale limón*, Caribe Productions 9458, 1992

José Luis Cortés y NG La Banda, *En la calle*, Qbadisc 9002, 1992

Juan Formell y Los Van Van, *30 Aniversario*, 2-CD Set, Caribe Productions 9555, 1999

Juan Formell y Los Van Van, *The Legendary Los Van Van: 30 Years of Cuba's Greatest Dance Band*, 2-CD Boxed Set Complete with 106-page Booklet, Ashé 2007A/B, 1999

Juan Formell y Los Van Van, *Live in America: The Exciting U.S. Premiere*, MNL 001, 1999

Juan Formell y Los Van Van, *The Best of Juan Formell y Los Van Van*, Tumi 063

Juan Formell y Los Van Van, *Toda Cuba baila con...Juan Formell y Los Van Van*, Max 2085, 1998

Juan Formell y Los Van Van, *The Best of Los Van Van*, Milan/BMG 35799, 1997

Juan Formell y Los Van Van, *Llego...Van Van / Van Van Is Here*, Havana Caliente 83227, 1999

Juan Formell y Los Van Van, *Te pone la cabeza mala*, Metro Blue 21307, 1997

Juan Formell y Los Van Van, *¡Ay dios, Ampárame!* Caribe Productions 9475, 1996

Juan Formell y Los Van Van, *25 años...¡Y seguimos ahí!*, 2 vols., Caribe Productions 9431/9432, 1994

Juan Formell y Los Van Van, *Lo último en vivo*, Qbadisc 9020, 1994

Juan Formell y Los Van Van, *Dancing Wet - Bailando mojao*, World Pacific 80600, 1993

Juan Formell y Los Van Van, *Azúcar*, Xenophile/Green Linnet 4025, 1993

Juan Formell y Los Van Van, *Aquí el que baila gana*, fonomusic 1080, 1991

Juan Formell y Los Van Van, *Esto está bueno*, Caribe Prodcutions 9452, 1991

Juan Formell y Los Van Van, *De Cuba*, Caribe Productions 9468, 1990

Juan Formell y Los Van Van, *Al son del Caribe/La Titimanía & Eso que anda*, Fonomusic 3042, 1990

Juan Formell y Los Van Van, *Los Van Van*, Vitral 4118, re-issued 1989

Juan Formell y Los Van Van, *Songo*, Mango 9825, 1988

Juan Manuel Ceruto, *A Puerto Padre: Tributo a Emiliano Salvador*, Unicornio 9009, 2001

Juan Pablo Torres, *Son que chévere/A cool son*, Circular Moves 7005, 2000

Juan Pablo Torres, *Cuba swings*, Universal 160 501, 2001

Juan Pablo Torres, *Descarga Afrocubana*, Caiman 9044, 1998

Juan Pablo Torres, *Together again/Juntos otra vez*, Connector 15857, 2000

Julio Barreto Cuban Quartet, *Iyabó*, Connector 15852, 2001

Julio Padrón, *Buenas noticias*, Sunnyside 1094, 2000

Julio Padrón y los Amigos de Sta. Amalia, *Descarga santa*, Real-Rhythm 50001, 2000

Klimax, *Oye como va*, Eurotropical 00529, 2000

Klimax, *Mira si te gusta*, Manzana 017, 1996

La Charanga Forever, *La Charanga soy yo*, Caribe Productions 9571, 2000

Los Surik, *Alma musical*, Magic Music 0003-3, 1994

Los Terry, *From Africa to Camagüey*, Tonga 9703, 1996

Lucrecia y su Orquesta, *Me debes un beso*, Magic Music 0001-3

Lucrecia y su Orquesta, *Prohibido*, Universal 40071, 1996

Malena Burke y NG La Banda, *Salseando*, Artex 15, 1990

Manolín El Médico de la Salsa, *De buena fé*, Metro Blue 21306

Manolito y su Trabuco, *Para que baile Cuba*, Eurotropical 0022, 2000

Manolito y su Trabuco, *Marcando la distancia*, Eurotropical 9, 1998

Manolito y su Trabuco, *Directo al corazón*, Bembé 2014, 1995

Mayelín, *Mayelín*, Eurotropical 17, 1998

Mayito Rivera, *Pa' bachatear...Chappotín*, BIS 173, 2000

Moncada, *El mundo al revés*, Egrem 453, 2001

Moncada, *Nueva Trova, Salsa y otros inventos*, Spartacus 22116, 1996

Moncada, *No puedo ser diferente*, Declic 50381, 1995

Omar Sosa, *Prietos*, Otá 1008, 2000

Omar Sosa, *Inside*, Night & Day MSCD 005, 1999

Omar Sosa, *Spirit of the Roots*, Night & Day MSCD 004, 1999

Omar Sosa, *Free Roots/Raices libres*, Night & Day MSCD 002, 1997

Orishas, *A lo Cubano*, Universal 159-571, 2000

Orlando Cachaíto Lopez, *Cachaíto*, Nonesuch 79630, 2001

Orlando Valle "Maraca" y Otra Visión, *¡Descarga Total!*, Ahi-Nama Records 1026, 2000

Orlando Valle "Maraca" y Otra Visión, *¡Sonando!* Ahi-Nama Records 1018, 1998

Orlando Valle "Maraca" y Otra Visión, *Fórmula uno*, BIS 120, 1996

Orlando Valle "Maraca" y Otra Visión, *Havana Calling*, Qbadisc 9023, 1996

Orquesta Aliamen, *Santa Clara*, Last Call 3046162, 1999

Orquesta Aliamen y Orquesta Havana Salsa, *Doble impacto cubano*, Mambo Express 0028, 2000

Orquesta Revé, *Rumberos latino-americanos*, Orfeon 16184, 2001

Orquesta Revé, *Arriba las manos*, Caribe Productions 9455, 1996

Orquesta Revé, *La explosión del momento*, Realword 2303, 1989

Orquesta Revé, *Mi salsa tiene sandunga*, Bárbaro 234, re-issued 1995

Orquesta Revé, *Papá Elegua*, Egrem 78, 1993

Osdalgia, *Mi harmonía*, Lusafrica 36552, 2001

Osdalgia, *La culebra*, Lusafrica 262862, 1999

Pachito Alonso y sus Kini Kini, *Traigo, Te Traigo*, Egrem 386, 2000

Pachito Alonso y sus Kini Kini, *¡Ay! Qué bueno está*, Caribe Productions 9512, 1997

Paulito y su Elite (Paulo FG), *Una vez más... Por amor*, Promusic 00013, 2000

Paulito y su Elite, *Con la conciencia tranquila*, Nueva Fania 108, 1997

Paulito y su Elite, *Sofocándote*, Universal 40070, 1996

Peruchín Jr. & the Cuban All Stars, *Descarga dos*, Lusafrica 362212, 1997

Peruchín Jr. & the Cuban All Stars, *Malanga amarilla*, Egrem 0428, 2001

Roberto Carcasses, *Invitation*, Velas 2004, 2000

Rojitas y su Orquesta, *Soy salsero, soy cantante*, Caribe Productions 9593, 1999

Rompesaragüey, *Entra y sale*, Tumi 078, 1998

Sin Palabras, *House of Drums*, Piranha 1259, 1998

Sin Palabras, *Orisha Dreams*, Globe Music B 11992, 1999

Sin Palabras, *KMO*, Audivis/Naïve, Y 226194, 2001

Son 14, *Grandes éxitos*, Egrem 0235, 1998

Son 14, *La Máquina musical*, 20th Anniversary, Tumi 086, 1999

Son 14 with Tiburón, *Cubanía*, Candela 4284242, 1997

Son 14, *Son para un sonero*, Caiman 3601, 1995

Son 14, *Y sigue el son...* Artex 54, 1991

Son 14 with Adalberto Álvarez, *Son, the Big Sound*, Tumi Cuba Classics vol. 4, Tumi 053, 1995

Son 14 with Adalberto Álvarez, *Y se baila así*, Bárbaro 237, re-issued 1995

Son Candela, *Llega, pero no te pases*, Cuba Chevere 0500, 2000

Tata Güines & Miguel Angá, *Pasaporte*, Enja 9019, 1995

Tiburón Morales, *La voz del Son*, Timba Productions 15872, re-issued 2001

Tony Martínez, *Maferefún*, Blue Jackel 5033, re-issued 1999

Tony Martínez, *La Habana vive*, Blue Jackel 5026, 1998

Tony Pérez, *From Enchantment and Timba... To Full Force Jazz*, Universal 160507, 2001

Yumurí y sus Hermanos, *Olvídame...Si puedes*, BIS 170, 1999

Yumurí y sus Hermanos, *Cocodrilo de agua salá*, Magic Music C-0002-3

# Glossary

*Abakuá*: system of worship of slaves supposed to come from Calabar region, and an initiate of the Carabalí brotherhoods.

*Akpwón*: solo singer of Yoruba rituals.

*Arará*: generic name of Fon groups of the kingdom of Allada (now Benin).

*Bailes de cuna*: popular neighborhood dance halls patronized by populations of color during the colonial period.

*Barracón, barracones*: plantation slave dwellings: a building with one entrance opening onto a central courtyard, surrounded by corridors subdivided into minuscule dwellings.

*Batá*: three sacred, hourglass-shaped and two-headed drums used in *Lucumí*-Yoruba rituals: the *okónkolo*, (the smallest), the *itótele* (medium-sized), and the *iyá* (the master drum, always placed in the middle).

*Bembé*: secular entertainment offered to the deities in the Yoruba system of worship.

*Bocú, bocúes*: a drum used in the *congas* and *comparsas* of the Santiago de Cuba carnival. Designated according to their rhythmic function under the names *fondo, requinto,* and *quinto.*

*Bolero*: simple rhythm and dance, different from its compound Spanish counterpart on 3/4 meter. Appears in Santiago de Cuba at the end of the nineteenth century.

*Bombo*: creole bass drum of the Havana carnivals, narrower than its counterpart in military brass bands.

*Bongó*: a drum of Bantu inspiration, born in the eastern provinces, made of two small attached drums held between the knees. It has an improvisational function in the *son.*

*Bossale*: a slave born in Africa.

*Botija* or *botijuela*: an instrument serving as a bass in the old rural and urban *son*, made of a clay jar with a hole on one side through which one blows.

*Bulá*: a drum used in the *tumba francesa*; maintains a steady repeated pattern.

*Cabildo de nación*: an organization originating in the colonial period, which represented the *bossales* who were supposed to come
from the same ethnic or linguistic area.

*Cajón*: a drum used in the rumba and made of packing crates for
codfish or tapers.

*Campana*: in Santiago, a metal percussion instrument made of
brake drums, which accompanies the *conga* drums.

*Carabalí*: a generic term for groups of slaves said to come from
Calabar.

*Catá*: a hollowed-out tree trunk, struck with drumsticks, which
marks the base rhythm of *tumba francesa* music in Oriente.

*Cencerro*: cowbell with the clapper removed, struck with a stick.

*Chachá (or maruga)*: metal shaker mounted on a handle and decorated with ribbons, used in *tumba francesa* celebrations.

*Changüí*: a rural antecedent of the *son* (eastern region of Guantánamo).

*Charanga*: a type of orchestra that replaced the *orquesta típica*
at the turn of the twentieth century to perform the *danzón*. Includes piano, flute, violins, double-bass, *paila criolla*, also
named *timbales criollos* (that replaced the timpani of the *orquesta típica*), and *güiro*. *Tumbadora*, cello, and voice were added
later.

*Cinquillo*: a rhythmic cell originating in Saint-Domingue, a group
of five syncopated notes (quaver, semi-quaver, quaver, semi-
quaver, quaver) within one measure.

*Clave*: a syncopated base pattern of the main dancing forms of
Cuban music, a group of five syncopated notes structured in a
two-measure phrase. Also designates a sung type of musical
theater from which the *criolla* is derived.

*Claves*: small percussion instrument, two small cylindrical pieces
of wood struck against each other, the stationary hand forming
the sound-box.

*Cocoyé*: *comparsa* theme of emigrants from Saint-Domingue in the Santiago carnivals where the rhythmic cell of the *cinquillo* appears.

*Columbia*: one of the three styles of rumba, of rural origin; danced by a sole male dancer.

*Comparsa*: a carnival formation including musicians, singers, and dancers.

*Conjunto*: *son* orchestra established by Arsenio Rodríguez in the early 1940s. Derived from former septets by the addition of instruments.

*Conga*: a group of musicians in a *comparsa*. In Santiago, its instrumentation is different from that of Havana, and it roams the streets alone, followed by people, before the carnival march. Also designates a dance rhythm.

*Congo*: a generic term used to designate slaves said of Bantu origin.

*Contradanza*: a collective figure dancing and type of instrumental music descended from European court and salon dances; it is creolized in Cuba as of the mid-eighteen century. Ancestor to the cuban *danzón*.

*Contradanza habanera*: a Havana version still including the European compound rhythm, that will evolve to the simple rhythm in 2/4 meter of the *contradanza criolla* (Creole quadrille); will be replaced around 1850 by the Eastern quadrille, a simple rhythm quadrille with the rhtyhmic cell *cinquillo*, introduced by the immigrants from Saint-Domingue to Santiago.

*Controversia*: a sung argument in ten-line stanzas, between two improvisers in the rural music of *punto guajiro*.

*Corneta china*: a small wind instrument with a high-pitched tonality and nasal timbre, specific to eastern *congas*.

*Coro de clave*: a mixed singing group with a repertoire including lyrical or popular songs, which roamed the streets at Christmas around the end of the nineteenth century. In the twentieth century these neighborhood groups include a *guaguancó* repertoire. Disappeared around 1940.

*Cuarteta*: a stanza of four octosyllabic lines, derived from the Spanish *copla*. In the Cuban Oriente it is called *regina*.

*Danza*: another name for the simple creole quadrille. Also designates a semi-formal musical composition, written in 6/8, or sometimes in two parts, one in simple time, one in compound time.

*Danzón*: the first dancing genre considered entirely Cuban, in 2/4 time, slower than the quadrille, and divided in three parts. Originally purely instrumental, it will include singing in the 1930s under the influence of the *son*.

*Danzón nuevo ritmo*: a new form of instrumental *danzón* created by the Arcaño orchestra which gives the name mambo to the last segment, which is rapid, syncopated, and very danceable.

*Danzonete*: derived from the *danzón* influenced by the *son* and including a sung part (1929).

*Décima*: a sung stanza of ten octosyllabic lines, of Spanish origin, used by the improvisers of rumba and of *punto guajiro*.

*Descarga*: Cuban version of the jam-session, where the musicians improvise on a given theme.

*Diana*: a sequence of sung syllables which opens the three forms of rumba, comparable to the sounds of the *cante jondo*.

*Ekón*: a metal percussion instrument used in Abakuá rituals.

*Ekwé*: a sacred Abakuá drum, rubbed externally.

*Estudiantina*: a formation made up of very young musicians, which appeared in Santiago de Cuba at the end of the nineteenth century. Its original instrumentation (*tres*, guitars, *paila criolla*, *botija* or *marimbula* — now double-bass, *güiro*, maracas, and trumpet) allows it to perform all the dance genres.

*Galleta*: derived from the large bass drums of military brass bands used in the *congas* of Santiago. Narrower than the Havana *bombo*.

*Guagua*: a hollowed-out tree trunk, or a large bamboo cane, beaten with sticks and marking a constant rhythm in the rumba.

*Guaguancó*: a style of rumba of urban origin, danced in couples and miming seduction with highly erotic movements.

*Guaracha*: a type of accompanied singing, with a lively tempo and with satirical lyrics, originating from burlesque theater. It evolved into a dance rhythm influenced by the *son* and was included in orchestra repertoires.

*Guataca*: a metal percussion instrument derived from agricultural tools such as the hoe.

*Guateque*: a peasant holiday in the western and central regions.

*Guayo*: a corrugated metal cylinder that is scratched to accompany the eastern *changüí*. Similar to the *güira* used in the Dominican *merengue*.

*Güiro*: Bantu-inspired Cuban instrument, made from a gourd or calabash, corrugated perpendicularly to the axis and scratched with a stick, accompanies popular music when introduced in the *danzón*. In Havana it also designates a non-religious celebration of *Lucumí*-Yoruba rituals.

*Habanera*: appears in the first half of the nineteenth century; in Cuba synonymous with *contradanza habanera*, also named *contradanza criolla* (Creole or Cuban quadrille), distinct from the Eastern Quadrille that appeared at the same time in eastern Cuba. Outside of Cuba, name of the Creole quadrille to distinguish it from the European quadrille. From 1841, a genre sung in verse, popular in Spain and Mexico.

*Íreme*: a character of the Abakuá secular rituals who also appears in the *comparsas* of carnival. Also called *diablito* for his leaping moves and his costume.

*Iyesá*: generic name for Yoruba groups said to originate in the kingdom of Oyo (now Nigeria).

Kinfuiti: sacred drum of Congo-Bantu rituals, rubbed internally.

*Lucumí*: generic name for groups supposed of Yoruba origin.

*Makuta*: secular celebration of *Congos*-Bantu rituals.

*Mambo*: name given by Arcaño to the last syncopated segment of the *danzón nuevo ritmo*. A musical genre created and popularized by Damaso Pérez Prado in Mexico. Also designates an instrumental phrase repeated in unison and forming a brief section that connects different parts of a musical piece.

*Maracas*: a pair of gourds filled with seeds, with different sounds, that is shaken to mark a constant rhythm.

*Marímbula*: a tuned idiophone consisting of metal strips (lamellae) arranged on a flat sounding board and mounted on a resonator (a box), derived from the African *sansa o mbira (hand piano)*.

*Masón*: group of dances of the *tumba francesa* descended from the figure dances of the French colonists from Saint-Domingue. Also designates a percussion rhythm used by the eastern *congas*.

*Montuno*: improvisation section with soloist-chorus alternation in the *son*; climax of the musical piece.

*Ngoma*: generic name of ritual drums of *Congo*-Bantu origin.

*Orisha*: generic name of the deities of the Yoruba system of worship.

*Orquesta típica*: the first type of *danzón* orchestra including big brass instruments borrowed from brass bands, clarinets, double-bass, violins, timpani, and *güiro*.

*Oru de igbodu*: initial greeting of the *batá* drums to each divinity with the rhythms which correspond to each; not sung.

*Paila criolla (or timbales criollos)*: two small single-skin Creole kettledrums, joined and placed on one foot, and beaten with a combination of drumsticks and hands. They replaced the timpani in *danzón* orchestras at the beginning of the twentieth century.

*Palenque*: fortified encampment of fugitive slaves in the Oriente mountains and in central Pinar del Río province.

*Palo (regla de)*: generic name of the *Congo*-Bantu system of worship.

*Pilón*: third large bass drum of the Santiago *congas*, slightly thicker than the *galletas*. It leads the rhythm section. Also designates a rhythm and a dance produced by the Pacho

Alonso orchestra.

*Premier*: improvising drum of the *tumba francesa* orchestras.

*Punto guajiro*: sung genre of the western and central rural regions, with a compound rhythm, performed with guitar, *tres*, lute, and small percussion instruments. Includes different modalities, *punto libre, fijo,* and *cruzado.*

*Quinto*: drum used for improvisation in the rumba.

*Rayado, rasgueado,* or *rasgueo*: a guitar technique used for rhythmic sequences, achieved by extending all fingers on the playing hand in a fan.

*Regina*: name for the octosyllabic quatrain in the eastern regions (*trova, changüí, son*).

*Regla de ocha-ifá*: name for the *Lucumí*-Yoruba system of worship.

*Repentista*: improviser of the *punto guajiro,* also called the poet.

*Repicador*: a *cajón* used for improvising in the *yambú.*

*Santería*: Christianized name of the *regla de ocha-ifá.*

*Sartenes*: frying pans that are bolted to a flat piece of wood and strapped onto the player, who plays them with wooden or metal sticks.

*Segón*: a drum used in the *tumba francesa.*

*Shekeré*: a large hollow gourd enmeshed in a net of cowries or glass beads. Shaken idiophone used by the Yoruba. Used in a trio in the Havana *güiros.*

*Solar, solares*: a building divided into tiny abodes opening onto balcony passages around a large central courtyard; reminiscent of the structure of slave *barracones* on plantations.

*Son*: a sung and danced musical genre, rural at first, then urban, born in the eastern provinces and transformed in Havana. One of the major types of popular music.

*Tambora*: a drum used in the *masón* by the *tumba francesa,* used also in the *congas* of Santiago.

*Tango*: a rhythmic cell (pointed quaver, half quaver, two quavers) typical of the first Havanan form of quadrille (contradanza habanera).

*Tonada*: a melody sung in the *punto guajiro.*

*Tres*: a Cuban string instrument derived from the guitar; having three doubled strings, it accompanies the *punto* and the *son*.

*Tres-dos* or *tres golpes*: a *cajón* or *tumbadora* which accompanies the basic rhythmic pattern in the rumba.

*Trova*: a type of popular music of Oriente, created by author-composer-performers who accompany themselves on guitar.

*Tumba francesa*: celebrations by slaves from Saint-Domingue who immigrated to Cuba's Oriente province, where, with their percussion instruments, they performed dances derived from salon dances and songs in Creole. The name given to associations where they gather in urban areas.

*Tumbador*: the name of the *cajón* or of the *tumbadora* which provides the steady rhythm in the rumba.

*Tumbadora*: a barrel-shaped drum made of hoop-bound casks.

*Tumbao*: the manner of playing the musical phrase within the base rhythm on the piano and the double-bass.

*Vacunao*: a gesture of sexual possession specific to the *guaguancó*.

*Yambú*: the oldest urban style of the rumba.

*Yuka (drums)*: long, cylindrical drums used in secular celebrations of the Bantu system of worship (*caja, mula,* and *cachimbo*).

*Zapateo*: a dance of the western rural regions, derived from the Spanish *zapateado*.